If I Lived with Noah

By Pamela Moritz

Illustrated by MacKenzie Haley

APPLES & HONEY PRESS

To Ron and the kids

-PM

To my family, for always keeping me afloat

-MH

Apples & Honey Press
An imprint of Behrman House Publishers
Millburn, New Jersey 07041
www.applesandhoneypress.com

Text copyright © 2020 by Pamela Moritz
Illustrations copyright © 2020 by MacKenzie Haley
ISBN 978-1-68115-558-6

Library of Congress Cataloging-in-Publication Data

Names: Moritz, Pamela, author. | Haley, MacKenzie, illustrator.
Title: If I lived with Noah / by Pamela Moritz ; illustrated by MacKenzie Haley.
Description: Millburn, New Jersey : Apples & Honey Press, [2020] | Summary:
"A young boy imagines himself playing with the animals on Noah's ark"--
Provided by publisher.
Identifiers: LCCN 2019015851 | ISBN 9781681155586
Subjects: | CYAC: Stories in rhyme. | Animals--Fiction. | Play--Fiction. |
Noah's ark--Fiction. | Noah (Biblical figure)--Fiction.
Classification: LCC PZ8.3.M8138 If 2020 | DDC [Fic]--dc23 LC record available at https://lccn.loc.gov/2019015851

Design by Rina Schachter
Edited by Ann D. Koffsky
Printed in China

1 3 5 7 9 8 6 4 2

062031.7K1/B1506/A5

It's just a big rainstorm, so don't be afraid.
We're under the covers and warm.

Let's all close our eyes and pretend we're with Noah.
Imagine an ark and a storm.

If I saw the animals boarding the ark
As Noah stood by with his staff,

I'd say, "I can help with the animals, sir."
He'd welcome me on with a laugh.

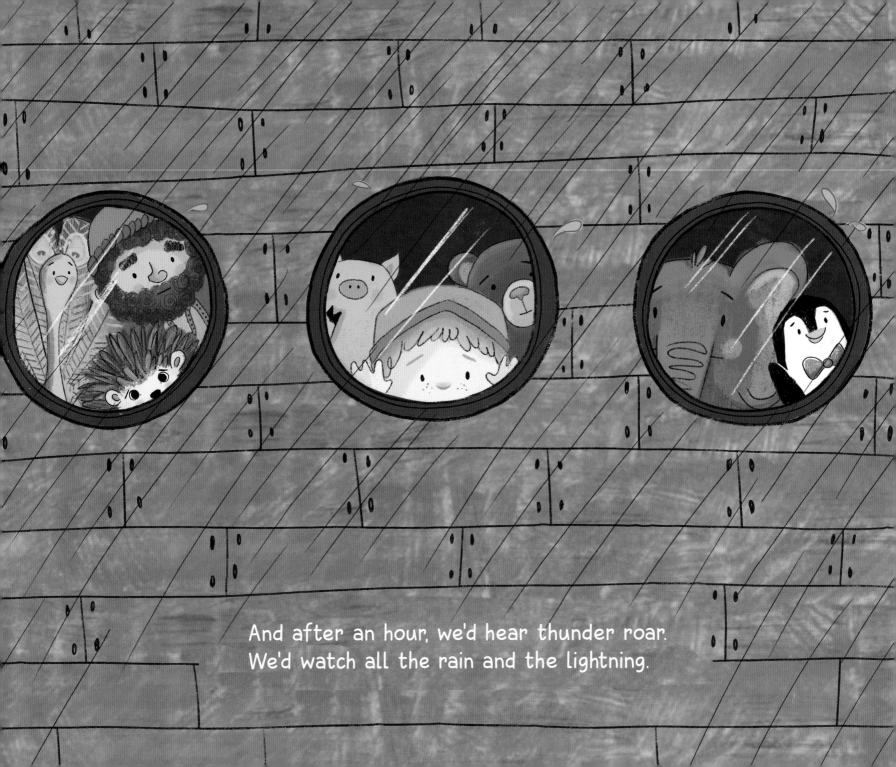

And after an hour, we'd hear thunder roar.
We'd watch all the rain and the lightning.

I'd comfort the animals hiding below.
"I know," I would say, "storms are frightening."

If I lived with Noah,
I'd sweep and I'd mop.

I'd work hard
And try not to tire.

I'd shower the animals out in the rain
And let them dry out by the fire.

roar!

tweet

I'd learn how to speak
Every animal's language
So we'd understand one another.

quack

At times we would argue,
But mostly we'd play.
I'd be like an animal brother.

But sometimes we'd feel there was nothing to do.
"This boat is so boring!" they'd shout.

"Does anyone care that we need some fresh air?
Please open the doors—let us out!"

So then I would build them
A great wooden board
And hammer it onto the rim.

The sun would peek out,
And I'd gather my friends.
We'd jump in the sea for a swim.

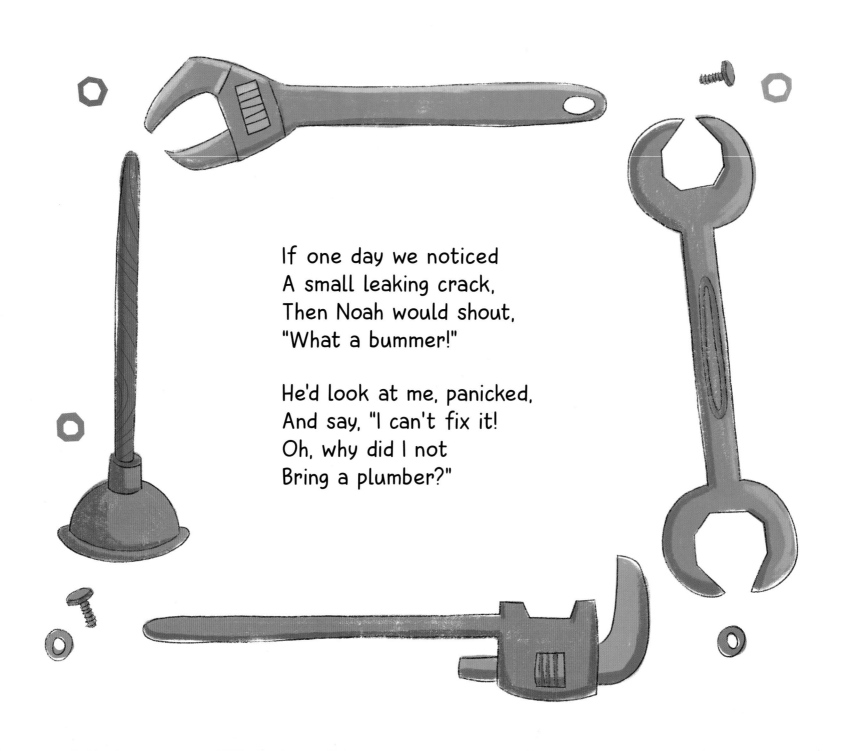

If one day we noticed
A small leaking crack,
Then Noah would shout,
"What a bummer!"

He'd look at me, panicked,
And say, "I can't fix it!
Oh, why did I not
Bring a plumber?"

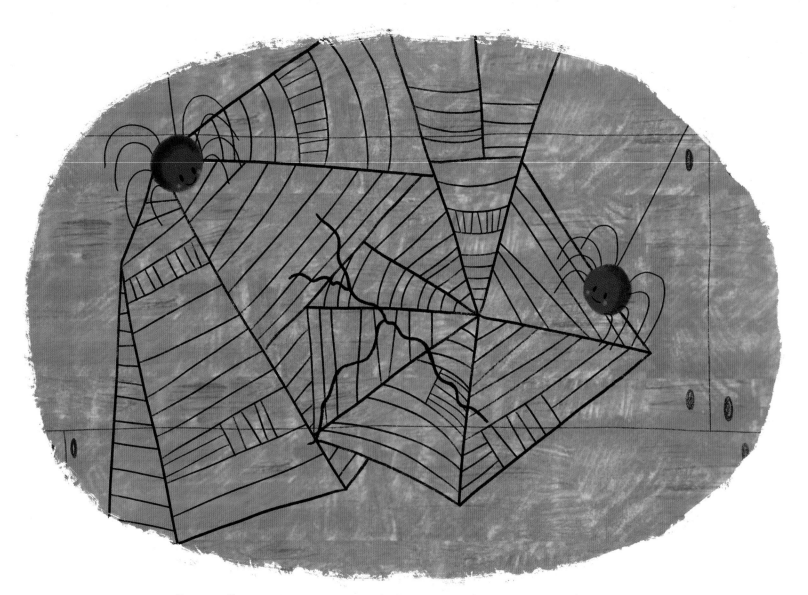

I'd first find the spiders! I'd call them together.
"We need sticky webs-save our ship!"

They'd quickly spin webs that would cover the crack.
Their patches would last the whole trip.

And then to the elephants, "Please use your trunks,
And suck up that water!" I'd cry.

They'd toss all the water right into the ocean
And make sure the flooring stayed dry.

Achoo!

And what if one day
Both the elephants sneezed?
The zebras and deer
Had sore throats?

And what if the cobras
And camels had coughs?!
The chickens! The turtles!
The goats!

If Noah were busy,
Then how could I help them?
Alone, I could not tend them all!

So then, in a flash,
I would realize the answer.

"Hey, monkeys, come help!"

I would call.

sniff

They both would come running and climbing to help.
We'd hand out the tissues and tea.

"I have the best animal friends," I would say.
I'm sure they would nod and agree.

If I lived with Noah,
I'd tell lots of stories.

They'd listen and
Ask me for more.

"Oh, no, now it's bedtime,"
I'd say. "Close your eyes."

"Tomorrow we'll look
For the shore."

And early each morning,
We'd all look together,
Till one day, "Hey, Noah!" I'd shout.

"What's that in the distance?
Is that a small speck?!
Quick, Noah, the dove—send her out!"

The dove would return with a branch from a tree.
I'd say, "You found land! Thank you, friend."

We'd steer the great ark toward the shore, and we'd know
Our voyage was now at its end.

The animals, slowly, would walk off the ark.
They'd look at me sadly and . . . *stay.*

"Please go," I would tell them.
"You must build your homes.
I'll miss you, but go. It's okay."

I'd look all around me,
At God's wondrous creatures,
And cry, "I'm so glad I was here!"

"I'll always remember our journey together.
I love you!" I'd say, and they'd cheer.

Then Noah would say,
"You brought laughter and warmth,
Even when it was rainy and dark.

And so, we have made you
A small parting gift."
And they'd give me
My very own ark!

A NOTE FOR FAMILIES

Noah and his family were kind to the animals on the ark. According to tradition, the family barely slept, because they had so many animals to feed and take care of. I'm sure Noah could have used some help!

Treating animals kindly is a mitzvah-a commandment and good deed. Just like Noah, we should be kind to God's creatures. If it's important to be loving to animals, think of how important it is to be loving to one another!

- If you got to live with Noah, in what way would you help?

- What are some ways that you can be kind to an animal in your own life?

- What are some kind words you can say to a friend?

Shalom,

A College
of
Magics

A College
of
Magics

Caroline Stevermer

TOR

A Tom Doherty Associates Book
New York

A COLLEGE OF MAGICS

Edited by Terri Windling

This book is printed on acid-free paper.

A Tor Book
Published by Tom Doherty Associates, Inc.
175 Fifth Avenue
New York, N.Y. 10010

Tor ® is a registered trademark of Tom Doherty Associates, Inc.

Design by Lynn Newmark

Library of Congress Cataloging-in-Publication Data

Stevermer, Caroline.
    A college of magics / Caroline Stevermer.
        p.   cm.
    "A Tom Doherty Associates Book."
    ISBN 0-312-85689-X
    I. Title.
PS3569.T4575C6   1994
813'.54—dc20   93-42997
                                            CIP

First edition: March 1994

Printed in the United States of America

0 9 8 7 6 5 4 3 2 1

This book is respectfully dedicated
to the inhabitants of
Denbigh's back smoker 1975–1977.
You know who you are.

Contents

And time is not a gulf, nor space a bar;
Our hearts are loyal, even when we're far;
As once we were, again tonight we are.

—Georgina Goddard King

A College
of
Magics

Volume One

The Structure
of the
World

1

Greenlaw College

🕷 FARIS NALLANEEN ARRIVED at the gates of Greenlaw on the same day winter did. It was late afternoon, just as gray daylight began to fade into blue twilight. Behind her brougham, hired in Pontorson to bear her on the last stage of her journey, the causeway stretched back to the coast, a spine of paved road amid the sands of low tide. Before the carriage and pair was the wooden gate of Greenlaw, and in it the gatekeeper's grille with its little green shutter, tightly latched.

As Faris watched from the carriage window, Gavren got stiffly down from the box to knock at the green shutter. Gavren was not an old man, not yet, but there was gray brindled in his hair, and the marks of a long journey were plain in his bearing.

The offshore wind blew steadily, an edge of frost in it. The coach horses shifted in harness, heads down against the cold. Daylight was failing fast. Soon the green shutter would lose its color and fade into the grays of sea, sky, and stone.

Gavren grimaced at the chill and knocked again. As he dropped his hand, the shutter snapped open and a face appeared at the grille. It was a round face, chapped red, its owner grim at the call out into the weather.

"Who goes there?" the gatekeeper demanded.

"The duchess of Galazon and her escort," replied Gavren.

The gatekeeper regarded Gavren for a moment, then looked past him at the well-worn brougham and its tired horses. He eyed Reed, the weary driver, who had remained on the box, and sneered at Faris, the only passenger. He glanced at the sky. There was at least a chance of sleet. His face folded into satisfaction. "We have no use for titles here." He closed the shutter.

Gavren let out a long slow breath and knocked again.

No answer.

Faris opened the carriage door. "Let me."

"We must put up the horses and I suppose we'll have to beg our way in to do it. But try to maintain some decorum. If you give in to them at once, you'll have no mercy from them," Gavren said. "Stay there and let me handle things."

Bunching her creased black skirts, Faris sprang down from the brougham and joined Gavren at the gate.

"You may be forbidden to use your title once you are a student, but don't abandon it before you've even seen the place. Don't sacrifice it before you make it do you some good."

Faris nodded at Gavren, her pale blue eyes serious, her brows knitted. Although she was eighteen, the black serge traveling suit she wore, twenty years out of fashion, in a style twenty years too old for her, made her look like a twelve-year-old playing dress up, in clothes nearly too small for her. Her red hair sprang untidily from beneath the brim of her uncompromising hat, and her bony wrists showed distinctly in the gap between frayed cuffs and worn leather gloves.

"Don't worry. They'll have no mercy from me." She smiled crookedly at Gavren. Her bitter smile revealed uneven, almost pointed teeth, and made her long nose look even longer. She glanced up at Reed, who was watching from the box, smiled again to herself, and knocked briskly on the shutter.

After a moment, the shutter snapped open. "Well?"

Faris put a hand against the gate to lean close to the grille. "It will be a cold night. My companions and I require lodging. We can pay well."

The gatekeeper studied her and sneered again. "Your name and business?"

"Both too trivial to concern you. I am but a humble acolyte, come to apply for a place at Greenlaw College. My uncle Brinker thinks I will prove an apt student."

The gatekeeper regarded her with loathing for an instant, then clapped the shutter closed. There was a hasty scrape and the wooden gate swung open.

Faris Nallaneen, duchess of Galazon, nodded again to Gavren. He rolled his eyes as he took her elbow, helped her back into the brougham, and took the seat beside her. Reed drove the carriage through the gates of Greenlaw.

Once on the other side, Faris put her hand on Gavren's sleeve. His rap on the ceiling called Reed to a halt. The gatekeeper closed the gate and barred it, then turned to the brougham with an expectant air as Faris opened her door and leaned inelegantly out.

"So this is Greenlaw." Faris looked about her at the courtyard and the narrow street before her, winding steeply up the stone mount. "And these are the gates, the visible built of oak, the invisible built of the Dean's will. But both guarded by the same man."

She gave the gatekeeper a faint smile of apology. "It's the custom to tip heavily, isn't it? I'm so sorry I can't oblige you. It would look as though I tried to bribe my way in. Absurd, don't you agree? But I can't risk it." She closed the carriage door and settled back into her seat.

From the box, Reed tossed the gatekeeper a coin. "See you do a better job keeping her in than you did keeping us out." He managed reins and whip and the carriage moved on.

"We're to stay at the White Fleece," Gavren told Faris. "Send word to us when you are accepted and Reed and I will go back to tell your uncle the news. If Reed can get this barge all the way up the street, we'll leave you at the door of the college. If not, we will escort you on foot."

Faris craned her neck to see what she could of the closely built street. "Which one is the White Fleece?"

"On our right, just ahead."

"Excellent." Faris rapped smartly on the ceiling of the carriage. Reed drew rein. Grateful to stop, the horses halted a few yards from the White Fleece.

"I will see the proctors when I'm ready," said Faris,

before Gavren could protest, or Reed enliven the coach horses. She opened the carriage door and sprang down into the street. "Just now I'm cold and hungry and I smell of horse. All three of us will put up at the White Fleece or I go not a yard farther. When I've had a hot bath, a decent meal, and a full night's sleep, I will consider the proctors."

Gavren let out a breath of slow control. "Very well. There is no need to make a scene in the street about it."

Faris smiled. "Great need. They must take me for a shrew, not a mouse. And see you don't forget to 'your grace' me."

"You put no stock in such things," Reed said. He looked at Gavren. "Does she?"

"They have no use for titles here, so if I don't use mine, they'll think I'm meek."

"God forbid," said Reed. As Faris looked down her long, red-tipped nose at him, he added hastily, "your grace." Since he dressed with the same severity as Gavren, he seemed far older than Faris, though the difference in their ages was barely five years.

Gavren folded his arms and sighed. "Then command us, your grace. Must we keep these nags standing much longer in the street, your grace? If they freeze in their tracks, doubtless the hostler at Pontorson will demand damages. Your grace."

"Stable them, by all means. If they freeze in their tracks, they'll make very evil-looking statuary and the rest of the street is pleasantly gothic. It would be a pity to spoil it with hired horses."

At the White Fleece, though titles were of no use, money secured them rooms and a large meal, served at one of the well-scrubbed tables in the common room.

Faris sat between her companions, oblivious of the stares of the other diners in the room. Gloves pulled off and crumpled in her lap, the cuffs of her suit halfway to her elbows, she was too hungry to worry about her appearance. She took up her spoon with exaggerated care, but after the first taste of soup she discarded her affected manners and devoted herself to the meal with enthusiasm.

When the bowls were cleared and the plates were empty, the innkeeper paused to ask them if they cared for a sweet or a savory to finish.

"Your grace?" asked Gavren, with heavy emphasis.

Faris put her mug down and nodded graciously at the innkeeper. "Yes, please."

"Which, your grace?" asked Reed, patiently.

"Both, please."

The innkeeper went away without acknowledging Gavren's signal to replenish their glasses.

"Greedy, aren't you?" Reed said to Faris. He turned to Gavren. "Was she born this way, or was she raised to it?"

"She was raised to know better, though she doesn't always behave the way she knows she should. Perhaps she'll learn better here."

Serenely, Faris began to butter a morsel of bread. "If the proctors accept me, this could be my last decent meal for years. If they don't, we'll have a long trip back to Galazon, and a longer explanation to make when we get there."

"The proctors will accept you." Gavren's voice was heavy and cold. "It's all been arranged."

"Of course it has. I don't know why I need to be involved at all. Everything's been arranged. Did you know, Reed, we have a spell at home in Galazon far more powerful than any I can possibly learn here? I used it to open the gates. Didn't you hear me? Just those three words—my uncle Brinker." She swirled the ale left in her mug and looked thoughtful. "I wonder how much the proctors of Greenlaw College cost him? I wonder how much bad behavior he was able to afford to pay them to overlook."

Gavren banged his mug on the table. "You put that right out of your mind, young madam. You're going to Greenlaw College and you are not, most certainly not, going to get yourself expelled." He gestured emphatically for more ale. When the mugs had been refilled, he turned back to Faris. "Do you think that failing here will get your uncle out of the wardship of Galazon? Do you think antagonizing the proctors will accomplish anything? What are you planning? Do you think you can fail your admission? If you expect us to wet-nurse you back to Galazon so we can be torn into strips by your uncle's observations, I suggest you think again—your grace."

The innkeeper returned with a flat dish of flan, creamy under a glaze of burnt sugar, and a reed basket lined with seaweed and heaped high with clams and snails and mussels, steamed in their gleaming shells. With the shellfish came a bowl of garlic butter and a handful of sharp implements of arcane design.

"I know you aren't overjoyed to be here," Gavren continued, "but it's more than I can do to figure out why not. There are those who would give a great deal to be in your place. Oh, you'll miss Galazon, I suppose, but it's for your own good. Behave yourself and you will do well here. At least you'll learn something besides when to plant oats and how to shoe a horse. And you and your uncle are spared the sight of each other for three years. That ought to be worth something to you."

Faris selected a mussel and probed it savagely. "If I don't like it here, I can always go home—I'm sure Uncle will let me, once he's squeezed every penny he can out of the land."

"If you don't like it," said Reed, "why don't you learn what you need to learn here so you can come back and do as you please, even if your uncle does wish you elsewhere?"

Gavren put down his mug with such violence that ale splashed on the table. "Mind your tongue, Drayton Reed. Talk like that is folly—talk like that before the duchess is worse. Who pays us? Lord Brinker Nallaneen is head of the clan."

Faris regarded Gavren with the same crooked smile she'd displayed at the gate. "Brinker Nallaneen is head of the family until I reach my majority," she said. "What then?"

Gavren frowned at her. "That isn't for years yet."

"Two years, twenty-three days," agreed Faris. "No, I'm

wrong. Next year is a leap year. Make it twenty-four days. What then?"

"In two years, and however many days it is," Gavren replied, "you will have learned that there's more to running Galazon than the legal right to try it."

Faris nodded. "Yes, but would you side with my uncle against me?"

Disapproval and suspicion were evenly mixed in Gavren's expression. "First I'd have to see how three years at Greenlaw College sat with you. Now don't you go pestering Reed to answer the same stupid question."

"I don't need to ask him. I already know what he'd say."

"Oh, you do, do you? I'd like to hear it."

Faris picked up a snail and set to work with the winkle pin. "You'd follow me against my uncle this minute, though it cost you your head."

"Why, you vain little baggage. Side with a carrot-haired gawk like you against the wiliest man in Galazon? I'd be a fool to consider it."

Faris kept her attention on the winkle pin. "Leave my hair out of it. If Gavren should follow me, it would be because I have the right. But when you follow me, it will be because you hate my uncle. Don't trouble to deny it. Those with the same ailment recognize the symptoms." She looked up and her calmness stilled his protest before it was uttered. "Don't rebel against him yet. I have a lot to learn before my name is as potent a spell as his. Three years worth, perhaps more." Faris discarded the empty snail shell and poked at the seaweed pensively. "It's a pity, though. I'll be homesick for Galazon the whole time."

The following afternoon, Faris Nallaneen arrived at the door of Greenlaw College. The night before and most of the morning, it had snowed. Faris had to step carefully to keep the worst of the dampness out of her worn shoes. Just inside the door, at the bottom of a flight of stone steps, lay a pool of water. Faris skipped across the snow melt in an unladylike fashion and deduced she was not the first visitor the proctors had for the day. Nor, probably, was she in the first one hundred.

At the top of the stairs, Faris found a great hall, furnished only with the simplicity of its design and the fine gray stone of its construction, illuminated only by a large window at either end.

Mindful of the tales of Greenlaw College, Faris did not try to find another door, nor to leave the room. Scholarship at Greenlaw concerned not only natural philosophy and social ingenuity, but the workings of magic. It didn't seem wise to meddle beyond the precincts the proctors opened to her willingly.

An hour passed. It was not unusual for Uncle Brinker to keep her waiting for an hour. She passed the time by pacing. Twenty-five steps forth and twenty-five steps back, in and out of the pallid shafts of light slanting through the great windows. On the tiled floor her steps were silent. The only sound she made was the rustle of petticoats.

Another hour passed. Faris kept pacing. Despite her activity, the room seemed as cold as if the floor had been carved of ice. When she had memorized the pattern of the tiled floor, she turned her attention to the carved beams of the ceiling. They were strap and garter work, picked out in gilt and polychrome, the details difficult to appreciate in the fading daylight.

The late afternoon light was just on the point of fading all colors into gray when the outer door opened and a young woman of about her own age climbed the stairs to join her.

Faris paused in her pacing to inspect the newcomer, who returned her scrutiny with interest.

"You aren't a proctor, are you?" asked the newcomer.

Even in the failing light, Faris could see the young woman was barefoot and wore a shabby dress, soaked at the hem with melted snow. She was very thin. Her black hair was pulled back and tied at the nape of her neck. Her hands, though the knuckles were chapped red, were long and narrow. At her wrists blue veins showed through milk pale skin. Despite her apparent poverty, she bore herself with straight-backed grace, head high and gaze direct.

Faris met the barefooted girl's fearless look and felt an instant, irrational rush of inferiority. "No, I'm Faris."

"I'm Odile. Are you a student here?"

"No. Are you?"

"Not yet." Odile came toward her across the stone flags. She left bare footprints from the puddle but seemed untouched by cold. "I hope to be." She looked around at the great room, filled with blue twilight. "I was to come this summer but harvest delayed me. I couldn't leave until the crops were in. I hope the proctors understand that."

"They should. Crops are important. Did you have to travel far?"

"All the way from Sarlat. I walked."

"Oh." Faris felt renewed inferiority. She had come almost fifteen hundred miles, by riverboat, train, and carriage. There didn't seem to be much virtue in that, certainly no topic for conversation. Faris stood silent, angry at her own embarrassment.

After all, what was there to be awkward about? This girl wanted to attend Greenlaw. Faris did not. The proctors could hardly honor an agreement with Brinker if she didn't give them a chance to do so. All she had to do was leave and let Odile have her place at college. If Gavren insisted, she could return the next day when Odile was safely accepted. There was not an unlimited supply of openings for applicants.

Faris eyed the stairs. As she did, the outer door opened again. This time the newcomer had an attendant, who bore a lighted lantern. A word at the threshold and the door closed. Alone, the newcomer climbed the steps, lantern in hand.

With a sweep of velvet the color of the sky outside the great windows, a golden-haired girl of their own age joined Faris and Odile. She wore slippers of the same deep velvet and ignored the puddle that had ruined them. She ignored Faris and Odile too, and walked straight across the great hall to an open door, where firelight shone against the failing of the day.

Faris and Odile exchanged stares.

"Was that door there a moment ago?" asked Odile.

"It's probably been there all along," said Faris glumly.

They followed the girl in the velvet gown.

In the next room was warmth and golden light, age-faded tapestries, and a marquetry table with a chair behind it. In the chair sat a plump woman with mouse-gray hair and tired eyes.

"You're the proctor," said the girl in the velvet gown. Her voice was melodious but her intonation made the words an accusation. She put out the lantern and placed it on the floor in front of the table. "I'm Menary Paganell."

Faris's eyes narrowed. Her mouth set in a hard line.

The proctor put her chin in her hand and gestured at Faris to close the door. "Stand over there, all three of you. That's better. Winter's just here and I'm already sick to death of drafts."

Unwillingly, Menary fell back to stand between Faris and Odile. Next to Menary's elegance, Odile's poverty was manifest, but she did not appear to notice it. She stood with the same proud carriage Menary displayed. Beside them, Faris knew herself to be graceless. More, she knew that next to Menary's determination and Odile's dedication, her presence was a sham.

The proctor sighed. "You know there's only one opening left, don't you? Officially, admission closed at Martinmas."

"I was afraid I was too late," said Menary, relieved. "We had ill wind for the voyage and a storm delayed us. We didn't put in to St. Malo until this morning."

The proctor opened her eyes a little wider and Menary fell silent. "I said we had only one opening." Her tone was polite but her weary gaze rested on Menary without interest. "You can count, can't you?"

"My family arranged for me to attend Greenlaw when I was four years old," stated Menary.

Faris recognized the intonation of the words "my family." It was similar to her own when it became necessary to mention her uncle Brinker. She regarded the proctor with pleased expectation. If there was only one opening, there was the certainty that someone's prestige would be insufficient, either her uncle's or the family Paganell. Either prospect promised entertainment.

"Then if I were to ask you to recommend someone for this single opening," said the proctor, "you would choose yourself."

"Well, of course." Menary glanced at Odile, then at Faris, then back to the proctor. Her beautiful gray eyes, the exact shade of her velvet gown, narrowed. "Unless it's a trick question."

The proctor stifled a sigh and turned her attention to Odile. "And you, Odile Passerieux?"

Odile's eyes widened. "How did you know my name?"

"We've been expecting you for some time."

Odile's eyes fell. She clasped her hands before her and twisted her fingers. "I know I'm late. I couldn't help it. My family needed me."

The proctor inclined her head graciously. "One opening, Odile. How would you have us fill it?"

Odile's eyes held the proctor's. "Choose me." Her voice was soft but ardent. "Oh, please. Choose me."

Faris altered her stance so that the toe of her left shoe was visible beneath the hem of her dress. She studied it for a long moment, until the quality of silence in the room told her the proctor had finished staring at Odile and had started staring at her.

"Well, Faris Nallaneen?" The proctor sounded very tired. "What have you to say?"

"Good afternoon. I didn't get your name."

The proctor sniffed. "We have one opening. How would you have us fill it?"

Faris took a deep breath. "Choose Menary Paganell. Let Odile stay on and scrub floors or something until Menary loses interest and goes home to marry someone better dressed than she is. Then let Odile take the vacancy." She let out what was left of her breath and looked at the toe of her shoe again.

"And what will you do, Faris?"

"I will go home." Faris was still inspecting the toe of her scuffed shoe. "And plant oats."

"Wild oats?"

Something in the proctor's tone brought Faris's head up swiftly. "All kinds. The one thing I could do here, I can do just as well at home in Galazon—get older."

The proctor laughed at Faris.

"I won't stay here, no matter what he's paid you to accept me."

"It seems he ought to have paid you." The proctor sobered slightly.

"He's tried," spat Faris.

The proctor made no effort to conceal her amusement. "Menary shall have the opening, what do you say to that?"

Faris's eyes widened as her thoughts raced. If Gavren could be persuaded to believe in her failure without consulting the proctors himself, she could leave in the morning. She could be home before the turn of the year. She looked from the proctor to Menary, who was triumphant, then to Odile, whose knotted fingers were the only sign of her distress.

"Will you take my advice about Odile?" she asked the proctor. "Even scrubbing floors is better than walking home barefoot in the winter. If you let her go, they'll only keep her home for lambing season, or some other chore. Let her have the next vacancy."

"What do you say to that advice, Odile?" asked the proctor.

Odile unclasped her hands and took a step closer to the marquetry table. "A fine idea. But what matters is what you say. Is Faris accepted?"

The proctor sniffed again. "Despite her uncle's best efforts, she is."

"Wait—" Faris looked from Odile to the proctor and back. "*I'm* accepted? What about you?"

"What about *me*?" Menary gave Faris a look of pure dislike.

"Oh, fear not," said the proctor. "You're both accepted. Along with the students who came on time. Allow me to introduce you again to Odile Passerieux. She is in her third year here."

"I'm glad that's settled," said Menary.

Faris fixed Odile with a cold stare and spaced her words deliberately. "Oh, please. Choose me."

"Contemptible, isn't it?" Odile replied affably. "I did walk here though, two years ago."

"Did they make you scrub floors?"

"They made me wear shoes." She pulled the ribbon from her hair, shook her head and let her black hair go free around her shoulders. "I humored them. You can humor them too."

"Do they make you relive your dramatic past for every applicant?"

Odile shook her head. "I volunteered. Your uncle's efforts to assure your admission made you sound fairly odious. And then your arrival confirmed the impression—your grace."

"I thought that might rankle."

"It made you seem like an ass."

Menary looked bored.

Faris said darkly, "My uncle is going to be very pleased about this."

"He should be," said the proctor. "He's rid himself of a minor nuisance for three years."

"If he gets a major nuisance back, will he still be pleased?" Odile asked.

"I wonder." Faris turned to the proctor. "I'd like to send word to my traveling companions. I don't have much baggage but I need to collect it from them before they return to Galazon."

"Your bodyguards will be notified," said the proctor. "They can communicate the news to your uncle for us. Perhaps they can also convey your uncle's letter of credit safely back to Galazon."

"Oh, the bribe—" Faris shook her head. "Don't do that."

The proctor's brows lifted. "Aren't they trustworthy?"

"Gavren and Reed are entirely trustworthy. My uncle isn't. You'd better keep the money."

"Hardly," exclaimed the proctor. "Greenlaw College would be perceived as having taken a bribe."

Faris smiled bitterly. "The damage is done. You've accepted me. No one will think for an instant that I got in on merit alone. This way, when my uncle is late paying school fees, Greenlaw needn't be inconvenienced."

"We could hold it in escrow, I suppose." The proctor looked amused. "Merely a formality, of course."

"Of course." It was a small thing, an inconvenience Brinker might not even notice, but it cheered Faris.

"Your escort will be notified and your baggage brought here at once. Menary, we have made arrangements for you, as well. In the meantime, Odile, will you show them both to their quarters?"

"Certainly. If we hurry, we will make it to the dining hall in time for dinner. It's the only meal of the day worth eating."

By the time Odile gave them a cursory tour of the college and showed them their places in the dormitory, Faris's single trunk had been delivered, along with a message that Gavren and Reed were on their way back to Galazon. Menary left them at the earliest opportunity, ostensibly to supervise the arrival of her luggage.

Her head spinning with long corridors and dimly lit stairs and the infinite jumble of gray stone buildings stacked nearly to the sky, Faris set off with Odile in search of the dining hall and dinner.

"Was all that playacting the exception or the rule? Do the proctors test everyone who applies for admission that way? Or am I a special case?"

Odile did not slacken her stride. "Why should you think you're special? It isn't usual to interview two applicants at a time, I admit. But you were both late and I suppose the proctors felt you and Menary were similar cases."

"What do you mean, similar?"

"You're from the same part of the world. You're from the same sort of background. Not like me. I'm as plain as a potato. At my interview, the proctor made me promise faithfully to keep my shoes on and to stay no matter how desperately homesick I feel. And that was that. I was accepted."

"Are you homesick?"

Odile smiled. "Not really. It's too flat here and they have the wrong kind of trees and not enough of them. But I'm not desperate."

Faris sighed.

Odile regarded her closely. "You aren't either, you know. There's no excuse for being homesick yet. You have far too much to do these first few weeks. After the novelty wears off, you might be on your guard. But for now, don't think about trees. Think about Greenlaw."

2

"What do you think standards are for?"

WITH ODILE'S HELP, Faris made her way into the pattern of life at Greenlaw College. She followed steep staircases and winding corridors from lesson to lesson: grammar, logic, rhetoric, natural history, natural philosophy, Latin, Greek, algebra, geometry, dance, and deportment.

The sheer amount of work would have overwhelmed her if she'd felt obliged to do any of it. But she had noticed with relish that no one seemed to care what she did or when she did it. Within the confines of Greenlaw College, she was quite free.

"No one expects anything of new students," Odile confided, over the evening meal at the end of Faris's first full day of classes. "If you turn your work in promptly, you'll be all right."

Faris refrained from mentioning that she had no intention of turning work in, promptly or otherwise. "But what if it isn't finished?"

"Turn it in anyway." Odile stirred the gray soup in her bowl and frowned at the residue on her spoon. "I hear we are to have an English cook this year. I see it must be so. Pass the bread, if you please."

Faris passed the basket of bread. "What if it isn't any good?"

Odile inspected the bread carefully. "It's from the bakery in the High Street, same as ever. Of course it's good." She selected a roll and broke it over her bowl of soup.

"Not the bread. My work."

"Oh, don't be an idiot. Of course it won't be any good. How could it be? You don't know anything." Odile gave Faris a swift and brutal summary of those in the student body she considered to be from backgrounds similar to Faris's.

Faris sheltered her thoughts behind her habitual expression of composure.

"Some of them are all right, I suppose," Odile conceded. "But most are like the Roman. She's third-year, mercifully. A Russian grand duchess, if you please. They say even her family can't bear her and I don't blame them. They also say the proctors tried to send her down during her first year but it made no impression on her. She couldn't get thrown out if she tried and she's too lazy to try. The pity of it is, she has a voice. She just can't be bothered to practice. A wasted space." Odile shook her head sadly. "I don't know why she bothers to honor us with her presence."

Odile's diatribe made Faris think again about the merits of doing nothing. If it were difficult to get expelled, it might be tempting to accept the challenge. But although it might bother her uncle a trifle to have her sent down, Faris knew it wouldn't inconvenience him for long. The world was full of finishing schools. He'd find one that would take her, no matter what crime she contrived to try the patience of the proctors.

But to Faris, failure at Greenlaw would be dishonor, whether she was sent home in disgrace or—far worse—kept on condescendingly, as a wasted space. It would be good to be home in Galazon, true. But it would be better to come home a witch of Greenlaw.

"Do you think I'll be able to catch up with the other students?"

"You are at a disadvantage, arriving so late in the term. What possessed your uncle? Anyone would think he wanted you to fail."

"Harvest was late this year. School fees don't just materialize out of thin air, you know."

"I know. Oh, I know." Odile nodded sagely. "It's not impossible to catch up, if you stay out of trouble. Do your reading. Leave the other students alone, particularly second-years. They've been here long enough to know how to get into trouble, and they still have the energy to bother."

What Faris liked best about Greenlaw was that no one paid her the least attention. She took Odile's advice about keeping to herself. Also on Odile's recommendation, Faris cut classes judiciously and used the free time to make up her work as it was called in and graded. The first lecture of the day was the only event that required attendance, the rest were subject to the students' discretion. There was far too much work assigned in each class to make attendance at all of them possible.

Her fellow students at first had given Faris the impression of high intelligence and strange intensity. Even slight familiarity taught her that this impression was, if not entirely mistaken, sadly incomplete. In fact, her fellow students were simply exhausted. Fatigue took strange forms.

One day in the dining hall, Faris sat across the table from a first-year student who stared blankly at the single artichoke on the plate before her.

"That looks good," said Faris. The artichokes had vanished before she'd arrived and she cherished a faint hope that her classmate disliked them, perhaps enough to barter for it.

"Extremely good," agreed the first-year, dashing Faris's hopes. Wearily, she added, "if only I could remember how to eat one."

Faris tried to follow another piece of Odile's advice and ignore the lack of proper trees in Greenlaw. She found it hard. Though the milder climate was pleasing, she could never quite accustom herself to the utter lack of severe weather. She found herself bracing for what could not come—no blizzards ever visited Greenlaw. Even so much as a hail storm was rare. It was like waiting for a stern lecture that never came.

The gardens of Greenlaw were a source of wonder to Faris. Some were mathematical in the precise arrangement of herb and simple, some were loose and profuse with merely attractive flowers and shrubs, some were noble in proportion and venerable for antiquity, all held some unfamiliar plant. Anything that did not grow wild in Galazon struck Faris as foreign and probably unnecessary, but since her own presence at Greenlaw was certainly foreign and very likely unnecessary, she tried to be tolerant.

The best place at Greenlaw, in Faris's opinion, was the Dean's garden, named for its location between the walls of the college and the Dean's residence. The oaks which shaded the Deanery windows and overhung the college wall reminded Faris of Galazon. She stopped there often, sometimes just for a moment between classes. If she closed her eyes and listened to the wind in the branches, the rustle of dry leaves remedied her homesickness.

Much of her free time was spent in pursuit of news of Galazon. There was very little, though reports from Aravill appeared in the press occasionally. She grew adept at picking out an Aravis dateline as she scanned *Le Monde*, *Figaro*, and the *International Herald Tribune* in the library. The *London Times* was her steadiest source of information.

The British ambassador to Aravill led a busy life, attending a wide variety of social functions to commemorate this or that event. Perhaps the widower King Julian of Aravill, who had attained his father's throne after fifty leisured years, aspired to a marriage with one of English Edward's profusion of eligible daughters or nieces.

Poor bride, if he succeeded in flattering the English enough to consent. He brought two eligible daughters of his own to the match. Menary was one of them: The *Almanach d'Ostrogotha* had given Faris Menary's precise pedigree. No wonder Menary's faith in the power vested in the family Paganell had been so complete. Faris could find it in her heart to pity any theoretical stepmother of hers, however utterly starched with nobility.

The pace of the class lectures proceeded without interference from the students. The instructors at Greenlaw seemed to speak for their own entertainment, without regard to how many or how few came to listen. Such indifference was soothing. When she was able to spare the time to attend class, she sat at the back of the room and let the sound of learned voices lull her. This pleasant pastime was possible in every class save dance and deportment. In dance she had enough technique to go ignored by the instructor.

The deportment lessons were not difficult in a muscular sense. Yet Faris found them strenuous. Nothing was more certain than that she would be reprimanded.

Though she had been drilled in the arts of courtesy for as long as she could remember, her knowledge did not suffice. Any other student, Faris felt, might curl fingers into fists and Dame Brachet would but murmur reprovingly and glide on. But Faris's shortcomings brought Dame Brachet to her side to stay, to hold her errors up before the class, to lecture at length on her elbow, her chin, the hang of her pointed sleeves.

"Point your toe," Dame Brachet would say to the class, and every student tried. Then Dame Brachet would glide slowly along the rows of earnest girls in their rumpled black poplin robes.

"Remember, Eve-Marie, you are a pearl necklace. Relax

your hands, Jane. No, don't curl your fingers. Just relax them. Now remember, your elbows are heavy. Don't let them stick out. They ought to drop down. Not like that, Faris."

Faris was mistress of her facial expression but not of her posture. She could stand before the class for an afternoon at a stretch without altering her mask of composure. But every criticism made her more conscious of her flaws, until self-awareness blossomed into genuine clumsiness, and by the end of the class she would find her hands were shaking.

"Shoulders back, Faris," Dame Brachet said one day. "Why are you doing that?"

"Doing what, Dame Brachet?" Faris murmured through stiff lips. By some miracle, her tone was civil.

"Doing that with your chin." Dame Brachet seized Faris's chin in cold fingers and thrust it into the proper position. "You must learn to learn, Faris. If you apply yourself, you will find it comes in time. Some day you will delight in the proper deportment of every bone in your body. In the meantime, take this opportunity to earn that delight with the work of learning."

Faris put her chin out and set her mouth in a hard line.

Dame Brachet lifted her hand to push Faris's chin back into position.

Faris moved her head aside. Very distinctly, she said, "Deportment is a sterile discipline. Habit built on superstition."

"Criticize it if you please. You are still no good at it."

"There's nothing to be good at. It's just an arbitrary set of standards. Why should I waste time learning to point my toes in a way that went out of fashion three hundred years ago? Why shouldn't I set my own fashions?"

"You must form your own fashions in a way which demonstrates that you flout the standards from knowledge, not from ignorance," replied Dame Brachet. "When you leave Greenlaw College, you may or may not be able to practice magic. That is a matter of talent and skill. But you will certainly be a witch of Greenlaw, and that station in the world carries expectations with it. You will be expected to speak with those of high degree and to speak fair to high and low. Your manner will be as vital as your matter, and in some sad cases, your matter will not amount to much. So you had better learn a manner to make up for your other shortcomings."

From the first words, Faris followed this speech with eyes narrowed. "But I may flout the standards?"

"Of course," said Dame Brachet, with some asperity. "What do you think standards are for? Now drop your elbows and tuck your chin. Very good, Faris. Now point your toe."

From that day, Faris's hands shook no more.

The only instruction given in magic took place at the mandatory lecture each morning. This series, delivered by the Dean herself, was known simply as "The Structure of the World." It was theoretical in the extreme, but it was all that Greenlaw offered. There was no practice allowed. Ever.

Faris listened attentively to the Dean's instruction and attempted to sketch the armillary spheres used to model the relation of the world to the celestial order. She recorded the sources the Dean cited in her arguments, pursued them through the stacks of the library: Ptolemy, Cicero, Lucan, and the rest.

Faris was not in the hunt for scholarship, but for details of doctrine that might prove useful to her among the credulous. By the time the term ended at Whitsuntide, she had a good grasp of the Dean's "Structure."

It puzzled Faris, at first, that the students were neither encouraged to study magic outside the Structure lectures nor permitted to practice it at any time. She decided that the rule was meant to prevent students from discovering there was no magic at Greenlaw to learn. Every student knew that whether or not magic existed within the gates at Greenlaw, it was exceedingly rare outside.

The Dean explained that this was because the rocky promontory of Greenlaw was warded in such a way that magic was easier to perform within its bounds than without it.

Given the dearth of magic among the students, Faris felt the Dean's words owed much to the tale of the Emperor and his new clothes. Apparently, all it took to learn magic at Greenlaw College was a willingness to claim one knew it when one left.

In theory, there was the world, the lowest, most mundane sphere in the model. Divided into overlapping hemispheres, north, south, east, and west, the world was theoretically protected by four wardens, whose theoretical wardships enfolded one another.

The warden of the south watched over her dominion almost unhindered by the wardens of the east and west. Most powerful, but most remote, ruling the ocean-guarded south, she never impinged on the warden of the north. The warden of the east was visited only by the wardens of south and north. He never touched on the wardency of the west. Of the wardens of the north and west, the Dean did not speak.

From her reading, Faris concocted theories of her own. The warden of the north, she calculated, might communicate with the wardens of the east and west but not the south. The warden of the west could call on the wardens of the north and south but not the east.

For the rest of the model, the Dean explained, the world lay at the heart of nested celestial spheres. The highest degree of magic in the world was lower by far than the lowest of that in the next sphere of the model. But nothing linked the spheres. There was no passage from one to the next in life. Within the precincts of the world, the wardens held the mundane sphere in balance.

Without the wardens, the mundane sphere would soon distort. Once disfigured, it would upset the balance of the other spheres.

Try as she would, Faris could not keep from thinking of the spheres as soap bubbles, floating one within another. She gathered that if there were no wardens to rectify the balance, the entire model would vanish, to go wherever soap bubbles go, just about as suddenly. Since the world showed no signs of vanishing, Faris presumed this was more of the Emperor's wardrobe.

The lectures ended, without climax or conclusion, when classes did, at Whitsuntide. Those students who were qualified took their comprehensives. All students left at the end of term. Those who passed their comprehensive examinations were entitled to call themselves scholars of Greenlaw, and to be referred to as witches behind their backs. Those who didn't pass, such as the Roman, withdrew and the crooked passages of Greenlaw College saw no more of them.

Those first- and second-year students who were not yet qualified to attempt the comprehensives went home for the summer and early autumn. Not until Michaelmas would they return, and not until they were at their studies for a fortnight would the first of the first-year students appear.

Her uncle had made it clear to Faris that she was not to return home to Galazon for the long vacation. Had she the means, she might have traveled elsewhere, but lacking funds, Faris stayed at Greenlaw, where her keep was paid.

As the classrooms closed and the dormitories emptied, Faris found she had the college nearly to herself. Even Odile was gone, permanently. She had passed her comprehensives, slept off the resulting exhaustion, packed her belongings, said her farewells, and set off for Sarlat, a fully-fledged witch of Greenlaw.

Faris did not notice much difference in her days after the term gave way to the long vacation. She had always spent more time in the library than in company, and the library's hours were unchanged by the season. She read, at first with an eye toward her classes, soon for pleasure alone. She took her meals in the dining hall, same as ever, but she was one of half a dozen boarders, instead of one of a hundred. What conversation there was at the table was stiff and civil.

To her surprise, Faris found she missed the grumbles, shrieks, and giggles of the regular term. She began to sleep late in the mornings and the long afternoons passed more quickly out of doors than in the library. She ventured out of the confines of the college and explored the steep streets of Greenlaw village. Wound around the base of Greenlaw like ribbons, the streets led to the seawall that circled and protected the place. At the foot of the promontory lay the great gate. Beyond that, the encircling rocks and sand flats ringed the seawall.

One hot afternoon, Faris was sitting on the rocks at the base of the north wall. Tempted by low tide, she kilted up her skirts, took off her shoes and stockings, and went for a walk along the cool gray sands. Fine bubbles broke on the surface as every step fizzed against her bare soles like champagne. Ahead she spied a larger bubble, where something lived beneath the sand. A clam, a winkle? She bent double to peer more closely.

"Come back. Come away from there."

Faris frowned over her shoulder to see who addressed her.

On the rock where she'd left her shoes and stockings stood a blond man with a broad, rosy face. He was dressed in badly cut black, very different from the light and elegant flannels of the usual summer visitor. He frowned back at her and called, "I think you'd better return at once."

Faris straightened so that she could look down her nose at him. "Who are you?" The look had no effect.

"These sands aren't safe. You could be pulled down."

"Thank you for the warning. I won't go out any farther." In the face of his silent disapproval, she added, "You can see I'm perfectly safe."

"I can't just leave you there."

"Why not? It's no business of yours what I do."

The man opened his mouth and shut it again without speaking.

"Is it?" asked Faris, suddenly suspicious.

"Certainly not. Good day to you." He turned on his heel and walked away, as quickly as the footing on the rocks allowed.

Faris returned to the rocks as soon as he was out of sight.

Lost in thought, she brushed the sand off her feet and replaced her stockings and shoes, frowning.

The next time Dame Cassilda took the cart to Pontorson to meet the train, Faris made it her business to go along.

"It's a long drive for a hot day. I wouldn't bother if it weren't for the baggage. There will be student trunks coming on nearly every train now. And some of them come from the ends of the earth." Dame Cassilda favored Faris with a sidelong glance.

"Any trunks that arrive today will be in good time for the beginning of term," Faris observed. "Nearly two months early."

"You're not expecting a parcel yourself?"

Faris shook her head.

"You'll maybe want to see the seamstress then." Dame Cassilda eyed the ragged hem of Faris's gown. "It often happens that you young people have a growing spell when you spend the summer here. It's the air of Greenlaw, the fresh sea air. You'll be wanting some alterations done."

Faris smoothed her skirt. "No, I have no business in Pontorson. I'm just along for the change of scene. Do you mind?"

"Glad of the company. I don't blame you for getting fed up with Greenlaw. If it wasn't for the work, we'd all go round the bend in a week."

Once at the station, Dame Cassilda kept a wary eye on Faris, but her charge contented herself with examining the people on the platform. After a brief wait, the train pulled into the station and halted in a magnificent billow of steam.

Faris craned her neck as passengers left the train to mingle with onlookers at the station. Departing travelers climbed aboard. When the last parcel was unloaded, the train lurched and drew away. After the porters had lifted the lone student trunk into the back of the cart, Dame Cassilda resumed her seat.

"You haven't even gotten down from the cart. Don't you wish to explore Pontorson now that you're here?"

"No, that won't be necessary," said Faris. "Tell me, do you know that man standing beside the ticket kiosk?"

Dame Cassilda inspected the man Faris referred to. He stood barely an arm's length from the ticket grille, his back against a poster-covered wall. Despite his hat, his blond hair was plain to see. It was hard to judge his features, for he was reading an illustrated paper with great concentration. His dark clothing was ill tailored. "No, why?"

"I've seen him somewhere. Or perhaps he only resembles someone I met once."

"A chance likeness can often be quite startling." Dame Cassilda took up the lines. At her signal the Greenlaw team set off at the amble which would eventually bring them back to the college.

As they left the station, Faris glanced back, frowning. "Quite startling."

Faris spied the blond man again at the very end of summer. It was a cool clear day, with little white brush strokes of cloud so thin and fine they let the blue sky show plainly behind.

Faris was at the vegetable market at the foot of the high street, trying to distract herself by looking at leeks and cabbages. She was homesick for Galazon, where such wide blue windy days brought in just such a harvest, along with a dozen other useful sorts of produce. When she saw the man, she turned to the owner of the leeks, a rangy woman with her black hair tucked up beneath a red scarf.

"Do you know who that is?" Faris asked. "The yellow-haired man so absorbed by that basket of turnips? Have you seen him before?"

"I have," said the leek-seller. "He rents a room from my godmother and takes his meals there. He's foreign."

"Do you know his name?" Faris knew that anyone not born in Greenlaw and living there anyway was considered to be foreign by the villagers. "Do you know how long he's lived here?"

"He rented his lodging a week before the new year." The

leek-seller gazed skyward for a moment. "It's just come back to me. He calls himself Tyrian. Foreign sounding name, isn't it?"

"It is." Faris gave the woman the last of her money. "Your leeks are lovely but I've no way to cook them. This is for your trouble."

"Would you like an introduction?" The leek-seller pocketed the coins. "My godmother might oblige."

"No, thank you. I don't care much for foreigners."

"Wise girl," said the leek-seller, and turned back to her vegetables.

3

At the Glass Slipper

❧ By the time second- and third-year students returned to Greenlaw, Faris was miserably homesick. Odile had written from Sarlat. Faris knew she ought to take comfort from her friend's happiness, but it seemed to make things worse.

Every sign of harvest that she saw made her think of the harvest that she was not in Galazon to see. Every small thing that did not remind her of Galazon reminded her that she was far away and years from going home. Faris grew so homesick, she stopped a returning student in the corridor for no better reason than the embroidery on her shirtwaist.

"Pardon me," said Faris. "That's Galazon white-work, isn't it? Have you come from Galazon?"

The student, a girl who would have been taller than Faris a year ago but was now an inch shorter, glanced down at the fine embroidery, snow white on the snow white of her blouse. "You have excellent vision," she said politely. She regarded Faris a moment, her clear gray eyes curious. "I've never been to Galazon. This was a gift."

"Oh," said Faris.

Something in the flatness of her tone melted the student's reserve slightly. "Have you been to Galazon?"

Faris shook her head. "I'm from Galazon. I haven't been back since I came to college a year ago." She broke off as she felt her reliable mask of composure alter. To conceal her embarrassment, she became absorbed in an examination of the toe of her shoe. One more word and her voice would betray her.

The student eyed Faris curiously. "You didn't go home for the long vacation?"

Faris shook her head.

"You'll know better next year. But think of it this way—you're lucky you have somewhere to go that's worth being homesick for. Not everyone has a home better than Greenlaw. Hardly anyone, I should say."

Something in her clipped words made Faris look closely at the girl. "Do you?"

"I suppose I must, mustn't I? But I don't wish to live anywhere but Greenlaw. If you don't like it here, you ought to go home." With a rustle of faultlessly tailored charcoal serge, she brushed past Faris and stalked away up the corridor.

Next morning, as she left Hall after breakfast, Faris felt a hand touch her sleeve. She looked around to find the gray-eyed student, immaculate in crisp academicals, black over a blue frock, her silky brown hair pinned up with precision in a neat Psyche knot.

"Yes?"

"I must apologize," said the student. "I'm terribly sorry for what I said yesterday. My only excuse is that I had no idea who you are. I didn't know until just now, when I asked the Pagan. I am sorry."

Faris frowned. "What are you talking about?"

The student looked perplexed, then chagrined. "I thought I'd dropped the brick of the century. Has the Pagan misled me? Or are you just being chivalrous and pretending I didn't drop it at all?"

"Who's the Pagan?"

"Oh, dear. Look here, I can't explain now. I'm already late, of course, and my tutor will slay me if I'm any later. You'll have to come to tea. I promise I'll explain everything. Are you free at four o'clock?"

"I think so," Faris replied, warily.

"Good. Number five study. Don't be late." She touched Faris's sleeve again and hurried away, black poplin billowing behind her.

Faris watched her go, wide-eyed.

At the appointed time, Faris made her way to the door of number five study. She was puzzled and inclined to misgiving. Only third-year students, and not all of them, had study privileges.

Odile had scorned study privileges as clubby, cliquish, partisan, and distracting. She had often told Faris that third-year students were a moody lot, and first-year students ought to steer clear of them as a rule, lest they be distracted into wasting time before their required courses were complete. But of course, Odile had her moody moments, too.

Faris knocked. Her hostess answered the door so promptly she might have been lurking in wait on the other side. Faris followed her into the study, a high-ceilinged room with a fireplace, a mullioned window, and a view of the sea. The room was furnished only with a table and four chairs. On the table, the tea service was solid silver and the china was old and fine.

Faris stopped with her back to the door. Perplexed, her hostess turned from the tea service. "What's wrong?"

"For one thing, I'm not certain I ought to be here. I don't know who you are and I'm not at all sure that you know who I am."

Her hostess winced. "So much for my manners. I'm Jane Brailsford. We were in deportment together last year. I have a very forgettable face."

Faris was silent for a moment. The name was familiar, though the face wasn't. Jane Brailsford was English, the daughter of a determinedly respectable family. Finally, Faris said, "My name is Faris Nallaneen."

"I know. The Pagan told me—Menary Paganell. I ought to have recognized you from class but I'm afraid my memory for faces is perfectly shocking. I was always worrying about pearl necklaces, too. Oh, dear. It was dreadful of me to say you should go home, but I had no notion of your circumstances. You must believe me."

Faris stiffened. "I beg your pardon? What circumstances are you referring to?"

"Menary told me you'd been sent here because you couldn't—er, because you might, ah, press your claim to the duchy." Jane raised her brows. "My, what good posture you have when you bristle. I'm sure Dame Brachet would be pleased to see it."

"What else did Menary Paganell tell you?"

Jane frowned. "Is it possible that Menary has taken liberties with the truth? All too likely, I expect."

"What else?"

"You'll forgive me for repeating it? She told me you are the duchess of Galazon's natural daughter by a sea captain, and that you were exiled to Greenlaw for the good of the duchy and for the improvement of your character." Jane looked apologetic. "If it is any consolation, I didn't believe the part about the sea captain. Menary seems to have a fondness for all things nautical."

Faris stared at Jane. Jane sustained her angry gaze, her eyes level and calm.

"I have two questions," Faris said at last. "One for you and one for Menary Paganell. Before I ask her why she slandered me, tell me why you asked her who I was. I scarcely know her."

"You come from Galazon. Galazon is in Aravill. Menary never ceases boasting about her family back in Aravill. She's the only student I know from that end of the world. So I asked her."

Her answer provoked another wordless stare from Faris. Jane returned it courteously.

"If it matters," said Faris finally, her tone icily polite, "Galazon is an independent principality. Aravill claims suzerainty but they are wrong to do so. My mother was the duchess of Galazon. Until I reach my majority, my uncle rules the duchy. To honor my mother's last wish, he claims, but really because we do not agree, he has sent me here to age, like cheese—" Faris paused to steady her voice. "In two years, I shall return to Galazon and turn him out. Perhaps after that I shall travel to Aravill, even attain the heights of Aravis itself, and insult Menary Paganell as she has insulted me." Faris whirled and threw the study door open.

Jane caught at Faris's poplin sleeve. "Are you going to find Menary now? It's tea time."

Faris froze, staring at Jane's hand as though it were made of raw liver. "Of course."

Jane's voice held only calm interest. "What will you do when you find her?"

Faris met her eyes. "I don't know. Deliver the same lecture to her, I suppose."

"Dry work. I'd hate to miss the spectacle but I'm perishing for my tea. Just sit with me for a moment while I drink a cup and then let me come along to watch you murder Menary." She closed the study door and led Faris back to the table. "Though of course, we'll have to queue up for the privilege. She does love to do an ill turn when she sees the chance."

"Do you speak so highly of all your friends?" asked Faris, coldly.

"Menary doesn't have any friends. She doesn't want any. She's more interested in servitors. I merely asked her a few questions. And don't snipe at me for my shocking geography," Jane added. "If it isn't the Empire, it's all the same to me: Galazon, Aravill, Graustark, or Ruritania. You really can't expect me to keep all those little countries straight. I'm not ignorant, just English. Milk? Sugar?"

"Can you tell Wales from Finland?"

"Don't sulk, it's not becoming. The tea's a bit stewed, I'm afraid, but that's your fault for distracting me. The milk may render it palatable. Now, tell me about this wicked uncle of yours."

Faris glared at Jane but accepted the cup and saucer Jane offered. "If you were in my place, would you sit here and drink your tea?"

"In your place, I would challenge Menary to pistols at dawn."

"May I call on you if I should need a second?"

Jane inclined her head graciously. "I am at your service. Now sit down. I have a stem ginger cake from Fortnum's."

"Very well. But I won't tell you about my wicked uncle. You're going to tell me what you meant yesterday, when you said you didn't want to live anywhere but Greenlaw. Ever?"

"Oh, dear. I talk too much, don't I?"

"Not yet," said Faris, and took her place at the table.

By the time the last morsel of cake was gone, Jane had given Faris two pots of tea and a fair notion of her circumstances. She had several uncles, none of them wicked by Faris's standards, a father, and three brothers with no higher ambition than to shoot as much game as possible as frequently as they could. She also had a mother, whose goal was to marry her children to the most chinless aristocrats available.

"I wanted to go up to Oxford," Jane explained, "but of course Father and Mother think only bluestockings go to Shrewsbury, so that could never be."

"What persuaded them to send you to Greenlaw, then?"

"My cousin Henry attended Glasscastle. Greenlaw and Glasscastle are nothing more than a matched pair of ridiculously expensive finishing schools, as far as my parents are concerned. If Glasscastle was unexceptional for Henry, Greenlaw was unexceptional for me. Henry came out of Glasscastle so highly finished, no one notices that he never uses any magic. No one knows whether he's capable of it or not. Not even Henry, I suspect," Jane added. "I wasn't enchanted with the idea of a French finishing school, but when Papa suggested it I thought three years of Greenlaw might be worth it, if only to give Mama more time to find me a husband with a chin. So here I am."

"Here you are, and you don't want to go back again."

Jane shook her head. "The first day I saw Greenlaw was the first day I ever truly saw anything. The sun shines differently here. Even the tides are different, lower and higher than anywhere else. It was as though I'd come home to my own country, in a place I'd never visited before. These months since Whitsuntide were torture. Now that I'm back, I never want to leave."

"But this is your last year. What will you do next Whitsuntide?"

Jane inspected the depths of her tea cup. "Travel, perhaps. But even if I go back to Brailsford, it won't be the same. From the first time I stepped into the great hall to see the proctor, Greenlaw has been home to me."

"If the Dean asked you, would you stay and teach? Then you'd be able to live here as long as you liked."

"If they asked me, I'd accept. My family would consider it eccentric but I don't think they'd disinherit me."

"What subject would you teach?"

Jane put her cup down. "I'd tutor if I could. What interest is there in lecturing? That's just window dressing for the finishing school."

Faris looked surprised. "Fearsome window dressing. Is tutoring so different? I don't start with Dame Villette until tomorrow."

"Don't you know? Hasn't anyone told you? Don't you ever gossip?"

"My friend Odile graduated last term. She told me to think carefully about what topic to choose for my thesis and to hope for a tolerant tutor."

"Oh, the slyboots. As though there's any topic that doesn't lead to magic eventually. That's what you're tutored in, Faris. Choose what thesis you like, it's magic you study. After all, this is Greenlaw, not Shrewsbury."

The following day, as Menary Paganell left her tutor's study, Faris Nallaneen eased out of the next doorway and fell into step beside her.

"On your way back to the dormitory? That's the way I'm going. I'll walk with you."

"I'm going to the library." Menary did not waste a glance at Faris.

"I've just come from there, but I'll walk with you anyway. I was reading the *Almanach d'Ostrogotha*. Are you familiar with the *Almanach*? It's like the Structure of the World. I'm sure the Dean would love it. A place for everyone and everyone in her place."

Menary uttered a wordless exclamation of scorn and walked on.

"Perhaps you ought to refresh your memory before you discuss my family again. Or should I say our family? My grandmother married your grandmother's uncle. My father's mother, I mean. He was no sea captain. I don't know how you could make a mistake about that, unless you were misled by the fact that he died at sea."

Menary walked faster. Faris matched her stride.

"It's confusing to foreigners, all these little duchies and kingdoms and protectorates. The names are longer than the census rolls. I think Jane Brailsford finds it quaint."

Menary stopped abruptly and sneered up at Faris. "What interest does Jane Brailsford take in you?"

"What interest do you take in me? Why confuse someone about our kinship? I'd be distressed if it happened again."

For the first time, Menary looked at Faris as though she were perfectly visible to the naked eye. "Say I distress you. What of it?"

"Distress me, and prepare to hear the whole history of our families discussed from one end of Greenlaw to the other.

I will provide genealogical charts, if necessary. It will be boring and inconvenient, but it ought to clarify our kinship."

"There is no kinship."

"No? Let us repair to the library. I will show you the *Almanach d'Ostrogotha*. I even know the page number."

"Are you trying to threaten me? You'll regret it."

"Do you find the truth a threat?" countered Faris.

Menary walked away without answering, golden head held high. Warily, Faris watched her go.

On her first visit to her tutor's rooms, Faris was startled to discover Dame Villette was the woman with tired eyes she had met on her first day at Greenlaw.

"I thought you were a proctor," Faris blurted.

Dame Villette looked up from the stack of papers spread across the desk before her. "I am. Once I was merely a tutor, but I found that didn't afford me scope to discipline callow youth. So I became a proctor, too."

"What will you tutor me in? Will you teach me magic? Or will you just hint about it, as the Dean does?"

Dame Villette stifled a sigh. "What subject have you chosen?"

"Does it matter? I've been told all subjects lead to magic in the end."

"Such candor. Such insouciance. I'll try to match you. Some things can't be taught. Magic is one such. You may or may not learn it. That is entirely up to you. Greenlaw is warded to make magic likelier here than in the world outside. We have one or two traditions which may make learning more likely, too. But just in case no one has told you, or just in case you weren't listening when they did, no student performs magic at Greenlaw. To do so is grounds for expulsion. Do you understand that?"

"No. How can Greenlaw claim to produce scholars of magic when magic is forbidden here?"

"Magic is not forbidden here. But in order to ward Greenlaw, the scholars here have been given charge of the use of magic within our precincts. If we wish to live exempt from the natural laws balanced by the wardens of the world, we must maintain the balance within our walls. Thus, students are forbidden to practice magic."

"If I were studying medicine instead of magic, I would be given some practical instruction in medicine."

Dame Villette put her palms together and exhaled slowly. "If you were to study law instead of magic, you would not be permitted to practice until the authorities were satisfied that you were qualified to do so. Perhaps once you qualified, you might still choose not to practice."

"If I were studying law, I would study law. Not deportment, not geometry—law."

Dame Villette put both hands flat on the stack of papers before her. "If you studied law, you might master what you studied. Your work from last year shows little sign of such mastery. Many students show sufficient expertise at this stage of their studies that they attend only the early lecture and devote the rest of their time to work with their tutor."

Faris looked bemused. "Oh? Only the backward attend class after the first year? Yet Odile was worse than I at Greek. And Jane Brailsford took deportment with me. Or is it as Odile said, we are assigned work until we have no time to spare to attend classes?"

Dame Villette widened her eyes very slightly. "Shall we put that theory to the test? Take back this paper you wrote on the *Georgics* last term. Think through your points again. Find sources to support you. Let me see it when you've finished."

Faris accepted the paper Dame Villette handed her. It was one she had written for her Latin class, a little dog-eared at the corners and much marked in blue pencil. "When should I turn it in?"

Dame Villette looked mildly surprised. "When you're finished."

Virgil occupied Faris through the month of October. By that time, most of the first-year students were settled in at Greenlaw, oblivious to the tutoring the more advanced students received in addition to the lectures. When the *Georgics* paper was turned in, Faris began to discover that there was more to life at Greenlaw than studying and sleeping and complaining about the food. And there was more to being Jane Brailsford's friend, she learned, than eating ginger cake and drinking poisonously strong tea.

Jane Brailsford's acquaintance was wide, her friends drawn from every year. There was wide-eyed Gunhild, a newly arrived student homesick for the village on the Raftsund that she had left for the first time in her life. There was calm Eve-Marie, who would probably take her comprehensives with record high marks, and even more probably stay to lecture at Greenlaw in years to come. And there were Charlotte and Nathalie, second-year students who spent nearly as much time in number five as Jane did. Charlotte, Faris recognized. She had once been so tired she'd forgotten how to eat artichokes.

Faris learned that to be Jane's friend was to be invited into the lair called number five study to criticize three-volume novels of romance and adventure with as much gravity as if they were Latin texts. To be a friend to Jane and Jane's friends meant sharing the contents of the parcels they received from indulgent relations, and arguing over the best way to roast apples and chestnuts over the study fire. Rather to her own surprise, Faris took to this behavior. Rather to her own amazement, Faris found that Jane's friends took to her.

Too busy to be homesick, Faris found that diversion and scholarship sorted well together. There was nothing so entertaining as the amusements that beckoned when she had something extremely pressing to do in the way of scholarship.

If she had done all her work as soon as it was assigned, she would have been free to enjoy the roasted chestnuts, the melodramatic novels, and the part-singing with a clear conscience. Yet, straightaway, the chief charm of their simple amusements would have vanished, for there was nothing forbidden in them, save that they required time, and time was always at a premium in their studies.

Thus scholarship improved diversion at Greenlaw, but Faris found that the reverse was also true.

Greenlaw, grave and scholarly, was filled with music. Greenlaw had stored up years of music from the students who had gone before, and it had music for every day in the college calendar. There were Greek hymns sung on Lantern Night, and Latin aubades for May Day Morning. There were madrigals and part-songs, rounds and catches. There was the occasional music of the world outside, imported by students who had returned from their holidays with a crank gramophone or a sheaf of sheet music. But the greatest part of the music at Greenlaw came through the voices of students like Jane and her friends, and it was as diverse as the students themselves.

As a student at Greenlaw, Faris learned melody and harmony, found occasional tunes that suited her limited voice, spent the rest of her time in descants that let her sing without damaging the music. "Not the music of the spheres," Jane observed, after a Lantern Night spent singing the usual Greek hymns and a Norwegian drinking song Gunhild had just taught them all, "but perhaps the music of the hemispheres."

Even after Virgil ceased to plague her every waking moment, Faris spent many a late night over Latin texts. One night in the library's reading room, her abstracted thoughts upon the structure of the world were broken by the sound of voices calling her name.

From the little topiary garden outside the library, merry voices called her until she unlatched the nearest window and swung it wide. The November night air fluttered the pages of her open books and every student in the reading room stared at her reproachfully.

Faris ignored the cold breeze and the cold looks and leaned out into the darkness. The light from the library's green-shaded lamps reached far enough to show her four upturned faces, hardly more than pale masks in the gloom, but she recognized Jane, Eve-Marie, Nathalie, and Charlotte.

It was not merely their voices she recognized, nor their relative heights, nor the attitudes they struck, with their bat-sleeved academic gowns rustling around them. It was their immense gaiety that betrayed them, their blithe confidence that hailing her from her books at just this particular moment was the best and most hilarious thing they had yet contrived to do.

From the geometrically neat garden below, four voices rose in wobbly harmony:

The moon's my constant mistress,
And the lovely owl my marrow;
The flaming drake, and the night-crow make
Me music to my sorrow.

"*The isle is full of noises,*" called Faris, trying not to laugh.

Behind her in the reading room, throats were cleared, papers were shuffled, books were slammed on desks. A cross voice called, "Some of us are trying to study."

The harmony struggled on, half submerged at times by stifled hilarity.

With a host of furious fancies,
Whereof I am commander:
With a burning spear, and a horse of air,
To the wilderness I wander.

"Some of us want to study, not freeze to death," the cross voice called again. "Close the window!"

Faris marveled for a moment at what kind of life these strict scholars must have led to make them so indifferent to that thread of song from the garden. She had never dreamed college would hold anything half so dear to her. Perhaps it was different when the song was for someone else.

"*With a knight of ghosts and shadows,*" Faris sang, or tried to sing, as she climbed from her chair to the sill. "*I summoned am to tourney: Ten leagues beyond the wide world's end; Methinks it is no journey.*"

She swung out and dropped feet-first into the garden, narrowly missing the topiary.

Jane said, "Just yesterday, you told me you didn't understand conic sections, yet here we find you, trying to make yourself into one." She and Charlotte picked Faris up and brushed the gravel off her skirts. Eve-Marie made sure the topiary was not damaged.

Nathalie called up to the reading room, *"Tee hee, quod she, and clapt the window to."*

Before she finished speaking, the window was slammed shut. For a moment, the five of them looked up in silence. The lights of the reading room shone forth undimmed.

"Thank you," Eve-Marie called.

Then Nathalie took up the song again, and as they left the garden, the rest joined in:

> *I know more than Apollo;*
> *For oft, when he lies sleeping,*
> *I behold the stars*
> *at mortal wars,*
> *And the rounded welkin weeping.*

Autumn at Greenlaw offered its share of discomforts. Bathwater, never entirely warm, chilled with amazing rapidity. Clothing sent to the college laundry returned clean but damp and had to be dried before the hearth, garment by clammy garment. Reading lists grew long, tempers grew short. Competition for space at the study fireside grew keen.

One night in number five study, Faris was supposed to be reading *Metamorphoses*, but in fact was merely nursing a cold and staring absently into the fire. Charlotte was at the table, working on an ink-and-wash illustration for the college's occasional literary magazine, *The Green Book*, while Jane attempted to dry her favorite black woolen stockings on a toasting fork over the fire.

"I think someone sold Menary a bill of goods," Jane said.

"This coal is supposed to burn different colors, like driftwood. But it looks like common or garden coal to me."

"What does the Pagan know about coal?" Charlotte inquired lazily.

"Nothing, apparently. She bought a scuttleful of this stuff at the market. I happened to walk back with her and she gave me a few pieces. So we've both been hoaxed."

"As long as it burns."

Faris blinked sleepily at the blaze. It had colors enough to please her, not just scarlet and gold but sometimes a pale green too, like a touch of the northern lights.

"Give it a poke, will you? I've just found the perfect spot and I don't want to move the fork."

At the heart of the fire, the coals snapped and shifted. A spark leaped and caught in Jane's lace cuff. Jane dropped the toasting fork and jerked her hand back.

Hissing, the damp stockings began to burn. Acrid smoke billowed. Jane slapped at her wrist and the sparks spread to the other lace cuff. "Oh, dear."

Charlotte sprang to her feet, knocking her chair over and upsetting the ink. Faris sneezed, dropped the hearth rug over Jane's arms, and set to slapping vigorously.

After a moment, Jane pushed her away. "Stop that. You'll break both my wrists." Cautiously, she emerged from the hearth rug and examined her shirt cuffs. "Ruined."

Faris helped Jane to her feet. "You can mourn your wardrobe on the way to the infirmary."

"Oh, there's no need to trouble the infirmary." Jane held out her wrists. "Not even singed."

In astonishment, Faris seized Jane's wrist for a closer look. "No damage at all." She released Jane, eyes wide. "You *are* a witch."

"I didn't do anything. It must have been the luck of the Brailsfords."

Deftly Charlotte extracted what was left of Jane's smoldering stockings from the hearth and displayed them, neatly impaled on the toasting fork. " 'What work is here, Charmian? Is this well done?' "

Jane looked past the toasting fork and spied the ink, trickling disastrously across Charlotte's illustration, over the table, and on to the floor. "Oh, dear."

Charlotte sighed. "More ink, less wash. One less illustration."

Late one November night, Faris was in number five study reading *The Prisoner of Zenda* while Jane performed prodigies of mathematics to present to her tutor the next morning. Eve-Marie knocked at the door and Faris admitted her and Portia, a first-year student who was friendly with Gunhild. Jane looked up from her work as Eve-Marie brought Portia to the table and sat her down in Faris's chair.

"Now," said Eve-Marie, gently but firmly, "tell Jane what you told me."

"Gunhild went down to the town," said Portia obediently. "I couldn't stop her."

Jane and Faris exchanged a glance of concern.

"After curfew? Why would she do that?" asked Jane.

Helplessly, Eve-Marie lifted her hands. "She's been terribly homesick ever since she arrived . . ."

Portia interrupted, "She keeps going on and on about the scent of pine in the frosty air . . ."

"I know," said Jane. "How well I know."

"She misses the scent of aquavit, too," Portia continued. "She found a man down in the town who promised to give her a bottle of the stuff if she came herself tonight to fetch it. I caught her slipping out of the dormitory and made her tell me where she was going, but I couldn't stop her."

Jane looked harassed. "Doesn't she know one doesn't accept gifts from strangers? It simply isn't done."

"I tried to tell her," said Portia. "But where she comes from, there aren't any strangers. She laughed at me and off she went. I don't know what to do. Even if we tell the proctors, by the time we've explained, she may be in terrible trouble."

"So she came to me," Eve-Marie said, "and I came to you."

"Alarums and excursions," said Jane pensively, "and quite possibly expulsions as well. What jolly fun." She looked at Faris. "Do you find that book absorbing?"

"Young Rupert's all right," Faris replied, "but on the whole, no. Are we to go a-roving?"

"It would be slack to stay in, I think." Jane turned to Portia. "Where is Gunhild supposed to meet this man?"

"At a brasserie near the gate. It's called the Glass Slipper."

"Very well, then. To the Glass Slipper."

Mathematics discarded, Jane led Faris, Eve-Marie, and Portia out of number five study, down a crooked staircase, over a window sill, and into the night. It was cloudless, with moon enough to cast shadows.

Between the dormitory and the Cordelion Tower, as the others clambered through the window, Faris paused beside Jane and forgot anxiety for Gunhild and worry about breaking curfew in her delight with the darkness. Since she had arrived at Greenlaw, Faris had not been outside the confines of the college at night without a reliable escort. By every measure Faris had ever heard of, her companions failed to qualify as a reliable escort. She drew a deep breath, savoring the chill of the evening, the scent of the sea, and her unaccustomed freedom. When the others joined her, she followed Jane and the rest to the Dean's garden, where an oak tree provided means to cross the college wall.

Free in the dark, Faris felt her delight shape itself into a small bubble of hilarity, which lodged at the base of her throat. Oak leaves rustled in the night breeze as they passed.

The garden below belonged to one of the houses of Greenlaw town. They slipped from the garden to an alley. Silently, down twisting streets, they came at last to the brasserie nearest to the great gate of Greenlaw.

"This is the place," said Portia, shivering. "We were here

this morning to ask if they sold aquavit. This is where we met that man."

Inside, the Glass Slipper was not much different from the common room of the White Fleece. A bit smaller, a bit dirtier, it held a few wooden tables flanked with benches. On one side of the room was a spacious fireplace, where dying embers cast enough light to give the room a sullen glow. On the other was the bar, deserted. At the far end of the room stood a sailor with a dark green bottle in one hand, and in the other, Gunhild's wrist.

At the sight of her rescuers, Gunhild stopped struggling and glared at the sailor. "Now you *must* let me go."

Wide-eyed and mercifully silent, Portia stayed in the doorway as Jane and Eve-Marie advanced toward Gunhild. Faris crossed immediately to the fireplace and helped herself to the poker from the rack of tools beside the hearth. Some of her reckless delight was still with her and this did not seem an appropriate place to be delighted. Without haste, she put more wood on the fire and stirred the coals judiciously.

"Aquavit is filthy stuff, Gunhild," said Jane. "You'd best come with us."

Gunhild tossed her sheaf of golden hair angrily. "He won't let me go."

"Let her go," Eve-Marie advised.

The sailor laughed. "Cinderella's step-sisters," he observed. "I think I've got the pick of your litter right here. The two of us made a bargain, and I intend to keep it."

"Don't be absurd," said Jane. "All we need do is raise hue and cry against you. You wouldn't care for that."

"Go ahead," said the sailor. "Call my friends. I'm not greedy."

Faris left the fireplace and joined Jane, poker at her side. The small bubble of hilarity made it hard to keep her voice steady. Carefully, she said, "Let Gunhild go." The words sounded normal enough, but Faris wondered if her hilarity could possibly be the first step toward hysteria.

The sailor eyed Faris. "You're too big for a little lad like me, carrots. You'd better call my friends."

With a quick tug, Faris kilted her skirts out of her way.

"Look at that, tearing her clothes off to get at me. I'd better call my friends myself."

Faris heard her own voice as though it belonged to someone else entirely. It was perfectly level, perfectly assured. "Let her go, before I make you."

The sailor lifted the dark green bottle high. "You come any closer, you'll get to taste this."

Gunhild twisted aside. Eve-Marie and Jane stepped forward. The sailor pushed Gunhild into them and brought his bottle down hard on the edge of the table. A crash, a thick scent of caraway and raw spirit, and the broken neck of the bottle was steady in his hand. Portia gave a squeak of alarm.

The sailor smiled. "Come on, then, sweetheart. Let's have it."

Faris was already on guard. Before he stepped toward her, Faris lunged. The tip of the poker caught him on the breast bone with a noise like thumping a melon. The sailor staggered but slipped aside. Glass glinted as he slashed. Faris parried with a blow that snapped bone. The sailor dropped the bottle and fell to his knees, cursing.

Faris felt Jane's hand on her sleeve, but her voice seemed to come from far away. "Let's go. Hurry, let's go."

"Get up." Faris's voice grated in the silent room. Her bubble of hilarity was gone. It took no effort to speak steadily.

The sailor looked up. At her words, he groped for the bottle neck with his good hand.

"Don't do that," said a man's voice as smooth and cool as buttermilk. "Stand back, your grace, and put the poker down."

Faris blinked and stepped back. At the door, beside Portia, stood a blond man, dressed in badly cut black. In his hand was a small but formidable looking pistol.

"Let the man alone, your grace. You've alarmed him sufficiently, I think."

Portia gaped at him. Eve-Marie looked relieved.

"Who are you?" demanded Gunhild.

"Consider me a witness," replied the blond man. "If you have any influence with the duchess, will you use it to persuade her to leave?"

"Duchess?" Gunhild looked bewildered. "What duchess?"

"Do put the poker away, Faris," said Jane. "Whoever he is, he's perfectly right."

Faris lowered the poker slowly. "His name is Tyrian." Her voice sounded distant but otherwise quite normal. "I think he works for my uncle."

"How nice," said Jane. "May we go now?"

Gunhild began to sniffle slightly.

Eve-Marie put her arm around Gunhild's shoulders and shook her gently. "Idiot."

"I know," said Gunhild, hanging her head.

Jane produced a flawlessly clean handkerchief and gave it to Gunhild. "Must we discuss it here?"

"Yes, let's go," said Portia.

Gunhild blew her nose.

The sailor cursed comprehensively.

"I believe that makes it unanimous. Or would you prefer to stay and explain to the authorities?" Tyrian asked Faris.

Faris eyed him defiantly. "I'll go. But I'm keeping the poker."

"By all means," said Jane. "A most useful object, the poker. I had no notion."

Tyrian bowed them out, paused on the threshold to threaten the sailor, and closed the wine shop door softly. "I suggest we hurry."

4

"If you can't speak sensibly, you can leave."

❧ DAME VILLETTE STOPPED Faris after the first lecture the next day. "The Dean asked me to send you to her office."

Faris's eyes widened. She thought, *Does the Dean know everything that happens within the gates of Greenlaw?* "Do you know why?" She hoped her expression held only innocent surprise.

"No, but I'm sure she will mention it at some point in your conversation. Come to see me when she's finished with you."

Faris left the lecture hall reluctantly. Had someone told the authorities that she had broken curfew? Or did the authorities know things without the need to be told?

Once away from the Glass Slipper the night before, Tyrian had insisted on escorting them to the college. Jane led the way back to the garden. Under the oak tree, she paused. "Gunhild goes first," Jane whispered. "If anyone is waiting for us, she ought to be the one to greet them."

Tyrian helped Gunhild up into the rustling branches, then Jane, Portia, and Eve-Marie. When he turned to Faris, she stopped him with a touch of her hand.

"First tell me," she said quietly, "did my uncle hire you?"

Tyrian's soft voice was surprised. "Weren't you told?"

Faris didn't answer.

"Obviously not. He hired me as soon as he had certain knowledge that you were a student at Greenlaw. He wanted to be sure you stayed at school."

"Stayed where he put me, rather. So you are my guard."

"Your bodyguard, should circumstances ever require

one. I am surprised that my services weren't needed tonight. I had no idea Greenlaw College provided such a liberal education.''

''They don't teach that at Greenlaw.'' Reluctantly, Faris handed the poker to Tyrian. ''Nothing so direct.''

''Perhaps they should. Our nautical friend may think twice before he approaches another student.''

The thought cheered Faris. For the first time since the fight, she felt her heart lift. ''A useful object, the poker,'' she said.

''I'll handle it with care,'' Tyrian said.

Faris jumped to catch the oak branch and found Tyrian's hands at her waist as she reached the top of her leap. Aided by his strength, she caught the branch and let the spring of it swing her over the wall.

The oak leaves rustled around her as she looked back down into the garden. Tyrian was gone. For a long moment, Faris let the tree branch rock her in the darkness, listened to the November wind sort dry leaves with a fitful rustling shiver.

''Faris?'' hissed Jane, from the darkness on the Dean's side of the garden wall. ''Are you all right?''

Faris climbed down the oak tree and joined her friend in the shadows. ''Absolutely.''

All the way to the Dean's office, Faris expected to encounter Jane or Gunhild or another fellow culprit. She had the feeling she ought to be riding in a tumbrel. Instead, she walked the maze of corridors alone, climbed the stairs alone, and finally stood alone before the Dean's desk.

The Dean, a woman of formidable height, with a glint of steel in her manner, did not look up from her work.

Faris reminded herself that she was a string of pearls and fell into the perfectly balanced posture Dame Brachet had taught her. It was tempting to steal a glance around at the book-lined room but she kept her attention focused on the Dean instead.

The Dean put down her pen. "I've received a letter, Faris Nallaneen. I want to know the meaning of it." She selected a sheet of paper from the stack before her and held it up. Her dark eyes caught Faris's pale ones. "Have you blackmailed many of your classmates, or is Menary your first attempt?"

Faris felt her jaw drop. After a moment's stunned silence, she managed to say, "I beg your pardon?" with only one stammer.

The Dean's stern expression eased slightly. "Or was it inadvertent?" She held the letter out to Faris.

Faris took the letter, read it through, and looked up at the Dean, horrified. "I didn't threaten her. I didn't say anything of the kind. It didn't happen this way at all . . ." She paused to collect herself.

The Dean arched an eyebrow. "Yet you are very short of funds. And as Menary's father makes abundantly clear, the Paganells are an important family. And important families are almost always wealthy families."

Faris took a deep breath and let it out as slowly as she could. When it was gone, she took another and told the Dean the story of her conversation with Menary. "I feel as though I should carry a piece of chalk and a slate with me to draw diagrams upon request," she finished.

The Dean regarded the Paganell letter with lifted brows. "Tell me, why do you suppose Menary says—what she said—regarding your parentage?"

"I was born six months after my father's death. It—it occasioned comment."

"Apparently so. Could you be a trifle more explicit?"

"Very well. Galazon and Aravill were two of a group of four duchies that were once ruled by the kings of Lidia. Geographic and economic interests in common made the four duchies—Cenedwine and the Haydocks are the other two—into a loose trading unit that outlasted the Lidians. The informal alliance lasted well into the eighteenth century. Then the dukes of Aravill began to style themselves kings of Aravill. A ridiculous conceit. There's no such title and there never has been, no matter what Julian Paganell likes to call himself."

The Dean lifted her hands. "I have changed my mind. Be less explicit. What has all this to do with you?"

Faris smiled grimly. "My father's mother had the poor taste to claim the throne of Aravill. After her death, my father pursued the claim. Eventually, he found a faction able to put him on the throne. For a while. Long enough for a coronation and a wedding. Another faction took him off the throne and exiled him and my mother from Aravill. I'm afraid that sort of thing is always happening there. It's not a very organized country."

"So I gather."

"The faction that deposed him didn't want him to recruit support and return to Aravill, but they didn't want to kill him publicly either. So they put my parents on a ship and never let them come to land. From time to time the ship put into harbor and the captain and his crew were changed, to keep my parents from winning their loyalty." Faris paused to clear her throat. "My father died." She cleared her throat again. "My mother was the duchess of Galazon. Our laws of primogeniture don't exclude the female lines. In Galazon, women have always held titles and property. So she was someone to be reckoned with, even before her marriage. Even after she was widowed. With the help of her family, she gained her release on the condition that she return to Galazon and never leave it. That was a condition she was very willing to fulfill. But she was—" Faris hesitated, considered various euphemisms, and settled for the unvarnished word she'd started to say, "pregnant. Had that fact been known, her imprisonment would have had no end."

"But it ended," said the Dean. "And then you arrived. That must have been a trifle difficult to explain."

"I am my mother's child. Her legitimate child. It doesn't matter to me what my father was, however briefly. But it matters to some people in Aravill."

"Hence the sea captain. Had your mother died childless, who would hold her title now?"

"My uncle Brinker. If I die without issue, he will become duke of Galazon."

"Have you never considered pursuing your claim to the throne of Aravill? Has no one ever tried to persuade you to do so?"

Faris's chin came up. "I am the duchess of Galazon."

The Dean's mouth quirked. "Just so. Why settle for second best? But be certain that the factions of Aravill don't see the matter that way. So tell me, why haven't they killed you?"

"They're much more likely to try to marry me to some feeble relation. To be safe, my uncle Brinker arranged an amendment to the act of succession. I'm barred from the throne."

"Was it in your best interest to be legally disinherited?"

"It was in *his* best interest. The amendment cost a little money but one of the factions paid him handsomely for his trouble. And I am still duchess of Galazon."

"The need for an amendment argues that at least someone in Aravill doubts the story of the sea captain."

Faris nodded. "There's the family resemblance, too. I don't look anything like my mother's family. But we have reproductions of almost all of the state portraits, among them my father's mother. Same nose. Eyes of no special color. She was very tall. My father had both the nose and the height. She was supposed to have had red hair, too. My uncle insists he doesn't see any similarity. That's what makes me think there's probably a strong resemblance."

"You and your uncle appear to understand one another very well." After a thoughtful pause the Dean added, "It seems to me that Menary misinterpreted your remarks. See to it that you don't say anything more that Menary can possibly misconstrue. And don't discuss your family tree with anyone. It isn't polite."

"I won't." Faris started to leave.

"One more thing." The Dean's dark eyes narrowed. Her

voice turned cold and crisp. "If I ever hear you gamboling about my garden again, on your way in or out of bounds, I will send you back to your uncle for good. Is that clear?"

Faris froze.

"And teach your friends not to call you by name when they're trying to be stealthy. Now, go on. Get out of my office."

When Faris had left the morning lecture to see the Dean, the sky was leaden. By the time she left the Dean's office, it was raining. Faris took the long way from the Dean to Dame Villette, partly to keep from getting wet, partly to think herself calm. By the time she walked through the north hall and into the cloister garden, it was raining hard. She paused in the eastern arcade of the cloister to lean against one of the cold gray marble columns.

Before her lay the neat square of garden, punctuated with a central fountain, its shallow stone basin empty but for a few limp yellow leaves. Abandoned to a winter that had not yet arrived, the garden lay fallow under the icy November rain. Glad of the quiet, Faris lingered.

At times, in the course of the year Faris had spent at Greenlaw, her own history seemed remote to her. Much more vital were the ideas she struggled with in the library. Much more useful were the terms and techniques she learned in class. What she had learned of Jane's history, and the history of her friends, told Faris that everyone had a family story, whether a tragedy, a comedy, or a romance. Hers was merely gaudier, not grander.

It had made Faris extremely uncomfortable to sum up the bald facts for the Dean. In the severe calm of the Dean's presence, she felt as though she'd invented the entire unlikely story to get attention. At the same time, her recitation of personal history made Faris realize how remote it all was for her now. After a year at Greenlaw, Galazon still lay bright in her mind's eye, burnished in her heart, but the rest of her story seemed distant and uninteresting.

The silence of the garden quieted Faris. She let the discomfort go and took refuge in the thought of Galazon.

Without closing her eyes, Faris could see Galazon Chase as it would be on this day of November, at this hour of the morning. Instead of gray pillars, gray trees surrounded her. Instead of the tidily staked garden, she could see thickets of bramble and briar, wild meadows of ungrazed grass and weeds, hip high and burned dry by frost, bleached sallow brown, gold, and gray. But by this day, Galazon's year would have turned to winter. Sky of the same iron gray would bring snow, not rain, and there would be frost in the ground underfoot, a taste of ice on the wind.

Faris watched the steady fall of rain in the cloister garden soak into the earth of Greenlaw. She was far from home, but she would not always be away. Time, that had brought her here to Greenlaw, would bear her back again to Galazon.

As if in answer to her thought, the rain slowed. It did not fall less steadily. Only, as Faris watched, the rain fell more leisurely, fell white, fell at the angle the wind wished, fell as snow. On this day of November, at this hour of the morning, as it did in the woods of Galazon Chase, snow fell at Greenlaw.

Faris came in to dinner late. The dining hall was full. Her customary place, one chair down from the far end of the corner table, was taken. As she approached, she recognized the student sitting there. Menary. And around her, warily polite, sat Jane, Nathalie, and the rest. There was one empty chair, just across the table from Menary. Faris sighed and took it.

"The Dean called Eve-Marie to her office," Nathalie was saying, despite a mouthful of stew.

Faris stiffened but kept silent.

Portia looked anxious. "Not to talk about last night?" She glanced at Menary and blushed.

"Vigil," said Nathalie, paused to swallow, and continued. "Isn't that always the way? Eve-Marie is short on sleep anyway because she insists on studying. Then the infant here gets in trouble and Eve-Marie makes the lot of you turn out for the rescue." Gunhild smiled sheepishly but said nothing.

Nathalie went on. "The very next day, Eve-Marie gets called up for her vigil, short on sleep and hollow with hunger."

"Hard cheese for Eve-Marie," Portia said. "The Dean does it on purpose."

"Well, now we know where Eve-Marie is. What about you?" said Jane, filling Faris's water glass. "Where've you been?"

"I've spent the afternoon smiling at Dame Villette while she tore thin strips off me. What have you been doing?"

"Nothing singular," said Menary. "Why was Dame Villette angry with you?"

"Grammar, same as always," said Faris. She looked up from her plate into Menary's gray eyes and found her appetite had vanished.

Menary lifted her eyebrows and smiled faintly.

Faris started to return the smile, knowing the expression didn't reach her eyes. But as she began her artificial response, something in Menary's small porcelain smile provoked Faris to genuine amusement. She grinned at Menary. Menary kept her mask of arch amusement intact. Faris returned her look for look, hardly able to keep from laughing aloud. The other students at the table glanced from Faris to Menary and back, felt their own expressions lighten.

"*Lambkins, we will live,*" Faris murmured.

Menary's brows drew together as her smile faded. She glanced from Faris to Jane, then up the table. With great dignity, she rose and left the dining hall.

"Now," said Jane, when the door was firmly shut and the diners had all gone back to their plates of stew, "what was that all about?"

Faris shrugged. "I'm blessed if I know. After staring at Dame Villette, my expression is out of control. Dissect my thought processes if you must but don't hold me responsible for my appearance while you do so."

"Menary doesn't like you," Gunhild said.

Nathalie fixed Gunhild with a disapproving gaze. "Odious child, didn't we tell you not to speak until you're spoken to?"

"Who says so?" Faris asked Gunhild.

"Don't encourage her," Jane said. "It's taken us most of the day to bring her to a proper sense of her own idiocy."

"Menary did," Gunhild answered. "She says you brag about your family too much."

"She's the one who brags about her family," said Portia, "and all their possessions. Do you think they really keep lions in the house?"

"And just when has Menary ever wasted the breath it takes to tell a first-year student anything?" Nathalie asked.

"Or willingly eaten a meal at the same table with us," added Faris. "What brought her here today?"

"She said she had a whim to sit here," Portia replied. "There was an empty place and she claimed it. I haven't seen her so friendly in weeks. We could hardly discourage her. I don't think it's possible to keep lions indoors. What would one feed them?"

"She was nice to me at the Glass Slipper," Gunhild said.

"List, list," said Jane, holding up a hand to silence Nathalie's reproof, "O list. When was this?"

Gunhild blushed. "Yesterday. She was talking to Maxim."

"Who's Maxim?" Nathalie demanded. "As if I couldn't guess."

Gunhild drew a complicated design on her plate with the tines of her fork. The other students traded looks of exasperated impatience as they waited for her to speak. "You know," she said, finally.

"Menary knew that sailor?" Jane prompted.

Gunhild hesitated.

Nathalie said, "Don't simper, you aggravating little wart. Yes or no?"

"You knew that man with the gun," Gunhild told Faris.

"Don't try to change the subject," Faris replied. "Did Menary know the sailor?"

Gunhild nodded. "They seemed very friendly."

"I can just imagine," said Jane. "Did Menary put you up to that jest with the aquavit?"

Gunhild shook her head.

"Could Menary have stooped to put the sailor up to it?" asked Nathalie.

"Why would Menary waste her time with a sailor?" Portia asked. "She barely speaks to us anymore."

"Well, for one thing, the sailor is male," said Jane. "You may have noticed that the Pagan has interests in that direction."

"No," said Faris, "I hadn't. Go on."

Nathalie glanced around the crowded dining hall. "I wouldn't elaborate if I were you, Jane."

Jane's eyes narrowed. "Do the walls have ears?"

"They might as well," Nathalie replied. "And what do the Pagan's interests amount to? Nothing but rumors. It isn't wise to spread them."

"Or to figure in them," said Portia.

"I heard a rumor," Gunhild offered. "I heard Faris was called to the Dean's office."

Faris helped herself to a large bite of stew and thought while she chewed. When she was able, she said, "I was."

"I rest my case," said Nathalie.

"Dare I ask why?" Jane inquired.

"It had something to do with our outing last night," Faris answered.

Portia and Gunhild winced at each other.

Nathalie asked, "Why not all of you truants? Why just summon Faris?"

"The Dean only caught one name," Faris replied. "Mine."

Jane looked stricken. "Oh—oh, dear. I do apologize. Was it very bad?"

"Swift and nearly painless," Faris said. "Punishment suspended, unless I'm caught at it again."

"And if you are?" Jane asked.

"Summary execution."

"Sword, or silken rope?" inquired Nathalie.

"I didn't ask," said Faris. "Judging from her manner, I think the Dean had something like a firing squad in mind."

"Suitable for mass executions," said Jane. She glared at Gunhild.

"I know," said Gunhild hastily. "It's all my fault."

"Next time you get homesick," said Nathalie, "do us all a favor and go home, will you?"

Jane looked past Nathalie toward the door. *"Lo, where it comes again."*

"Finally," said Nathalie.

Charlotte paused in her entry to collect a plate of stew, sauntered to the place Menary had left, and sank gracefully into the high-backed chair.

"How's Eve-Marie?" Nathalie asked.

Charlotte slid Menary's plate into the middle of the table and put hers in its place. "Pass the bread, please. Ask not how, but where." She smiled slightly.

Portia passed the bread basket. "Where?"

"At the foot of the Gabriel Tower," Charlotte replied. "This stew is *extremely* cold."

"Don't eat it, then," Jane advised. "Does she seem all right?"

"I have to, I'm starving," Charlotte replied. "She's all right now. She wandered about for what seemed like hours before she hit on a place that suited her. At least she's out of the wind."

"She'll freeze anyway," said Nathalie. "It's far too early in the term for a vigil."

"But then, Eve-Marie's always been precocious," said Charlotte, between quick bites.

"Bad enough to watch the night through when it's warm," said Portia. "By morning she'll be an icicle. I hope I get called in May."

Charlotte looked thoughtful. "She ought to last out the

night pretty well. I bagged a goosefeather comforter out of the dormitory. She's wrapped up to the eyebrows."

"Eve-Marie is a queen among women and she's going to have the best vigil in fifty years, you'll see," Nathalie predicted. "No mice, no pigeons, nothing paltry for Eve-Marie. A tiger—a comet—something spectacular."

"I'm extremely glad to hear you say so," Charlotte said. "It was your comforter."

"I'd rather see something utterly mundane," said Portia. "I won't be tempted to boast about it."

"An ant," suggested Gunhild.

"I'd hold out for a spider, if I were you," said Nathalie. "What sort of spiritual guide would an ant make? Though I suppose it depends on your spirit."

"Must we really debate this now?" sighed Charlotte. "I've just spent the past two hours pursuing Eve-Marie from perch to perch while she muttered to herself about it. I think that's why she chose the Gabriel Tower. There's a view of the sea. Perhaps she hopes to see a fish. Isn't there *anything* else to eat?"

Portia passed the bread basket again.

"Leviathan," offered Gunhild.

"Crumbs," said Charlotte darkly. She emptied the bread basket and looked dolefully around the table. "Have I mentioned that I had no luncheon at all? I meant to make short work of my tutorial and just nip down to the patisserie after. But it was not to be. Dame Woodland came stamping in all rumpled and cross-looking, like my little brother after a bath. Seems they'd had a spot of bother with the anchors this afternoon. She was distracted enough to put me through my paces for an extra hour."

Faris looked pointedly at Menary's unfinished dinner. "Menary lost her appetite and left us."

"Menary, eh?" Charlotte eyed the plate for a long moment, then said regretfully, "I find I'm not so hungry as I thought, thanks."

"What sort of trouble with the anchors?" Jane asked. "I

thought Dame Malory seemed a trifle off her game this afternoon. Preoccupied with the underpinnings?"

Charlotte shook her head. "Dame Woodland wasn't dis-
posed to enlighten me."

"An owl," said Gunhild, after much earnest thought.

"It's early days for you to be worried about signs and por-
tents, isn't it?" Jane inquired. "Best be careful of such matters.
My cousin Henry went to Glasscastle with a man who saw a
white stag on his vigil. He was so excited he told his tutor.
Poof." She dropped her crumpled napkin beside her plate.

"I don't see how that superstition ever got started," Faris
said, as she handed Charlotte her own plate. "If no one can say
what they see on vigil, explain to me how anyone knows what
the vigil is supposed to accomplish."

Charlotte saluted Faris with her spoon. "Thank you. Extremely grateful though I am, I insist that if we bandy words,
we bandy the correct words. It isn't a superstition—it's a tradition. If you fast and keep watch from sunset to dawn, you're
bound to see something. Fast long enough and you'll *make*
yourself see something. You believe it helps you and it helps
you. If you don't believe in it, of course it won't work. That's
true of anything."

"And if you try to explain it, it won't work," said Nathalie. "The same way magic stops working if you try to explain it."

"Which is why none of our tutors ever teach us any
magic," Faris said. "I've gathered that much. But suppose I
don't believe in algebra. Algebra works just the same."

"Not for me," said Portia. Gunhild nodded agreement.

"Suit yourself," said Jane. "When the Dean tells you it's
your night to keep vigil, eat a hearty dinner and go to bed. As
for me, I believe it. When my night comes, I'll be out there
watching the wind, just like Eve-Marie."

"After all," said Charlotte lazily, "if there's nothing to it,
all that's lost is a night's sleep. No novelty there. If it works as
it's said to, it's magic."

"It's the Emperor's new clothes," said Faris. "Odile never mentioned any vigil."

"You know Odile didn't tell you everything. Take a long look at Eve-Marie tomorrow morning," Jane advised. "Make up your mind then."

"Will you admit it's superstition if Eve-Marie doesn't see her spiritual guide during the vigil?" Faris asked. "No, you'll claim Eve-Marie doesn't have the aptitude for magic. It's a double bind."

"What a scoffer you are tonight," Jane marveled. "Is it Dame Villette's baleful influence? Or the Dean's?"

"I just find it absurd that Eve-Marie is outdoors on a night like this, freezing for folklore," Faris said. "It snowed this morning, for pity's sake."

"Did it?" Jane looked surprised. "I sat by the window in logic and never noticed. I must have been paying more attention to the lecture than I thought."

Just past dawn, Eve-Marie returned from her vigil with a joyous expression and a bone-rattling cough. To her classmates' well-concealed exasperation, she attended the morning lecture, nodding smugly throughout. Afterward, she allowed Charlotte and Nathalie to escort her to the infirmary, where she took to her bed with seraphic patience.

"It was bad enough before," Charlotte observed at the midday meal. "Eve-Marie always looked as though she knew something I don't. Generally she does. But now that I *know* she knows, and she knows I know she knows—" She lifted her hands, exasperated. "I don't understand how anyone with a chest cold can manage to look so extremely complacent."

"Dame Brachet covers the topic in deportment," Jane replied. "Did she say anything pertinent about her vigil?"

"I should hope not," said Charlotte.

"Double bind," said Faris darkly.

"Think what you like," Jane replied. She nodded at Gunhild, who was silently absorbed in her plateful of cabbage. "Just try not to corrupt the young."

"Corrupting the young is not a pursuit I find appealing," said Faris.

"Any more upsets in the anchors?" Nathalie asked.

Charlotte shook her head. "Not a sausage. Last time I asked, Dame Woodland tried to tell me I misconstrued her."

Jane smiled. "Somebody fell asleep and dreamed the whole thing, I suppose."

"Seasonal adjustment. Quite routine. That's today's story, at least."

"I do love it when they try to explain things to us," said Nathalie. "Romance at short notice."

"That's only fair. They enjoy it so much when they catch us doing it to them." Faris put her napkin beside her plate. "Now, if you'll excuse me, I'll be off."

"Off where?" asked Jane. "Rhetoric isn't for half an hour."

"I'm going to the patisserie in High Street," Faris replied. "Somehow cabbage doesn't thrill me the way it used to do."

"We only do it to soothe their nerves, poor things," Charlotte said to Nathalie.

"I expect that's what they have in mind for us, as well. Grim thought, isn't it?"

"Extremely."

Faris left the others talking at the table. By the time she was out the college gate and walking into High Street, Jane was waiting for her.

"I'd be careful about using that oak tree," Faris advised, "particularly in broad day. The Dean's declared her disapproval."

"You forced me to it. Why go to a pastry shop when you never have any money? Vulgar curiosity got the better of me."

"What did the others think?"

"Nothing. I told them I was off to fetch a book from the study."

"Thank you for that. If you'd brought the whole pack along, I would have had to go to the patisserie after all." She set off along the street.

Jane fell into step beside her. "Where are we going, then?"

"To the Glass Slipper."

"Why?"

"To see Gunhild's sailor."

"*Why?*"

Faris shrugged. "He might prove useful for further reference."

"In case you decide to corrupt the young after all?"

"In case someone else wants to. Gunhild said Menary knew the sailor too. It might be interesting to find out how well they know one another."

"You think he'll tell you? After you maimed him? Ha. I can tell you more than he ever will. If he knows the Pagan at all, he knows her very, *very* well."

"How do you know?"

Jane looked exasperated. "Well, he's hardly the first. Why do you think we called her the Pagan?"

Faris blushed to the roots of her red hair, a painful contrast of colors. "Oh."

"It's pathetic, of course, but it's been going on almost since the day she arrived. If she didn't care for herself, you'd think she'd care for her reputation. And Greenlaw's. If word of this ever reaches my parents, they'll explode with mortification, and fetch me back that very day."

Faris frowned. "Greenlaw has rules . . ."

"And you know perfectly well how we keep them. Whatever two penny half penny court Menary came from, Greenlaw is a miracle of liberty by comparison. To give her some credit, she doesn't seem to break the rules to get attention. She just breaks them for her own amusement. So far, she hasn't harmed anyone but herself."

"What about Gunhild?"

Jane stifled a sigh. "It's our duty to keep an eye on her until she learns what Greenlaw is all about. After that, if it suits her to go her own way—or Menary's—it's our duty to let her."

Faris stopped at the Glass Slipper's doorstep. "You don't have a duty to me. I've learned what Greenlaw is all about. You needn't come with me."

Jane rolled her eyes. "I told you why I'm here. You needn't be quite such a giddy idiot."

"Vulgar curiosity." Faris eyed Jane curiously. "The Pagan. Why does only Menary have a nickname?"

"Oh, she's not the only one. I thought you wanted to go find that sailor."

"Who else has one? Do you?" Faris followed Jane into the Glass Slipper. "Do I?"

At their entrance, the host looked up from his customers and swept toward them. "No, no. No more of your kind in here," he said indignantly. "No more students. We don't serve students here."

"We don't wish to be served," said Jane primly.

"We're looking for a sailor called Maxim," said Faris, her voice low. "I was told to ask for him here."

The host regarded Faris with deep suspicion. "You are friends of his?"

"We only want to ask him some questions."

"I want to ask him questions too," the host said angrily. "I want to ask him why he left the room he rented from me without paying the reckoning."

"He's gone?" Faris looked alarmed. "Where?"

"If I knew that, would I be short the money?"

"When did he leave?"

"I don't know that either. If you see him, you tell him I'm looking for him."

"When did you see him last?"

"You are a very nosy young lady," the host observed. "Go away." He took Faris and Jane back to the threshold and shooed them out. "And stay away," he advised, as he shut the door.

Jane regarded Faris with interest. "Well, that was definite, at least. What next?"

Faris set off toward the gates at the foot of the street. "I wonder," she said, and fell into an abstracted silence. Jane at her side, she walked through the gates of Greenlaw and out along the causeway.

After a few hundred yards, Jane asked, "Are we going to walk to Pontorson? It's miles."

Faris looked up, startled. "You're right. That would take all afternoon." She turned back toward the gates, but before she reached them, left the causeway for the path that followed the foot of the seawall.

Jane followed, picking her way carefully across the rocks. "Just out of curiosity, when does the tide come in?"

Faris paused to look over her shoulder at Jane. The wind pulled her hair into snakes around her face. She put up her hand to clear her vision. "Tide?"

"I forgot, you're an idiot about things like that. Let me think. Yesterday, high tide was about half past one. So today it ought to be about three quarters of an hour later. What time is it now?"

"Two o'clock?"

"I asked you first. We'd better start back. Unless you expect to meet Maxim here?"

"Of course not."

"Then let's go."

"You go," said Faris. "That would probably be best."

"What? No, it certainly would not. Come on." Jane wheeled and took two steps, realized Faris wasn't coming, and turned to remonstrate with her.

Faris stood on the rocks, her back to Jane, her hair blown to a tangle, her hand up to brush it out of her eyes. Before her stood Tyrian.

Jane came to stand at Faris's elbow.

"I thought you might turn up if I tried to leave," Faris said to Tyrian. "I'd like your help."

"Of course." Tyrian glanced appraisingly from Jane to Faris. "Your friend is right about the tide."

"I mean to find out where that sailor Maxim has gone.

Can you make some inquiries for me? In an unobtrusive way. I want to ask him a few questions."

"In fact, I have already made inquiries. After you returned to the college, I went to the Glass Slipper to restore their poker. You broke the sailor's arm, your grace. I found him still nursing his injury." Tyrian looked rather pleased. "It was a challenge to find a doctor at that hour. I succeeded. His services, and his silence, have been paid for."

Faris looked anxious. "Did it cost very much?"

"My expenses will be reimbursed. The unfortunate Maxim agreed to leave here and go to Paris to recuperate. When he did not meet me in Pontorson this morning, I returned to look for him."

"Pontorson?"

"At the railway station, I'll venture," said Jane.

Tyrian gave her a small smile. "I intended to put him aboard the train before I paid him."

"But he didn't keep the appointment?" Faris looked puzzled.

Tyrian's satisfied expression gave way to faint discontentment. "No one has seen him since yesterday afternoon. His possessions are still in the room he rented. He's nowhere to be found."

"Scarpered," said Jane. "That's a relief, in a way."

"Before he collected the money?" Faris countered. "That doesn't seem likely."

"He might have been frightened. You were fairly brutal with him."

"Too frightened to pack?"

"I think he was more angry than afraid when I last spoke to him," said Tyrian calmly. "Someone may have frightened him subsequently. When I investigated his room today, I found a dead rat in his unmade bed."

Jane grimaced.

Faris's eyes narrowed. "That's interesting. The owner of the Glass Slipper didn't mention any rat."

"Bad for business, I should think," said Jane.

"Maxim left his belongings. He ignored an offer of money. He went off without a word, with a broken arm that will keep him from working for weeks." Faris frowned. "Where did he go? And why did he go there?"

Jane gazed out at the horizon, where the sky met the sea in a gray line. "Perhaps he is out there somewhere."

"I hope so." Tyrian regarded Faris gravely. "It means nothing, I am sure. But the rat had a broken foreleg."

Faris stared.

"How perfectly disgusting." Jane felt something cold touch her left foot. She gasped and looked down. The rock she stood on was half submerged. "Time is," she said, clambering to the next rock. "Tide is, too."

"So it is. May I escort you back to the college?" Tyrian asked.

"You are very kind," Jane said. "I confess that at the moment, I should simply hate to see a rat."

The three of them made their way back across the slippery rocks. Tyrian left them at the college gate. Despite Jane's questions about Tyrian, rats, and sailors, Faris said nothing on the way back, nothing on the way to collect their books, nothing until they reached the landing on the stair near number five study.

"You never answered me, Jane," she said at last. "Do I have a nickname?"

"You had one last term," Jane admitted cautiously. "Hardly anyone used it. I'm sure it's forgotten now."

"Well?" Faris eyed Jane warily. "What is it?"

"Ferret."

Faris looked annoyed for a moment, then amused. "I suppose it could be worse. Who was responsible for that?"

Jane's ears turned a delicate shade of pink. She did not answer but Faris did not need to ask again.

Menary made no trouble for Faris that winter. Gunhild found no more scrapes to fall into. Her sailor was never heard of again.

Eve-Marie became so proficient at her studies that she traveled in a tangible mist of magic, like the scent of wet earth in springtime. To keep her from some involuntary use of magic, her tutor prevailed on the Dean and the proctors to administer her comprehensives at Candlemas. Eve-Marie passed them, accepted her degree with shining happiness, and departed for the lucrative position she'd won with the Foreign Office. Her friends made envious remarks to conceal their emotions, and took up the threads of the school routine again, but Eve-Marie's strand was sorely missed.

Charlotte and Nathalie applied themselves to their studies so strictly that they nearly vanished from the routine, too. Even Portia displayed some signs of academic ability. Which left Faris and Jane alone in their study of three-volume novels, Faris because she didn't believe in learning things no one taught her, and Jane because she didn't want to learn too swiftly.

"Think about it," Jane said over the teacups, one gloomy afternoon in early March. "Five months of Greenlaw Eve-Marie stole from herself. And why? To show off."

Faris was at the window, elbows on the sill, chin in her hands. "Does the first snow goose north in the spring fly to show off? Or does it answer a call it can't resist?" A flight of geese had gone over in the night, their wild cry waking Faris from a dream of Galazon. She'd sat up in bed for the rest of the night, arms clasped around her knees, shivering with homesickness.

"Oh, don't speak in metaphysics. It's bad enough when the Dean does."

"I can't help it." Faris stared out at the empty gray sky. "It's all Dame Villette wants to hear. I've gotten quite fluent at calling a hawk a heron."

"The doctrine of signatures," said Jane with loathing. "Every single thing in the world symbolizes something it isn't. It's a wonder anything gets done."

"Does anything get done? Isn't it all part of the divine

struggle of order and chaos, rising to fall, falling to rise again?"

"If you can't speak sensibly, you can leave."

"Is there any tea left?"

"No. And that was the last of the Darjeeling. I'll have to write away for more and Mother probably won't send it because I'll be home from school so soon." Jane sighed. "Three months left."

Someone knocked at the study door.

Faris turned away from the window to meet Jane's surprised look. The first-year students of their acquaintance were all virtuously in class, and few of the older students stood sufficiently on ceremony to knock at doors.

Jane opened the door. No one was there. Puzzled, she crossed the threshold to look up and down the hall, then stooped to retrieve the paper dropped outside the door.

Faris watched Jane closely as she unfolded the sheet of paper, read it, reread it, and folded it again.

Jane looked at Faris. "It's tonight," she said, her voice perfectly prosaic.

"What's tonight?"

"My vigil."

Faris did not sleep that night. It wasn't merely the knowledge that Jane was outside, huddled in every blanket she could borrow, shivering at the very top of the Gabriel Tower. It wasn't just the flight of geese that went over at midnight, their faint cry like hounds hunting overhead. It wasn't only the south wind, which had been blowing steadily for days, bringing the fragrance of plowed fields with it.

All these things conspired, but most of all it was time that kept her awake. Faris realized that her stay at Greenlaw was not an interminable exile from Galazon. It would come to an end, inevitably. Unlike Jane, Faris welcomed the end of her time at school, longed to go home. There was no doubt that she had been ignoring a great deal that Greenlaw had to offer. If it was too much to expect to learn magic, and apparently it was, it was likewise too much to expect her to spend three years in a place, any place, and learn nothing.

But it seemed to Faris, lying wakeful in the quiet darkness of the dormitory, that nothing was precisely what she'd managed to learn. She could stand at ease for hours, graceful as a strand of pearls. She could look complacent with a head cold. But that was as far as her education went.

Bitterly, Faris tolled over the days that she'd been away from Galazon. She'd spent half her time there prodigally, reading novels. In that time, her uncle could have cut down every tree in Galazon Chase.

By dawn, Faris was red-eyed as a ferret and nearly as cross. She met Jane at the foot of the Gabriel Tower and helped her bundle up blankets.

"Thank you," said Jane, when the last blanket was folded.

"Any luck?" Faris was surprised at how gruff her own voice sounded.

Jane looked pensive. "The story of Puss in Boots makes much more sense to me now."

"You're not supposed to tell me."

"Oh, it isn't a cat. What does it matter? You don't believe in it."

"You do. I suppose you're going to the morning lecture now?"

"Well, yes. After that, I will probably start to study. Unless I take a bit of a nap first."

Faris sighed heavily. "I will probably start to study, too. Everyone else does. It will help to pass the time."

"Yes, indeed, it's just the thing for that."

Side by side, they took the blankets back to the dormitory. Neither of them looked happy.

5

News from Home

🦋 FARIS SPENT THE rest of the term wrestling with Greeks in general and Aristotle in particular. For Dame Villette, she read *Metaphysics*. For herself, she read *Politics* and anything else that seemed likely to be of use to an aspiring ruler. By the time comprehensive examinations were administered to the third-year students, she was virtuously annotating the *Metaphysics* structure of the world in the light shed by the Dean's lectures.

Jane set her sails to bear her deep into the uncharted seas of mathematics and magic. The place on the staff tacitly reserved for Eve-Marie was now free to all comers. Jane considered such an opportunity to be a gift straight from heaven and studied accordingly. She emerged from her comprehensives victorious. Not only was she a graduate of Greenlaw, she was invited to remain at the college.

On an afternoon in May, when most of the students were accompanying their trunks to the Pontorson station, Jane and Faris met on the seawall near the Cordelion Tower. Fully recovered from the torments of scholarship, Jane was as neatly turned out as ever. Faris had attempted to pin her hair up into a copy of Jane's neat coiffure, but the offshore breeze was doing its best to unknit the untidy knot she'd achieved.

Faris had a book under her arm. Jane carried a bottle of champagne in one hand and two dining hall glasses in the other. In companionable silence they clambered up the ramparts and sat atop the wall. Faris took the glasses while Jane struggled with the champagne cork.

"Finally," Jane exclaimed. "Hold out the glasses."

Faris obeyed, and admired the play of sunlight on the

wine as Jane poured. At the sight of the label, Faris drew a breath of admiration. "I had no idea the shops of Greenlaw held such luxury."

"They don't. I brought this with me when I came back to school this year. I thought that if I passed my comps, I'd want to celebrate, and if I didn't, I'd jolly well need something to cheer myself up."

Faris handed Jane her glass and lifted her own. "Here's to the celebration. Congratulations."

Jane returned the salute. "Here's to the chinless lads of England."

"Here's to that notable witch of Greenlaw, Jane Brailsford."

"May they never meet again." Jane touched her glass to Faris's.

They drank. Jane smiled blissfully out at the horizon where the seagulls dived and circled. "A fair end to a fine year. May your last year go as merrily."

"Not much merriment these past months."

Jane took another sip. "I'm gratified that you've noticed a change, but you know it is largely your own fault. You've been far too studious. You'll have to mend your ways next term. I bequeath number five study to you and Charlotte and Nathalie. You'll have to indulge in cakes and ale occasionally, just to keep up the tone of the place."

Faris's eyes widened. "Thank you. Will you pay us a call now and then to keep the merriment up to standard?"

"If I'm invited."

"You may join us for tea and three-volume novels, provided you have any left I still haven't read."

"Too kind." Jane poured champagne. "What have you been reading lately?" Her tone was elaborately casual.

"Whatever Dame Villette thinks I ought."

"No, I mean *reading*."

"Oh. Well. Let's see. *Three Men in a Boat*."

"What, again?"

"Ah, no."

"Faris, you read that in February. Do you mean to tell me you've been doing no reading but schoolwork since then?"

"What about you? You're the one who's spent the past six months sleeping two hours a night and spending the rest of your time in the library preparing for your comps."

"Ah, but that's the rightful pursuit for third-years. I intend to spend my life around libraries, if I can contrive it. You, on the other hand, have been there every day this week and classes concluded ten days ago."

Faris studied the bubbles rising in her glass. "Why do you sound so shocked? All I've been doing is a little serious reading to counterbalance the novels I soaked up at the beginning of the school year."

"My, how prim you've grown while I wasn't looking. How long do you propose to sustain these virtuous habits? Is it too much to hope you'll indulge in a little holiday traveling?"

Faris kept her eyes on the bubbles. Most of them knew their mission and fizzed up dutifully to the surface of the wine. What became of them then, poor bubbles? Or worse, what became of the laggard bubbles that lurked in the bottom of the glass? Faris put the question firmly away. Jane in an inquisitive mood required her undivided attention. "My uncle wrote to the Dean. My board is paid until next Whitsuntide. Here I stay."

Jane looked grave. "If you keep on at this rate, you'll never last until then. They'll send you to Switzerland to learn to breathe again."

Faris grimaced. "What's the matter with me, anyway? Everyone else studies. No one says a word. I flounder about for months, getting cold looks from the proctors daily, and no one thinks a thing about it. Then, once I finally do set to work, you lecture me as though I'd gone off my head. Do you think my intellect can't manage the strain? Do you think my brain has turned?"

"No more than anyone else's. If you spend all summer at your studies, however, I won't vouch for you. And if you grow any smugger about counterbalancing the three-volume novels, I won't speak to you."

"No studies? What shall I do instead? Count seagulls?"

"If you wish. Can't you think of anything more useful?"

"Studying is useful. Learning how to run Galazon is useful."

Jane threw back her head and stared into the depths of the sky, endlessly blue above. "Magic is useful." She gazed upward for the time it took to draw a dozen breaths, then looked at Faris. "Wouldn't you like to learn some?"

After a long silence, Faris asked, "Is this a trick?"

"No tricks. I don't think you believe in magic and I can tell you right now that if you don't believe in it, you'll never pass your comprehensives."

"Oh, come. I can't be the first skeptic ever to grace these halls." Faris put her glass down carefully. "Is belief a requirement? If it is, I must resign myself to failure."

"You needn't."

Faris clenched her fists. "Then why don't they teach us? Here we sit for three long years, waiting. Why don't they teach us anything?"

"Teaching is meaningless if you can't find your own way to it. If I can only convince you that it's true—that magic is here waiting—you can find your own explanations."

Faris frowned. "You don't need to convince me. Eve-Marie did that. A wooden block would sense something in her presence. Like a kettle about to boil. But it's one thing to know it's true for her, and something else altogether to believe it's true for me. If it were, wouldn't I know by now?"

Jane put down her empty glass. "It's probably against every rule ever written—but then, I'm not a student here anymore." She picked up the champagne cork and held it out on her open palm.

Unable to look away, Faris watched the cork tremble in Jane's hand. Slowly at first, but with increasing speed, the cork altered shape, detail by detail, until what sat on Jane's palm was a sparrow, feathers ruffled and black eyes bright with a fevered gleam. Jane breathed gently into her palm. The sparrow spread its wings, dropped from Jane's hand, and plummeted off the seawall.

Faris and Jane craned over the rampart to watch. Inches from the water, the sparrow's wings found purchase in the air. With fierce little strokes, it flew. Up it climbed in sharp swoops, to a level not much below their vantage, then away toward the open channel. Fifty yards from the seawall, in response to some change in the air itself, the sparrow's flight ended. The sparrow vanished. A champagne cork fell into the sea and bobbed lazily, tossed by the waves.

"That is how far the wards of Greenlaw reach. Beyond that barrier, magic exacts a higher price. The wardens of the world rule out there. Here, the witches of Greenlaw balance their own magic." Jane rubbed her forehead and frowned a little.

In silence, Faris watched the ceaseless, aimless motion of the waves.

Jane looked at the sky again. "I wish it had flown up instead of away. It would be interesting to know how high the barrier goes. Perhaps it extends over us like a glass bell."

"Why did you do that?" Faris's voice held no emotion, not even curiosity.

"I thought you'd be interested." Jane regarded Faris closely. "*Are* you interested?"

Faris was still watching the cork. "If I could do that, I could *own* Galazon." Her voice was small and dry.

Jane looked surprised. "I thought you did."

Faris shook her head. "My uncle rules Galazon the same way he rules me. If I come back to Galazon a witch of Greenlaw, then it will truly belong to me. I can care for it as Galazon should be cared for, as my mother cared for it."

"Is that all magic means to you? Power over your uncle?"

"You don't understand." Faris picked up her book, offered it to Jane. "*The Prince.* A very practical book. It demonstrates the futility of statecraft. Without the skill to read hearts, a ruler must always fear. A frightened ruler *must* rule through fear. Nothing else will serve. If my uncle taught me nothing else, he's taught me to fear."

Jane looked alarmed.

Faris waved a hand to dispel the concern in her friend's expression. "Oh, I don't mean anything melodramatic. But I must fear the things he could do, whether he chooses to do them or not. It isn't a question of me wanting power over him. It's a question of his very existence. I'd be a fool to ignore him. And now you ask me, ever so casually, if I'm interested in learning magic. Well, let me ask you this. Can the magic of Greenlaw teach me to read hearts?"

Jane took the book and put it down between them. "Think, Faris. Greenlaw has turned out witches for three hundred years. Diplomats, judges, ambassadors, mediators, magistrates—but no saints. We don't live in paradise. We live in the world, where there are still wars and plagues and anarchists and all manner of assorted mayhem. Greenlaw doesn't hold the cure. It teaches us to balance what we can, as best we can, as the wardens of the world balance our sphere within the great model."

"Just let me balance Galazon," Faris countered. "I'll show you such a paradise as will turn the heart in your breast to see it. We have soil rich enough to put a French garden to shame, and meadows enough to graze every sheep in Scotland."

"Is that what you'll do with what you learn at Greenlaw? Raise sheep?"

"And oats. All kinds of oats. Where there are horses, there should be oats. We have wonderful horses in Galazon, not big, but very strong. When the Haydockers were harrowing the rest of Lidia, it was our light cavalry that let many-times-great-Uncle Ludovic keep them out of Galazon. Mother used to say that we had the Haydockers to thank for our borders. If it hadn't been for them, Ludo might have had time to go knocking at the gates of Aravis himself. It's the grazing the horses get in the high meadows all summer long. There's limestone in the meadow country, good for bones. But the oats are what make the difference."

Jane held up her hand. "Spare me. Your point is taken. You needn't belabor the details. We have the summer before us to discuss these matters. I'll give you all the help I can."

"Won't you get in trouble with the Dean?"

"I don't think so. The Dean told me to tutor you."

Faris stiffened. "What?"

"It was that or go home. I knew my parents would never let me come back here, so I accepted the duty."

"In other words, I'm your first pupil."

Jane smiled. "The Dean tells me I don't know much yet, so you're unlikely to pick up too much from me. You need the attention because you may turn as early as Eve-Marie. In eighteen months here, you haven't been outside the wards of Greenlaw for more than a few hours. Living here all year round has its effects, you know. How much have you grown since you came here?"

"The seamstress told me five inches. She says I'm as good as an annuity." Faris's eyes widened. "That's because I spent last summer here? Do you mean to tell me that the Dean thinks I may turn earlier than I ought to because my uncle kept me here instead of allowing me to go home between terms?"

"It takes some people that way."

Faris laughed until her hair came loose and fell into her eyes. "Oh, how cross he'll be when I tell him."

After luncheon a few days later, Faris and Jane returned to their favorite spot near the Cordelion Tower. The tide was in, so they sat side by side, staring vacantly at the waves that slid tirelessly against the seawall.

At Jane's insistence—and expense—they had eaten at Greenmantle's, a restaurant in the village, which served many of Greenlaw's tutors and proctors, and was, as a result, strictly off limits for students. Jane had scoffed at Faris's fear that the Dean would catch her there, and Faris had to admit that the quality of the food was well worth the risk. Both the quality and the quantity led them to eat more than usual.

Very full, tranquil to the point of sleepiness, Jane and Faris sat in the sunlight. They spoke little, and that little almost at random. After a lengthy silence, Jane asked, in connection with nothing at all, "When will you marry, do you suppose?"

Faris stopped swinging her feet and looked at Jane. "Are you mad? I'm not going to marry."

Jane looked surprised. "Not at all? That's rather careless of you, isn't it? Who will you leave Galazon to, then?"

"Not Uncle Brinker."

"His children? What if they're worse than he is? Children often are, I believe. Look at Prince John."

"I don't have to look at his children, thank goodness. He's a bachelor."

"Bachelors marry. The world must be peopled, after all. Why don't you people it yourself? I'm surprised you don't already have an 'understanding' with some sprig of the nobility. What was your mother thinking of?"

"Very possibly she was thinking of her own 'understanding.' She didn't have a very high opinion of marriage."

"No doubt she had her reasons. I don't have a very high opinion of it myself."

"And how is it that you feel exempt from the necessity?"

"Brothers, Faris, brothers. They are good for something, you know. The Brailsford name can go sailing on down the centuries without my help. Come on, Tell All. Haven't you ever even considered it?"

"Have you?"

"Oh, I left that notion in the nursery. I remember the moment distinctly. I was four years old. The guest of honor at a birthday party I had been lured into attending took a fancy to me. The little blighter tried to kiss me. I bit him on the nose. By the time all the fuss was over with, I'd made up my mind it was just an expense of spirit in a waste of shame."

"Precocious, weren't you?"

"Weren't you?"

Faris sighed. "Quite the contrary. I've never been the sort, somehow."

"What, never?" Jane demanded, then answered herself merrily, "No, never!"

"Never," Faris insisted.

"What, *never*? Hardly ever!"

Faris blushed. "Well. I spent a few summers away from home when I was younger. There was a boy my age there."

Jane hooted. "I knew it."

Beguiled by her memories, Faris ignored the interruption. "The summer we were eleven, when we went fishing, he taught me to take my catch off the hook, but then he did it for me so I wouldn't have to. The summer we were twelve, he let me shoot his rifle sometimes. He stole a cigar from his father's humidor once, and when he'd turned quite green, he let me have a puff. We were sick side by side in the ornamental border. I liked him. I think he liked me, because at the end of the summer we were thirteen, he gave me his pocketknife."

"He sounds quite perfect."

"He'd gotten a much better knife for his fourteenth birthday, a few days before."

"Still."

"I never saw him again." After a thoughtful pause, Faris added, "I wonder if that was why they never sent me back. Just shows, doesn't it? One should never tell adults anything. Even mothers."

"Particularly mothers." After another lengthy silence, Jane added, "Perhaps you'll meet again someday."

Faris shook her head.

"You're right. It's better this way. Whenever you see a humidor, you'll think of him. Unfortunately, whenever he sees one, he'll probably think of you."

"I must admit, I've never cared for ornamental borders."

Faris thought she knew all about Greenlaw. But during the long days she spent at Jane Brailsford's heels, she learned Greenlaw from the marks of low tide below the seawall to the spire that crowned the college like a sword held up to heaven. The seawall ramparts were Jane's favorite retreat in sunny weather. The crooked streets of the village, they visited occasionally. Most of the rest of their time was spent in exploring the heights, the secret heart of Greenlaw.

Within the outcrop of granite that provided Greenlaw's foundation, under the piles of dressed stone, piers, and vaulting, lay the first chapel built at Greenlaw. Long buried by the ambition that had balanced a college atop a pinnacle of granite, the chapel was a single room, a simple barrel-vaulted space containing an altar and nothing more. In the heat of the summer, in the chill of winter, the chapel held a constant coolness, a balance of the seasons.

Standing beside Jane, just inside the door of the chapel, Faris felt the silence, as tangible as the temperature. In the dimness, relieved only by the lamp at the altar, Faris could sense the weight of time pressing in on her, just as her imagination told her she could sense the weight of masonry pressing on the barrel vault above.

"When this place was dedicated to St. Margaret, slayer of dragons," Jane murmured, "it was already old. It was old when the wardens of the world held court in splendor. It was old before that, when they walked abroad in the world, as free as minstrels. Time sings in the stones here."

"How very poetic."

"Don't even attempt to patronize me. I am a witch of Greenlaw, you lowly undergraduate, and I shall be as lyrical as I please. Now, pay attention. The ward that balances Greenlaw has two anchors. We're very near the lower anchor here. Because there is a difference between the balance within Greenlaw's bounds and the balance beyond, there's a silent spot near the anchors. That's what you don't hear."

"Then we're near Greenlaw's south pole."

"If you care to think of it that way. I prefer to think of Greenlaw and its wards as a bubble in a glass of champagne."

"Where is the other anchor?"

Jane looked pleased. "Follow me."

Faris followed Jane out of the chapel, across the nave of the new chapel, so called since it was a mere two hundred years old, and into the south transept. There, through a low-linteled door, Jane led Faris up a spiral staircase. And up. Swiftly at first, but slowly after three hundred steps, they climbed the dimly-lit stair.

Too stubborn to protest, Faris followed Jane in silence. As she climbed with her left hand on the central pillar of the stair, the spiral was so tight that Faris's right sleeve brushed the outer wall. There were narrow windows every hundred steps, just wide enough to shoot an arrow through, which gave them enough light to guess at the degree of wear of the stair wedges.

When Jane stopped, it took Faris a moment to realize they weren't merely resting. Jane stood on the top step, her hand on the latch of another low-linteled door. She lifted the latch and led the way through the door.

As she followed Jane out onto the roof, sunlight assailed Faris. She reeled as the world wheeled around her. She put out a hand to catch at the door and stood, eyes wide, panting and gaping at the view flung out before her.

To the east and far below, the sea made a silver skin across the bay to the blue hills of Normandy. Here and there, the shifting sands were visible beneath the shallow tide, like winding rivers running under the sea. From the perfect flatness of the bay, the seawalls of Greenlaw rose like a child's sand castle.

As she looked down, Faris admired the tidy stack of gardens, dovetailed with slate roofs, that marked the village wreathed around Greenlaw's base. At her back was the neat pepper-pot tower that sheltered the stair. At her right was Jane, squinting against the sunlight as she gazed into the depths of the sky. At her left was the sheer face of the spire, spangled gold and silver with patches of lichen on gray stone.

Faris looked up at the faceted heights of the spire. At the tip, foreshortened into a tangle of wings and swords, she knew St. Margaret stood back to back with St. Michael, trampling the dragon tirelessly into a lump of green bronze. As she looked, the drift of clouds across the sky behind the spire made Faris dizzy.

"Welcome to the north pole. We can't stay long. Just standing here we upset the balance of the wards. But I thought you would like to see."

"Oh, yes," said Faris softly, eyes on the horizon, "I would like to see."

After twenty minutes of silence, Jane sighed sharply. "We must go."

"So soon? My heart is still pounding from climbing the steps."

"Shameful. I must see to it that you take healthful exercise this summer."

"Climbing steps?"

"Climbing trees. Come along."

"Must I?"

"Don't whine. Follow me."

"You *English.*" Faris cast a last wistful look at the view and followed Jane back to the spiral stair. "You're so *strict.*"

Obedient to Jane's orders—or the Dean's—Faris spent the rest of the summer enjoying Greenlaw out of season. With help from Jane's purse, she was able to experience the joys of the patisserie. Though she climbed the more convenient trees of the Dean's garden, Jane spent just as much time slumbering in their shadow as she did in healthful exercise. Faris learned what it was like to watch the pattern of shadow cast by tree leaves until the random scatter of sun and shade made her sleepy.

Most days, the weather was good, and walks along the causeway or at the foot of the seawall were inviting. When the weather was not, there was refuge from the rain to be found in the library. There, on one of the last days of the summer term, Faris actually found herself reading Greek for pleasure, an il- luminated manuscript of *Works and Days.* She put the book down hastily the instant she realized her transgression but it was too late. The season had turned. Summer gave way to autumn.

At Michaelmas, the other students returned. Faris found herself sharing number five study with Charlotte and Nathalie, but all three of them were so intent upon their studies that they scarcely spoke to one another.

By November, Faris had almost grown accustomed to hearing her friend referred to as Dame Brailsford.

"There's a message for you," Nathalie said, when Faris came into number five study one night in late November. "Jane—that is, Dame Brailsford—left it. She was on her way to the Common Room."

Faris put her books down and picked up the folded page. The crisp paper, the elegantly illegible slant of the Dean's handwriting, told her the contents before she read it. Jane had received an identical message. On their vigil nights, Eve-Marie and Odile and every qualified third-year student had received just such a summons. Faris unfolded the sheet of paper.

The Dean of Greenlaw College invites
Faris Nallaneen to keep vigil tonight, the
twenty-eighth of November, until the
rising of the sun on the twenty-ninth.

"It's my vigil." Faris folded the sheet of paper in half again, then into quarters, and so on, without thinking, until she could fold it no more. She put the resulting untidy wedge of paper down on the table without realizing she did so.

"I thought it might be." Nathalie didn't look up from her book. "Is it cold out?"

"Of course. May I borrow your goose feather comforter, the one Eve-Marie used, just for luck?"

"What about your double bind, then?"

Faris laughed. "May I?"

Nathalie closed her book. From behind her chair she produced a shapeless armful of folded comforter. "I thought you'd ask."

Wearing Nathalie's comforter over her shoulders like a cloak, Faris left the dormitory and stepped out into the night. The evening air was chill but Faris was too excited to be cold. She had spent most of her time at Greenlaw being skeptical about magic. In the past few months, she had set aside skepticism, but no conviction had replaced it.

Now, although she could not find words to describe the feeling, even to herself, Faris found herself possessed of a peculiar restlessness. Since the arrival of the message from the Dean, she had known that something had changed for her. She was certain of the change, though nothing else was clear. At any other time, such irrational certainty would have worried her. On this night, it delighted her. She was a student of Greenlaw, this was her vigil, and on this night, of all nights, magic was afoot.

In planning for her vigil, back before she really believed she'd have one, Faris had determined that on a cold night the best place to be was the Dean's garden, in the shelter of its walls.

Once she made her way there, Faris found it hard to stand still beneath the oaks. It soon became plain she would find no peace in the garden. She turned away, with a sudden vivid memory of Eve-Marie's vigil. No wonder she had fidgeted her way almost all across Greenlaw. The vigil made its own demands, independent of the weather.

Faris reached the garden gate and halted, startled, as Menary Paganell stepped into her path. Menary carried a small lantern, its candle sheltered from the wind by panes of thick glass that gave the light a greenish cast. She lifted the lantern high and peered into Faris's face.

"Where are you going?" Menary asked. "Better yet, where are you coming from?" In the odd light, her face seemed to hold more than ordinary interest.

"I don't know," said Faris uneasily. "I'll know it when I reach the right place."

"It's your vigil too, isn't it? Stay with me. We'll watch together."

Faris drew back, disconcerted by Menary's unexpected friendliness. At her expression Menary smiled widely. The night wind lifted her hair into a mane that caught uncanny light from the lantern and stirred her academic robes around her like great wings. Though she wore no cloak, no hood, she seemed untroubled by the cold.

"This is a good place to keep vigil." Menary lifted her lantern and glanced around at the empty garden.

"Not for me." Faris moved forward.

As she brushed past, Menary caught her wrist. "I meant it. I want you to stay with me."

Menary's fingers on her wrist were so cold they stung. With a sharply drawn breath, Faris pulled free. "I can't stay."

"You will." Menary reached out again.

Faris stepped backward and bumped into someone. Her first thought, strangled before she spoke aloud, was *the Dean!*, then she heard Tyrian's voice, reassuringly calm, in her ear.

"Is this young person troubling you, your grace?" His level tone hinted at boredom.

Faris turned. In the wan light of the lantern, Tyrian stood at the gate of the Dean's garden, somberly dressed, exuding competence. Faris let out a breath of relief, started to speak, and glanced back at Menary.

Menary, her hair a wild pale aureole, her eyes wide, stared hungrily at Tyrian. "Is that where you came from?" she whispered to Faris.

Faris glanced apologetically at Tyrian. "I must go."

"Of course," Tyrian agreed. "Go on."

Faris left them. This time Menary made no attempt to stay her. She regarded Tyrian with rapt delight.

Faris let the restless feeling drive her, first to the foot of the Cordelion Tower, then to the cloister garden. She paused there, but the restlessness persisted. From the cloister she crossed the parvis to the new chapel. Then, more sure of herself, she hurried to the spiral stair.

All the way up, Faris hurried, though she had to feel her way up the steps by touch in the darkness. With each step, the restlessness built within her. It drove her toward something, a moment or a place or a moment that belonged to a place. The urgency was so great that Faris climbed the last steps as furiously as the first and burst, gasping, at last out through the low-linteled door of the pepper-pot tower.

After the stair, the roof was cold, raked with the night wind. Faris staggered, dizzy from the spiral stair, and caught herself at the wall. There was nothing before her but wind and darkness.

Faris stood quietly, hands braced on the low wall, and listened to the sound of her laboring breath. All urgency gone, Faris let her heart find its accustomed pace. She could hear every nuance of the wind in the pinnacles and towers around her. She could see nothing. Finally the cold conquered her stillness. With Nathalie's comforter huddled around her, Faris tucked her skirts close and crouched at the foot of the wall, taking what shelter she could from the wind. At last, her vigil had begun.

The hours were long. In the darkness, Faris waited. The cold became a part of her. She became as still as the stones beneath her. She felt the college and the village far below grow quiet as the peace of the night held them close. She sat at the heart of the world. Silent and serene, she balanced in the void.

During the last hour before dawn, the wind raked the clouds away and Faris saw the stars. She craned her neck to gauge their progress against the spire overhead. Above her, St. Michael and St. Margaret guarded one another's backs. She could not see them. Only the bulk of the spire, black against the sky's blackness, was visible against the stars. She did not have to see them. They were there. All was right with Greenlaw, she could feel that was so. Arms around her knees, chin nestled in the softness of the feather comforter, Faris felt sure of every stone in Greenlaw. All was well.

Out of the north, faint and far off, came the call of a skein of geese. Faris sat up straight. The call came closer, like a high wild song, like hounds hunting. Faris saw nothing of their passage against the stars. Only her heart could see them. Her memory showed her wild geese over Galazon. Faris swallowed hard. It was not that they were leaving winter behind. It was not that they were going somewhere Faris wished to be. It was the very fact of their passage that stirred her, the fact that something drove them across vast distance.

The wild geese did not merely heed the call that moved them. They answered it with a call of their own. The wildness of that call met the wildness of her longing for Galazon.

Vigil forgotten, Faris hid her face in her folded arms until the last faint notes of the call had faded. When the sky was empty, she looked up. Eastward, over the dark line that marked the hills of Normandy, the sun was rising. Faris looked up. The spire was still a featureless bulk against the sky. The stars had faded completely. In the rising light, the world was merely quiet. The utter silence of the night was gone. Faris shivered suddenly. She got stiffly to her feet, teeth chattering with the cold she had all but forgotten during the vigil.

When the long shadows of dawn had moved into place, when the sun was full up, free of the horizon, Faris made her way slowly down the spiral stair. She knew she did not display Eve-Marie's joyous expression. She wondered about Jane's grave response after her vigil. She had seen nothing but stars, heard nothing but the geese going over. But if Jane's vigil had been as uneventful as her own, it had done nothing to impair her skill at magic. Faris resolved to keep a calm countenance and say nothing.

Good policy in any circumstance, Faris told herself, and yawned convulsively.

With the deliberate pace of extreme fatigue, Faris started to return Nathalie's feather comforter to the dormitory. On the way, she saw the college stirring to life. It would soon be time for the Structure lecture. Resignedly, Faris left the comforter in number five study and turned toward the lecture hall. If she came too close to her bed, she would not have the heart to leave it again.

In the hall Faris saw Jane, who was frowning as she listened to Dame Villette's corner-of-the-mouth conversation. Near the front of the room, Menary sat, resplendently smug, among Gunhild and the younger students. Faris found an inconspicuous place in a far corner and braced herself to stay awake one more hour.

The Dean, the steel in her manner more noticeable than usual, delivered a lecture on the wardens of the world. Faris was feeling a little worried about having spent an entire night near the upper ward of Greenlaw. She told herself that she was imagining the Dean's cutting emphasis on the necessity of balance, but resolved to avoid catching the Dean's interest in any way for the next fortnight. The possible double meanings in the lecture had one good effect. By the time the hour was up and the speech over, Faris made her way to the door completely awake and on her guard.

As she reached the door, Jane joined her, looking grim. "You're wanted in the Dean's office."

Faris thought of her bed and set her jaw to suppress an involuntary protest. "Now?"

Jane nodded. "Or sooner."

When Faris presented herself at the Dean's office, the door was open and the Dean was already at her desk. She looked up as Faris entered and held out a sheet of paper.

"I have received another letter," she said crisply. "I think you had better see it at once."

Faris took the letter warily. It was not, as she had instantly feared, from any of Menary's family. Written in a clear, clerical hand, signed with her uncle's untidy scrawl, it read:

> Greenlaw College will permit the withdrawal of
> Faris Nallaneen. Her presence in Galazon is
> urgently required.

Stricken, Faris looked up. The Dean met her eyes gravely. When Faris said nothing, the Dean folded her hands and spoke.

"What Greenlaw College will or will not permit is no matter for your uncle to dictate. If you choose to obey him and return to Galazon, be aware that the nature of your studies here cannot be lightly interrupted. If you ever choose to return to finish your work here, you must begin at the beginning. You will not be permitted simply to resume where you left off." The Dean glanced down at the inkstand on her desk, then reached out to adjust it minutely. Without looking up again, she added, "Should you choose to stay here and complete your studies, Greenlaw College could inform your uncle that your withdrawal is not permitted."

Faris blinked. She had heard barely a word of the Dean's well chosen statement over her deafening thoughts. Galazon needed her. Or was it Brinker who needed her? Or *did* he need her? Was this something else altogether? She folded the letter and surprised herself by asking levelly, "Is there any message for me?"

"That missive was delivered here by a courier from Galazon. He wishes to speak with you as soon as possible. He is staying at the White Fleece."

"If he has some more explicit message for me, I wish to hear it," said Faris. "It might make my uncle's motives more clear."

"That seems perfectly reasonable. Please return when you've explored your uncle's motives sufficiently. We must discuss this further."

Faris managed to keep herself in hand until she was out of the Dean's presence. The instant she was in the corridor, she ran. Down the hall, down the steps, out the college gate, and through the streets of Greenlaw, Faris ran to the White Fleece. Her black robe billowed behind her with the speed of her passage. She ran, frowning fiercely, and the students she met on her way scattered before her.

A summons home was unlooked-for good fortune. Wasn't

it? Yet she did not feel the delight she should have. Even at the beginning of Michaelmas term, she would have been glad to go home. Now she felt as though she'd been shoved out of a vivid dream, jostled rudely by her uncle's summons. The wording of his letter to the Dean was characteristically opaque. If he'd sent along a message for her, very well. But if she was to leave Greenlaw for Brinker's convenience, some explanation was required.

Inside the White Fleece, Faris remembered that she didn't know who to ask the innkeeper for. Just as she decided to ask if a foreigner had recently arrived so she could sort out the candidates by their accents, she saw Reed. He was at a long table in the dining room, his nose buried in a pewter tankard. As she crossed to join him, he glanced up, snorted, and slammed the tankard down as he shot to his feet, choking.

"Sit down." Faris clapped him on the back, which only seemed to make the choking worse, and took the seat beside him. "Please sit down."

At her elbow, possibly summoned by the expression on Reed's face, the innkeeper appeared. "Is this young lady bothering you, sir? We do not generally encourage the students of the college to socialize with our guests."

Without troubling to rise, Faris looked down her nose at the innkeeper, who fell suddenly silent. Reed blushed and protested that the duchess was not bothering him, that is, he was not bothering her, that is, in short, they knew one another.

The innkeeper gave Faris a look mingling suspicion and resentment, sneered at Reed, and withdrew reluctantly.

"*Now* will you sit down?"

Reed regarded her with narrowed eyes as he resumed his place. After a moment, he took another long draught from his tankard, and ran one hand over his close-cropped hair. "You've changed, your grace."

"No, I haven't. When did you arrive? Did my uncle send any message for me? What's he hatching this time?"

"All I know is that I'm to fetch you home. I arrived last night. I have no message for you. And God forbid I should know what schemes best please Lord Brinker." Reed hesitated. "Look at you. You're as tall as I am."

"Taller, I'd guess, by at least an inch. Let's stand back to back and make the innkeeper measure." For an instant, Reed looked as if he were going to stand up. Hurriedly, Faris changed the subject. "Am I to be fetched immediately or only eventually?"

"Immediately. If you won't come willingly, I'm to order Tyrian to help me." Reed eyed the innkeeper. "If you speak to him again, he'll make me leave. And I haven't even started eating."

Faris pushed his plateful of fish stew toward him. "Don't stand on ceremony. What news from home? How does the harvest look?"

Reed busied himself with fork and spoon. "All is well. A good harvest. Gavren wished to come for you but your uncle wouldn't allow it. The journey is too much for a man of his years."

"Bilge. Uncle doesn't trust Gavren not to take my side, that's all. What does Tyrian say to orders from you?"

"I have no idea. I left a message at the address Lord Brinker gave me but he hasn't acknowledged it. You haven't asked after your family's health."

"Oh, very well, how does my esteemed uncle?"

Reed kept his eyes on his plate. "He is well. You ask only after him?"

Faris looked surprised. "Who else am I to ask news of? He's all the immediate family I possess, more's the pity."

Reed looked up. "What of his lady wife and their child?"

Faris regarded Reed quizzically. "I trust they do as well as my husband, our children, and all their get. The feast of fools is months off, Reed. Save your wits until then."

Very carefully, Reed put down his cutlery. His voice was gentle. "I feared you had no word from home and so I find it. Your uncle was married a year ago. His daughter is nearly three months old."

Faris blinked at him. Before she spoke, Reed had time to

take up his fork and spoon again. His stew was nearly gone when Faris repeated faintly, "Married?"

Reed nodded. "You sent gracious regrets at missing the wedding ceremony. For the child's christening gift, you presented your own silver cup."

"Did I? That was kind of me." Faris's blank expression gave way to one of calm calculation. Had she been studying so hard she missed mention of this ceremonial alliance in the newspapers?

Reed looked relieved and slightly amused. "Your generosity caused much comment. The child was christened Prosperian."

Faris's eyes flashed. "By what right? Why choose my grandmother's name? Aren't there enough names in Galazon?"

"I believe Lady Brinker chose the name," Reed replied. Gingerly he put his fork and spoon down. "She is a distant connection of your father's family, I believe."

"Oh? And who is Lady Brinker, when she is at home?"

Reed cleared his throat. "Her Royal Highness, Princess Agnes of Aravill."

6

"Where is Tyrian?"

🌟 FARIS SAT VERY still. She was aware, beneath the stillness, of her profound fatigue. It would be good to go on sitting at the table for a long time. Not thinking. Not talking. Just sitting.

"That would be Agnes Paganell, sister to Menary Paganell, I imagine?" Her voice didn't sound tired at all. She sounded calm and, in a small dry way, amused. Faris permitted herself to feel proud of that calmness. Perhaps Greenlaw had changed her a little after all.

"Princess Agnes is Princess Menary's elder sister, and so heir presumptive to her father, King Julian." Reed sounded apologetic.

"King Julian," repeated Faris, as though the words tasted spoiled.

"She seems quite decent, for an aristocrat from Aravill. She doesn't even use her own title. Just Lady Brinker. Not that any of us would ever remember to call her anything else."

"If Brinker has his heir, what does he want with me?"

"I haven't the slightest idea. Why not go home and ask him?"

Faris rubbed her forehead. "Asking does no good. If you need to find out what Brinker has in mind, you must just wait until it becomes painfully clear. Greenlaw College, for example. Greenlaw is far away and it takes a long time to finish. Probably the only reason he ever agreed to the terms of Mother's will and sent me here was to negotiate a match like this. Only I would have guessed he'd negotiate my marriage before his own."

"It *is* far away. The sooner you leave, the sooner you can be home in Galazon. There's a train from Pontorson at five this afternoon. You'll have plenty of time to pack."

"I'll leave Greenlaw when I'm ready, not before."

"You leave today. I admit you may have grown a bit, but together Tyrian and I can manage you."

Faris eyed him thoughtfully. "Do you think so?" She rose. "Come along."

Reed stood up. "I'm glad you're being so sensible."

"Don't be glad. I have no interest in being sensible." Reed's eyes were precisely level with her own, a detail that she found obscurely annoying. She turned for the door and glanced back over her shoulder. "Are you coming?"

"Where are we going?" Reed fell into step with her.

"To talk with Tyrian. We'll see what he says to your orders."

* * *

At Tyrian's lodging, Reed's message waited undelivered. No one had seen him since the evening before. In troubled silence, Faris led Reed back out into the street. When she led him through the gates of Greenlaw, he started to ask questions.

Faris ignored him. It was low tide. The empty sands stretched away from Greenlaw. Intently, she picked her way along the rocks at the foot of the seawall. The pace she set quieted Reed eventually. While she waited for Tyrian to interrupt her walk, Faris considered matters.

Her studies at Greenlaw, and her friendships, had cured her homesickness. It had been a long time since she pored over the pages of foreign newspapers and magazines for word from home. If she had only been more faithful to the tedium of the court circulars, she must have found some hint of her uncle's marriage. It was her own fault that she'd let herself be taken by surprise. Her love for Greenlaw had put her love for Galazon into the background and this was the price she paid for her faithlessness. Caught flat-footed by the news, without even a rumor to help her judge what to do next.

If Tyrian and Reed insisted, she would have no choice but to return to Galazon. It would certainly be annoying to obey her uncle promptly, but it might be wise to learn what was afoot at once. There was always the chance, however unlikely, that the summons concerned something of genuine importance.

On the other hand, if Tyrian and Reed could be set at odds, there might be means to delay her departure from Greenlaw. Under the Dean's auspices, some sort of comprehensive examination might be administered during that delay. But if it were administered, what was to say she could pass it? Faris was not sanguine about passing in May. To rush the test might merely serve to end any chance at her degree. Faris rubbed her eyes wearily.

"That was pleasant." Reed sounded puzzled but amiable. "I like a brisk walk after a good meal."

Faris looked up. They were back at the gates. There was no sign of Tyrian.

"Now shall we go and find Tyrian?"

Faris looked from the gate, to the gray stones of Greenlaw College rising above the little town, and to the spire that crowned all. "Yes," said Faris. Her voice was crisp and cold. Her eyes were worried.

At the college gate, Reed was stopped and given a place to sit on the guard's bench while Faris was within.

"I won't be very long," Faris promised him. "I last saw Tyrian with one of the students. If I can find her, she may be able to tell me where he is."

"If you aren't finished here by four o'clock, I'm going back to the White Fleece for supper. Look for me there in the morning. See you're packed and ready to leave on the nine o'clock train."

While she counted silently to ten, Faris regarded Reed with a look compounded of irritation and amusement. When she trusted her voice, she said pleasantly, "You don't understand. You don't issue orders here. Neither does my uncle. Whether I go or whether I stay, you're only a messenger. Remember that. The day may come you'll be grateful."

Reed shook his head. "You *have* changed."

Faris left him and headed, more or less at random, for the library. She had no idea where to find Menary, but the library seemed as good a place as any to start looking. As she passed the foot of the Gabriel Tower, she heard Jane call her name. Faris paused. Beaming, Jane hurried toward her from the direction of the Dean's garden.

"Why aren't you busy torturing your students with quadratic equations? Has the Dean declared a half holiday?"

"Thank goodness I found you. The Dean told me you're going home. I'm so glad for you. And as I've told you before, to a normal intellect, quadratic equations are elementary."

Faris uttered a small sigh of pure exasperation. "Don't be glad. It's my wicked uncle again. He's summoned me home without so much as a trumped-up excuse. I'm to abandon my education today."

Jane raised an eyebrow. "Well, perhaps that is rather sudden. But you do want to go home, don't you? It's all you think about. At the slightest excuse you wax agricultural and exude homesickness."

"You don't think he's sending for me because he misses the pleasure of my company, do you? No, he has some scheme in hand."

"You're so used to thinking of him as an ogre that you credit him with the worst motives out of sheer force of habit."

"What do you think are my chances of persuading the Dean to give me my comps before I have to leave?"

Jane arched both her brows. "Better than your chances of passing them. If you don't *want* to go home, don't go."

"I may not have a choice. Much depends upon Tyrian. Have you seen Menary since the lecture this morning? Where can I find her?"

Jane's brows drew down into a puzzled frown. "What do you want with Menary?"

"We spoke last night. She wanted to keep vigil with me, doubtless for some inscrutable reason of her own. Tyrian distracted her while I left."

"I should just think he would," said Jane, half to herself.

"He hasn't been seen at his lodgings since. I wonder if she knows where he went after I left them."

"I can't imagine that she'll give you a civil answer, but I suppose it can do no harm to ask. She's in the Dean's garden. I saw her when I passed."

With Jane at her side, Faris walked to the garden. In the gateway, she paused.

At the foot of the oak tree, Menary sat on the dry grass, her skirts spread wide. Blond hair loose down her back, she leaned her head against the trunk of the tree, and laughed at the animal in her lap.

To get a better look, Faris drew closer. The animal was a black cat, its tail bushed rigid. It spat at Menary, but neither clawed nor tried to flee. Ears flat, it seemed to flinch from her touch as she patted its head, but its legs were limp.

Faris frowned. Beside her, Jane said softly, "I've never seen a cat in that humor that didn't try to bite the first hand to come near it."

At her words, Menary looked up. "Come see my new pet. Isn't he handsome?"

Faris came nearer. She had always found it difficult to make polite conversation with Menary. This was no exception. "Did your vigil go well?" she asked finally.

Fierce enjoyment dancing in her fine eyes, Menary smiled up at Faris. "Very well, thank you. And yours?" She caressed the cat, ignoring its rising growl.

"Well enough." Faris regarded Menary's merriment suspiciously. Menary laughed softly, and dropped a kiss between the cat's ears. The cat spat again.

"You choose a strange season to sit and play in the garden." Faris studied the cat intently.

Jane looked warily from Faris to Menary and back, and said with false heartiness, "Why you aren't both sound asleep is more than I can explain. After my vigil, I felt as though I'd been laundered and hung on a bush to dry."

Faris stared. "What's the matter with that cat? He can't move his legs, can he?"

Menary tried to look grave but her eyes betrayed her amusement. "He fell climbing the tree. He'll be all right soon." Under her hand the wedge of the cat's head stirred. Menary moved her fingers soothingly, just enough so that Faris met its glaring golden eyes.

Faris experienced a slight sharpening of her vision. Weariness, hunger, and pique fell away before her sudden surge of anger. In a remote, calm portion of her mind, she thought how odd it was that people spoke of losing one's temper. Ordinarily, she was scarcely aware she had a temper. Now that she could feel it yielding like rotten rope, her temper was vividly present, like another person inside her skin.

With great detachment, she told herself that it was her temper that gave her leisure to examine the variety of her reactions. It was her temper that made time seem to run so slowly.

It was her temper that narrowed her field of vision to those golden eyes. And it was her temper that made Jane's voice sound far away, more distant than her recollection of Tyrian's words. That day the tide had come in as they stood on the rocks, his voice had been entirely businesslike: *I found a dead rat in his unmade bed.*

She heard her own voice, loud and rough, as she started toward Menary. "Where is Tyrian?"

Jane's hand brushed Faris's sleeve as she moved forward. Far off, she was saying, "That's not a cat—"

Menary's mouth curved with slow satisfaction. "Whatever he was once, he's mine now."

Faris stood over Menary, so close that she could see Menary's fair hair stir against the tree bark as the girl looked up and added, "What will you do about it, sailor's daughter?"

Very far away, Faris heard Jane's voice. "Oh, dear—"

Then Faris felt the silk of Menary's hair in her hands, and heard Menary's outraged shriek as Faris hauled her to her feet. The cat dropped free and fell in the grass a few feet away. Jane tried again to catch Faris's sleeve.

Faris ignored her and shifted her grip to Menary's shoulders. Her temper had made it hard for her to see. Her vision had shrunk until she could scarcely make out what her hands were doing. What little vision remained, anger tinted red.

Faris shook Menary until her head banged against the tree trunk. The impact traveled up Faris's arms. Satisfactory but not perfect.

Faris gathered herself for another try. Menary shrieked again, not a scream of pain, a scream of rage, a shriek with words in it. Dimly, the remote, calm portion of Faris's mind recognized the intent behind the words. Her hands loosened.

As Faris took a step back, Menary fell against the trunk again, and shrieked in earnest as the tangled silk of her hair caught fire.

It was not natural fire, Faris realized. It gave no heat, no scent of singed hair. It blazed pale gold and green, Menary's wild halo. In its own way, it was beautiful, as cold and strange as the northern lights.

Jane shouted, and thrust Faris aside. Her hands were on Faris's sleeve again. Irritably, Faris pulled away. Jane stripped the academic robe from Faris's shoulders, and fell upon Menary to smother the flames. Menary kept on screaming. The noise she made hurt Faris's ears.

Suddenly cold, suddenly shuddering with cold, Faris fell to her knees in the garden. Her anger was gone. Her vision was clear. Too clear. There was no way to avoid the sight of Menary huddled at the foot of the oak. Under Jane's hands, she sobbed and struggled. The cat was gone. An arm's length away, unconscious, naked in the brown grass, lay Tyrian.

At the sound of a soft footfall, Faris looked up. In the garden gate the Dean stood, resplendent in her dark green robes. She was flanked by Dame Cassilda and Dame Villette. With calm severity the Dean regarded the disarray of the garden, then looked back to Faris.

"You are going to have to tell me," she said, restraint in every syllable, "precisely what has happened here."

Faris swallowed. She could find no words to force through the tightness in her throat. Instead, she regarded the Dean with mute wonder.

"Dame Brailsford, tell the infirmary what's happened here, and have them send stretchers. Dame Villette, Dame Cassilda, see to the injured. Faris, come with me."

Uncertainly, Jane looked from the Dean to Faris, then down at Menary, who was weeping quietly at her feet. Dame Cassilda and Dame Villette came forward, and something in their brisk manner decided her, for she nodded respectfully to the Dean and left.

"Faris—" There was warning in the Dean's voice.

"I won't leave Tyrian," said Faris hoarsely. "I'm responsible for him."

"You are responsible for a great deal, it seems. Dame Villette?"

Dame Villette spoke up from her place at Tyrian's side. "He'll do."

Reassured, Faris rose to her feet and crossed slowly to the Dean. The backs of her knees seemed to jerk and quiver as she walked. She shivered.

"I want Menary Paganell sent to my office the moment she's recovered," the Dean said to Dame Cassilda, and left the garden. Faris followed her unsteadily.

In the Dean's office, which felt splendidly warm after the chill of the garden, Faris sank into the chair the Dean indicated. Surely there was solace in the offer, she reflected. Wouldn't swift execution take place standing?

The Dean spread her hands flat on the desk blotter. "Tell me precisely what happened."

Faris folded her hands in her lap, and noticed without much surprise that they were trembling. "I am not at all sure." Her voice was small and nearly peevish. She cleared her throat twice and continued more normally. "I was looking for Tyrian. He works for my uncle. He's here on my behalf, so I feel responsible for him. While I was looking, I found Menary. In some fashion, she had transformed Tyrian into an animal. A crippled animal. I lost my temper—"

"Before all that. Tell me what happened from the very beginning. You had your vigil last night. Start there."

Faris blinked. "From the beginning?"

The Dean nodded.

Faris cleared her throat again and began. By the time she had finished, the Dean was sitting very straight, gripping the arms of her chair until her knuckles showed white.

The Dean spoke very gently. "Tell me what else happened on the roof of the chapel. Northern lights?"

"Nothing else. It was cloudy. I heard some geese go over. I saw the stars when the sky cleared, just before dawn. Am I to be expelled?"

"You cannot stay at Greenlaw," said the Dean. "You are quite certain you experienced nothing out of the ordinary while you were up there?"

Faris closed her eyes in an effort to think more clearly. She was so tired they stung and burned, but this was not the time to betray fatigue. She squared her shoulders and returned the Dean's piercing gaze as directly as she could. "I didn't get as cold as I expected to."

"You were aware that you were near the anchor?"

Faris nodded.

"You realize that the presence of most individuals disturbs the anchor? And in turn, that the anchor disturbs them? How did you feel during your vigil? Did you have a headache?"

"I felt a little out of breath the first time I visited the place, that's all," Faris replied.

From a drawer of her desk, the Dean produced a card and wrote a few words on the back. "Time is of the essence. At the earliest opportunity you must go to this address," she handed Faris the card, "and ask for Monsieur Hilarion."

"Why?" Faris examined it, an ordinary visiting card, with the Dean's full name engraved on one side, and on the other an address written in the Dean's rakishly slanted hand: 24, rue du Sommerard, Paris. "Who is Monsieur Hilarion?"

There was a knock at the door.

"He will prefer to explain that to you himself." At the Dean's summons, Jane Brailsford entered. "For now, I must ask Jane some questions regarding the scene you created in the garden. Please give her your chair."

"Just a moment."

Oblivious to her, the Dean asked, "Jane, is Dame Cassilda finished in the infirmary yet?"

"No, but Dame Villette is in the hall."

"Excellent. Faris, go tell Dame Villette to keep you under her thumb until I need to speak with you again."

Faris gripped the arms of her chair. "I'm not going anywhere."

Jane came to stand beside her. "Your friend Tyrian is down at the infirmary. He's asking for you."

The Dean frowned at Faris. "I have told you that time is of

the essence. I have several important matters which I must discuss with Jane. After that, I must prepare to deal with Menary Paganell. The infirmary staff have wonderful powers of restoration, so my time is limited. Go tell Dame Villette to guard you."

"Why? After all, I'm going to be expelled. Why should I obey you?"

Jane regarded Faris with dismay.

"One might wish you had grasped the subtleties of language in the time you've spent here. I never said you were to be expelled. I said you cannot stay at Greenlaw."

Faris opened her mouth, and then shut it again without speaking.

The Dean seemed pleased with the effect she had produced. "Dame Villette may escort you to the infirmary. Go see about that young man. After all, you say you feel responsible for him."

Reluctant to obey but entirely unable to think of a reason not to, Faris rose. Jane still looked a little stunned as she took the chair.

As she closed the door, Faris heard the Dean's calm voice. "Now, Jane, tell me precisely what happened—from the very beginning."

With Dame Villette at her side, Faris walked into the infirmary. It was a small gray building that smelled strongly of carbolic soap. In the corridor, she encountered a harassed-looking young woman wearing doctor's garb.

"I'm here to see the man they brought in from the Dean's garden."

The doctor regarded Faris with interest. "The naked man? Are you indeed? So much the better." She offered Faris a bundled heap of clothing, all black. "They found his clothes under the desk in the Pagan's study. Makes you wonder, doesn't it? You can bring them in to him."

Faris took an involuntary step backward. "I certainly will

not. You take them in to him. I'll see him when he's himself again."

The doctor thrust the bundle of clothing into Faris's arms. "Who do you think you are, the Queen of Sheba? Do as you're told."

Faris took the bundle. The doctor left her. Faris stood in the drafty corridor, aware that her knees were quivering again. At her elbow, Dame Villette said softly, "This room to the left."

Faris turned and held out the bundle to her. "You take his clothes in. Please."

Dame Villette smiled. "I think not."

Faris found Tyrian's room typical of the infirmary, a white-washed space with one window, empty but for the narrow iron bed. Beneath the drab blankets, Tyrian seemed smaller than she remembered. His disordered hair was bright against the white pillow. He watched her enter, his blue gaze clear and steady, but said nothing. Faris put the bundle on the foot of the bed, and retreated until she could feel the door against her shoulder blades. He looked very young, almost her own age.

"They found your clothes," she said, unnecessarily. Her voice sounded nearly normal, so she added, "Are you all right?"

"Yes." It sounded as though it hurt him to talk. "Thank you."

"They said you asked to see me."

"Yes." He watched her intently.

Silence filled the room. He did not seem to notice. His eyes held Faris's.

Faris turned and opened the door. "I'll come back in a few minutes, then. You'll want to get dressed." His stare disconcerted her. She had to get away from it. There was something wrong with the intensity of his regard, something strangely childish, that had nothing to do with the man she had expected to see.

To her relief, he nodded.

"I'll wait in the corridor. Call when you're ready to talk."

When he called "your grace," Faris returned. This time, Tyrian was sitting on the foot of the bed, fully clothed. He was finishing with his boot laces as she entered. Faris could not see his expression, but the hunch of his shoulders suggested embarrassment or guilt.

"I have three things I must make it my duty to tell you." Tyrian's voice was soft and slightly hoarse. He did not look up from his boots. "First, I apologize. I have no excuse worth offering, only that she is so young. As young as you, your grace. I underestimated her. I am sorry."

Faris frowned. Tyrian, it seemed to her, spoke with the carefully measured phrases of a man in pain. "Are you certain you're all right?"

Without looking up, Tyrian continued, "The second thing is, thank you for breaking the spell. I underestimated you, too. Until you freed me, I thought I was hers forever." Tyrian paused. "When I agreed to guard you, I swore I would never let you come to harm. Instead, you had to rescue me. So, the third thing is my resignation." He did not look up.

"Oh." Belatedly, Faris recognized the misery that ran beneath his words. She was looking at a man ashamed. Wearily, she wondered how Jane would manage this situation. After a moment's thought, she came and stood beside him at the foot of the bed. "I'm sorry. I'm tempted to try sophistry but I won't. You know the sort of thing—I didn't hire you so I can't accept your resignation—" She held up a hand to still his protest. "I won't. And you didn't let me come to any harm. But I won't chop logic with you. If you've had enough of magic to last a lifetime, I understand."

Tyrian rose. "Thank you." Eyes downcast, he started slowly for the door.

Faris did not move. "Only, I consider it a great pity that Menary Paganell should possess the power to turn you from your duty."

Tyrian turned back to face her, his mouth tight. "It is a

great pity she possesses any power at all, but she does. Indeed she does."

"I am warned. I'll be wary of her. Although," she added carefully, "I doubt our paths will cross again. Menary will probably be expelled. And I must leave Greenlaw. My uncle has just sent Reed to fetch me back to Galazon."

Tyrian's eyes widened slightly. "Reed? Drayton Reed?"

"Why, yes." Faris looked surprised. "Do you know him?"

"Who else is with him?"

"Nobody."

"Your uncle sent him as your escort, just Reed alone?"

Faris nodded.

"Then your uncle is a fool, and Reed's another." Tyrian scowled at the floor for a moment. Then he looked back at Faris with sudden resolution. Indignation erased any strangeness in his manner. "I withdraw my resignation. I will go with you to Galazon. I must."

In her relief, Faris smiled broadly at him. "Then you do know Reed."

"Indeed I do. I don't wish to slight him, but he has had far less experience at this sort of thing than I. He shouldn't have to bear sole responsibility for your safety."

Faris studied him. "On my uncle's behalf, I accepted your resignation. I employ you now myself." She extended her hand to Tyrian. To her astonishment, he made a courtly bow over it.

"Command me, your grace." Tyrian smiled at her and Faris found herself smiling back.

"The Dean intends to conduct an inquiry into my doings with Menary. When that is finished, I'm told I must leave Greenlaw. Indeed, the Dean has asked me to pay a call for her in Paris." Faris frowned slightly, but continued with scarcely a pause, "After that, we will go home to Galazon."

"With great pleasure, your grace." Tyrian opened the door. Dame Villette stood there, fist raised to knock. He greeted her politely.

"The Dean has sent for you both. She has spoken with Menary and is ready to question Tyrian."

"Good," said Faris. "Time is of the essence."

At half past two, Dame Villette led Tyrian into the Dean's office and left Faris under Jane's supervision. In weary silence, Faris followed Jane through the angled sunlight of winter afternoon into the great hall.

"We're to wait here," Jane said quietly.

Faris looked around at the vast lacework of the windows, the polychrome ceiling, and the complicated tile floor. "That makes sense, I suppose. This is where I started."

"The Dean questioned me as though I'd witnessed a murder. This is no mere inquiry into a row between students. It's a full scale court-martial. What have you done?"

Faris sighed. "You were there. You saw it. I lost my temper. Do you think we might go look for a chair somewhere?"

"We're to stay here."

"Why?"

"Because you'll get me into trouble." Jane tried to laugh. The attempt failed, and she looked troubled.

"Oh, come now. I've been up all night. I've missed so many meals I may never catch up. I've been questioned by the Dean and I'm going to be questioned again. At least let me sit down. I'm going to need all my strength for this."

"I'm serious, Faris. We're to stay right here. I'm sorry there's nowhere to sit but it can't be helped."

"Graduation was the ruin of you, Jane Brailsford." Faris sat down on the floor.

"Get up. You can't be court-martialed sitting on the floor."

"I'll get up when the Dean comes, I promise." Faris stretched out on the floor, and yawned enormously. "Wake me up when it's time."

The outer door opened and Menary entered, Dame Cassilda at her side. In her severely cut gray frock, with the neat turban of white linen bandaging her head, Menary resembled a novice rather than a penitent. Her eyes were thoughtful, her expression serene. She seemed troubled neither by the events that had passed nor by the interview to come. She regarded Faris with amusement.

"Abase yourself before the Dean, by all means, but it's usually done lying on one's stomach, not on one's back."

"I yield to your greater experience in such matters." Faris rose. Menary smiled at her. It was a small, yet extremely nasty smile.

Jane stepped between the two. "Greenlaw's quarrel with you takes precedence over the quarrel between you. Wait your turn."

"A pleasure deferred," said Menary.

Faris sneered.

"Get your servant to explain the concept to you," Menary added.

"That's enough," said Jane grimly, as Faris bristled.

Menary laughed. "Be still, Dame Brailsford." She made the title a mockery. "You know nothing of this. This is a matter between the sailor's brat and me."

Belatedly, Dame Cassilda put a restraining hand on Menary's sleeve. Menary shook it off disdainfully.

From an inner door no one had noticed as it opened, the Dean said, "This meeting will now come to order."

As those in the room turned, the Dean swept forward among them. At the spot she deemed satisfactory, she halted. "Here, I think, Tyrian."

From the inner room, Tyrian emerged, bearing a lyre-backed chair which he set for the Dean. He bowed her into it with grave courtesy. At her gesture of dismissal he stepped backward to join the ring the others made before her. From her place in the ring, Faris regarded Tyrian closely. Whatever had passed in his interview with the Dean, his customary expression of calm indifference was back. Inwardly Faris rejoiced at the sight.

Through the outer door Dame Villette entered, Drayton Reed in tow. They joined the circle between Faris and Jane.

"I thought I left you waiting in the tumbrel," Faris whispered to Reed.

"You said you wouldn't be long," Reed replied.

Faris kept her eyes on the Dean and replied out of the corner of her mouth. "I tried to hurry. See where it's gotten me. Court-martialed."

"Wouldn't a simple notice that you won't attend any more classes have done the trick? Who's the dragon lady?"

"That's the Dean of Greenlaw College. She's in charge here."

"It figures. Trust Tyrian to ingratiate himself with the ruling class."

"Dame Villette, Dame Cassilda, Dame Brailsford, we are here today to deal with the transgressions of these two students." The Dean nodded at Faris and Menary as she named them in full. "The inquiry I have conducted has satisfied me that they were party to acts of magic as undergraduates. What they have done before, they may do again. If they attempt any action, physical or metaphysical, you are to do your duty and restrain them by any means in your power. Do you understand?"

Dame Villette looked mildly pleased, Dame Cassilda mildly wary, and Dame Brailsford mildly distressed. All nodded.

"Very good." The Dean turned from Menary to Faris. "Do either of you have a defense to offer for your extraordinary behavior? Do you?" There was perfect silence in the room. The Dean looked from Faris to Menary, her eyes blazing. "Speak up if you do."

Faris looked at Menary. Menary was staring with polite resignation at a point in the air over the Dean's head. She looked as if she were listening to distant music she did not much care for.

Faris met the Dean's steely gaze. "Very well. I do."

"Speak."

"I didn't try to do any magic. I tried to kill Menary, that's all. She harmed someone in my service. Send me away if you must, but know that I did what I did for a good reason."

"Do I understand you correctly? You admit you attempted to kill your classmate."

Faris nodded.

"You consider *that* a defense?"

Faris nodded again.

The Dean turned to Menary. "And you? Do you offer any explanation of your actions?"

Menary brought her gaze down to meet the Dean's. "No."

The Dean held Menary's gaze for a long moment, then Menary looked at the floor. The Dean said, "You are expelled from this college. You will both be gone by sundown today. Never return."

Menary bowed her head and withdrew from the circle with a gliding graceful step.

Faint impatience troubled the Dean's gaze. "Where are you going?"

Menary halted, gray eyes wide. "I was about to leave the college, never to return. I obey orders."

"Not invariably," said the Dean dryly. "Don't be so hasty. I have not quite finished speaking to you."

Menary returned to her place in the circle.

"For reasons of your own, concerned perhaps with vanity and spite," the Dean told Menary, "you have misbehaved almost from the moment of your arrival at Greenlaw. You brought with you not merely an insolent notion that because you had the inclination to question rules, the rules did not apply to you, a notion which a few of your classmates share—" Here she glanced pointedly at Faris for an instant. "—but a vicious habit of mind as well. You have done those things which you ought not to have done. It matters not at all how you did them. I grant that you did not use the magic of Greenlaw. Still, no matter how you contrived it, you have done those things."

Impassive, Menary returned the Dean's gaze.

"At first you showed great promise. Despite complaints, I allowed you to go your own way. I erred. I was loath to break your spirit merely in the name of manners."

"Fear not," said Menary softly. "I have resisted sterner efforts at discipline than yours."

The Dean looked sad. "I know it. It seems you are determined that your promise will go unfulfilled. But I must not allow you to leave just yet. You are half trained and wholly unreliable. Before you go, you must tell me what you saw on your vigil."

Menary's eyes widened, then narrowed. She said nothing.

"You understand. Tell me, or I will ask you again and you will have no choice about answering."

"I saw—" Menary hesitated. Her eyes slid from the Dean to Dame Villette and back to the Dean.

The Dean held up her hand. "Don't trouble to lie." She pointed at Menary and Menary seemed unable to take her eyes from the Dean's index finger. "For the third time, and the last time, and the time you must answer: *Tell me.*"

Menary paled until her eyes seemed nearly black in her white face. "Tyrian," she said softly, unwillingly.

Faris glanced at Tyrian. Unmoved, he was watching the Dean closely.

The Dean lowered her hand. "The damage your whim did him has been undone. He is free of the bond you laid upon him. Now, with your word, you are free of him. You are free of the power your vigil lent you. Go now. Never return."

Menary's color rushed back, a tide of scarlet that overwhelmed her pallor. She blushed but still her gaze did not fall. After a moment the high color subsided until it burned only in her cheeks. "I have nowhere to go. I must send for a ship from home."

"There are rooms to be rented in St. Malo. I do not want you within the gates of Greenlaw, not even down in the village. Dame Cassilda, attend her while she packs. See that you escort her to St. Malo."

Chalk pale, her bearing stiff but still proud, Menary withdrew, Dame Cassilda with her. When the door was closed behind them, the Dean spoke again. "Now for you, Faris Nallaneen. You are lucky to have such observant testimony in your defense. It is plain to me that you brought no magic to the encounter. Indeed, your primitive defense states the matter fully. You lost your temper and tried to kill Menary. Let me remind you that wrath is a deadly sin."

For the first time since she had left Dame Brachet's deportment class, Faris dropped her gaze and examined the toe of her shoe with minute interest.

The Dean continued. "You cannot remain at Greenlaw. Your uncle and I agree on that, if on nothing else. Yet I have no mind to set a half-trained witch of Greenlaw at liberty in an unsuspecting world. Tell me what you saw on your vigil."

Faris frowned. "I told you all that."

The Dean lifted her hand. "Tell me again."

"Very well. It was dark. It was cloudy. Just before dawn it cleared and I saw the stars."

"Come here." At the crispness in the Dean's tone, Faris came forward without demur. When she was an arm's length from the lyre-backed chair, the Dean halted her. "Kneel. Look at me."

Faris knelt and found she could look nowhere else. The Dean's dark eyes held her motionless and silent. She was only remotely aware of the floor beneath her knees, of the ache in her neck, of the stillness in the great hall. All she could see were the Dean's eyes. It seemed to her that their darkness took fire from the angled sunlight until they glowed golden.

"Now tell me."

"I saw the stars." Faris's voice sounded distant and sleepy.

"Name them."

From some distant lesson in natural history, the names came back. "Arcturus," Faris said. "Vega, Spica, the Northern Crown—"

"That will do." The Dean folded her hands.

Faris rose stiffly.

"You may go. You may not return. You have come too far to tread the student's path any longer." She sounded tired. Her eyes were merely brown.

Faris steadied herself. "I'm not ready to go yet. I have some questions and I want some answers."

"Inquire in the rue du Sommerard. It is Hilarion's business you wish to know. He would not thank me if I tried to enlighten you. Go to Paris."

For a moment, fatigue and impatience stirred the embers of Faris's temper. "Very well. Since I have been expelled, contrary to your word, and since I have been sent for by my uncle, and since it is on my way home to Galazon, I *will* go to Paris."

"You are very obliging." The Dean closed her eyes wearily.

"But I will not leave until you have refunded the balance of my school fees for the term—not to mention the balance of the funds held in escrow since my admission."

The Dean opened her eyes and fixed Faris with a glance of deep displeasure. Faris returned it. "Dame Villette, kindly inform the bursar she is to draw up a letter of credit for this young extortionist. Dame Brailsford, go and pack your things. I am not sending Faris Nallaneen away from here with a full purse unless I can be quite certain that she is properly supervised in Paris. She seems to listen to you. You will escort her. See she pays the call I require in the rue du Sommerard. It is of the first importance. Go."

Jane's eyes widened. "Go now, ma'am?"

"Now. Have Faris's things packed, too. Be certain she behaves herself. Paris is full of distractions, particularly for the well-to-do."

"Yes, ma'am." Jane departed.

The Dean rose, shook out her robes carefully, and regarded Faris, Reed, and Tyrian. "Stay here until Dame Brailsford fetches you. There should be no difficulty in reaching Pontorson in time for the Paris train. Be very certain you are on it." The door in the paneling was open. She walked through it and it was gone.

Reed and Tyrian exchanged glances of guarded relief. Faris sat down in the lyre-backed chair. However long the wait for Jane's return, she was far too tired to pace.

Volume Two

The Warden
of the
West

7

Hilarion

❧ By HALF PAST five, the train was well on its way to Paris, charging along in clouds of steam and a haze of soft coal smoke. Across the compartment from Faris, Jane sat with her gloved hands folded neatly in her lap, her expression unguessable behind the heavy veil she wore. Reed and Tyrian had solicitously installed them in a first class compartment, but both left without explanation a few minutes after the train's departure from the station.

Faris sat quietly, yielding to the steady sway of the railway carriage. The compartment smelled of cigars and managed somehow to be stuffy and cold at the same time. It was already dark outside and the yellow gaslight in the compartment was dim enough to make slumber easy for anyone. For Faris it was nearly irresistible. Although she had too much to think about, it was impossible to concentrate. She blinked and wished the brim of her hat allowed her to lean into the corner.

The compartment door slid open and Tyrian entered, dexterously balancing a tea tray. Awestruck, Jane lifted her veil to take a long look at the teapot and cups arranged on the tray. "Tyrian, you are a thorough brick."

She took the tray from him and added, "See if you can bring down my hat box from the rack without dislodging any of the other things, please."

"It's only railway tea," Tyrian said, with an apologetic air that surpassed mere boastfulness. "This hat box?"

"Yes. I packed up the last of Aunt Alice's plum cake. It was the only food I could find on short notice and it was much too good to leave for Dame Villette or the students." Jane pulled off her gloves and poured tea. She held out a cup to Faris, giving her a glance of appraisal at the same time. "Are you all right?"

Faris smiled and accepted the cup Jane offered. "Just about. Ask me again in a few hours."

"Don't worry. We'll manage everything." When she could spare attention from the teapot, Jane looked sharply across at Tyrian. "Who are you, anyway?"

Tyrian was slicing the plum cake with a large knife of alarmingly efficient design. "I beg your pardon?"

Jane addressed him sternly. "You know what I mean. You appear like the slave of the lamp just in time to stop Faris killing that sailor. You bring out the worst in Menary and the best in the Dean. You can make the French railway produce tea and you carry a knife better suited to cut throats than to slice cake. Who *are* you?"

Tyrian looked embarrassed. "I am no one, my lady. Merely a precaution on her grace's behalf while she is far from home. I have agreed to escort her back to Galazon. Reed intends to help, too. He is on watch in the corridor at the moment."

"A precaution, hm?" Jane looked dissatisfied. "Against what, precisely? Do you know of any particular threat against Faris?"

Tyrian shook his head. "Lord Brinker's chief concern was that her grace might leave Greenlaw. I think he did not wish her to be out in the world with no protection."

"Say, rather, he did not wish me to come home unexpectedly, to surprise him in his schemes." The tea was weak but hot, the cup's warmth comforting to Faris's cold hands. She accepted a piece of Jane's sticky dark cake, and thanked them both. "When do we arrive in Paris?" The cake was heavy, damp, and rather sparingly spiced. Traveling through the post had probably improved it. Faris could not remember when she had tasted anything so good.

"Too late to go out for dinner, even if you had anything suitable to wear. That's why I thought of the plum cake."

"Not before ten o'clock," said Tyrian, handing Faris another slice of cake as she finished the first. "I took the liberty of wiring to arrange a hotel. We have reservations at the Hotel Suisse."

Jane's eyes widened over the rim of her teacup. "The Hotel Suisse? I've never heard of it."

"It's quiet and close to the station. It's even clean."

Jane regarded Tyrian with consternation. "Who will believe that a duchess would stay at the Hotel Suisse? What *modiste* in her right mind would willingly send large purchases on credit to an address near the gare Montparnasse? What is wrong with the Hotel de Crillon? My family always stays at the Crillon."

"What sort of large purchases on credit?" countered Tyrian. "As soon as Reed and I arrange it, the duchess will return to Galazon."

Faris handed her tea cup to Jane. "You will kindly include me in this conversation."

Jane ignored her. "First she has a call to pay in the rue du Sommerard. Do you suppose she will be received dressed as she is now? She's a perfect ragamuffin. She must have new clothes."

"Am I a parcel?" Faris inquired to the compartment at large. "Am I a portmanteau? I will not be spoken of as if I am not here."

"The Hotel de Crillon is very elegant. It is also very large. Reed and I can't possibly secure the whole building."

"You needn't. You need only watch her."

Faris reached up and began to unpin her hat.

"You know better than that, Faris. No lady travels without a hat."

"No lady? But then, *I* am no lady. *I* am a ragamuffin, so let me be a comfortable ragamuffin. Since you persist in referring to me in the third person." Faris folded her cloak about her. "You leave me no choice but to ignore you both in return. Wake me when we arrive." She turned to Tyrian. "And when we arrive, we go to the Hotel de Crillon."

"To soothe the vanity of a dressmaker?" Tyrian glanced at Jane.

"To soothe the bankers. Before you arrange the train tickets, before Jane arranges my call in the rue du Sommerard, before we spend a sou on accommodations, we must first consider the bankers. They are sure to feel more at ease with a letter of credit from a young person who resides at the Hotel de Crillon than from a young person who stays at a hotel convenient to the gare Montparnasse."

Jane and Tyrian looked at one another. "You must admit she's right," said Jane.

"Of course she's right." Tyrian smiled angelically. "She is my employer."

Faris nestled into the corner and gave them a last exasperated look. "Wake me at the station. Not before."

On her first morning away from Greenlaw, Faris woke in time for the Dean's lecture. In the half-light of early morning, she lay in the unaccustomed luxury of a featherbed and considered matters. It took her a moment to remember that she would not need to rise early for that lecture, nor any other, ever again. Her time as a student was over. Despite her uncle's guardianship, she was the duchess of Galazon, and as such, was required to conduct business on Galazon's behalf while she was in Paris. There were bankers to see, urgent arrangements to make. And most urgently of all, there was a call to pay in the rue du Sommerard.

Duty called. She should rise and answer. Instead Faris pulled the coverlet up over her face and fell asleep again.

Faris woke the second time when Jane dropped a neatly wrapped box on her stomach. "Do you mean to sleep all day?"

Cautiously, Faris peered over the edge of the coverlet. "What time is it?"

The bedroom was filled with light. Jane was silhouetted against the windows, fussing with the drapes. "Past eleven. I've rung for rolls and coffee. If you hurry, you'll be finished in

time for luncheon." Jane turned away from the windows. She
was wearing a stylishly enormous hat, the veil still down. As
she neared the bed, Faris pushed herself up on her pillows in
surprise.

"Get rid of that veil, Jane. It makes you look a hundred
years old."

Jane stopped in front of one of the great gold-framed mirrors that flanked the fireplace and started to extract hatpins. "I
mean to look a hundred years old. A fine figure you'd cut,
larking about Paris with only a slip of a girl like me for a chaperone." Veil still down, she turned to Faris. The features behind the thin material were Jane's, but Jane's in forty years, or
fifty. She lifted the veil and her own young face returned. "I
was glad to find I could keep up the illusion once I left Greenlaw. But oh, how it makes my head ache and my face itch.
You've no notion."

"Where have you been? Where are Reed and Tyrian?"
Faris looked around the room, saw the stack of boxes on the
divan, and more boxes scattered across the oriental rugs.
"What have you *done?*"

"Don't sound so horrified. I just ran out to find a few
things for you to wear."

"A few things?" Puzzled, Faris looked at the profusion of
boxes again. "How did you know what would fit?"

"I didn't. That's why I had to bring an assortment. We'll
send back the rest."

"Oh," said Faris, relieved.

"I left Tyrian to stand guard here and took Reed with me.
They have the rooms on either side of our suite, so methodical
of them, don't you think? The instant I brought Reed back
here, Tyrian went racing off to make arrangements for the Orient-Express. I think he wants to snatch you away from my per-
nicious influence."

"He may have a point. How much have I spent so far this
morning?"

"For this?" Jane resumed the removal of her hat. "It's
only ready-made. Everything is on approval. If you like, I'll

send it all back. But you can't, honestly, Faris, you *can't* go about Paris dressed like an expelled Greenlaw student. And you must pay that call the Dean has arranged. If you go looking like a ragamuffin, you'll be treated like a ragamuffin. It isn't enough just to be a duchess. You must look like a duchess. These things matter."

The visit in the rue du Sommerard seemed less appealing than ever. "Oh, very well. But leave something of the school fees to pay for my train tickets."

"I knew you'd be sensible."

From the outer room came the sounds of room service, delivering rolls and coffee under Reed's supervision. Jane sighed and lowered her veil again. "Excuse me. I must see to this. Reed has no notion of *douceur*. He undertips scandalously."

Faris got up. It seemed wise to visit the bankers at the earliest possible moment.

By the time the coffee and rolls were finished, and by the time Jane considered Faris suitably dressed in her ready-made finery, it was past noon. All the banks were closed at midday, so there was nothing to do but retire to the hotel dining room and eat luncheon.

Jane referred to this as "making the best of things," but Faris appreciated the chance to take in the well-organized splendor of the hotel. It had been a mistake to fall asleep on the train. By the time she awoke, Jane, Reed, and Tyrian had arranged matters among themselves so efficiently that her removal to the Hotel de Crillon made Faris feel she was just another piece of baggage. Of her arrival, she remembered very little. She had a confused recollection of the chestnut panelling in the corridors and the brilliantly polished brasswork of the lift. But the profusion of chandeliers she remembered in the lobby was gone. Instead there were four noble crystal fixtures and a profusion of high-arched mirrors. The spring flowers she had glimpsed, extravagantly out of season, proved to be made of wax, and arranged with a strict symmetry of the most Parisian kind.

Into the restaurant—a vale of haughty waiters, tables draped faultlessly with shell-pink linen, and intricately wrought fruit forks—Faris followed Jane.

Luncheon took two and a half hours. Tarrying only for coffee and *profiteroles,* Faris and Jane set off on the day's errands, Reed and Tyrian in attendance.

The bank was easy. Greenlaw College employed the same bankers that Faris's mother had used, and they were delighted to be of service to the duchy of Galazon once again. Encouraged by their courtesy, Faris lingered until Jane became restive.

"Yes, by all means," Jane murmured, "renew your usual line of debt the instant you come of age. Build roads. Build railroads. But remember, the *modiste* waits for no one."

"Must I really visit Madame Claude? These clothes seem perfectly suitable to me."

Jane regarded her with dismay. "Have you ever in your life owned a piece of clothing that fit you? If you had, you'd know the difference now. If your grace has made your wishes known, there is no more to be said in the matter, of course. But just once, stop and consider. You are, however briefly, in Paris. You have, however briefly, a great deal of money to spend. While you are here, isn't there something you wish to do that you can't do as well anywhere else?"

Faris sighed. "Very well. On to Madame Claude's."

After an hour at the *modiste*'s, Faris was ready to leave Paris and never return. Jane was oblivious to Faris's discomfort. Veil down, she made shameless use of her apparent years and her fruitiest accent and most British French to order the staff about in a high-handed way. Utterly absorbed, she consulted with Madame Claude and nodded over the gowns displayed by the bored mannequins who stalked in and out of the fitting room.

Faris was thoroughly measured and thoroughly ignored.

As assistants brought in bolts of fabric for Jane and the *modiste* to consider against Faris's hair and skin, she tried vainly to make her wishes known. "I don't need very much," she said plaintively. "A traveling suit and something for afternoons. An evening gown, if you insist, Jane. That black silk was nice."

"Not with your complexion. Lift your chin a little. That's good. No, hold still. Show us that violet charmeuse again, Madame, if you please."

Out of the corner of her eye, Faris saw the violet charmeuse drawing near. "That's much too bright. I don't need it. One traveling suit. Perhaps that will do for afternoons, too. One evening gown. Oh, yes. And I'll need a riding habit. But that's *all.*"

Jane nodded absently. "Of course, your grace. I think the marocain may do for the dinner gown. That shade gives your eyes some color."

"The dark blue is all right, but that purple silk is too bright. I'll look like a clown. And I don't want any of that transparent stuff." Faris brushed aside the assistant hovering near her with a bolt of sheer shrimp-pink fabric.

"It's called tulle, your grace. What do you think of this one? You may turn your head now."

Faris turned her head and regarded the latest mannequin with horror. "No. Never. No feathers." She stepped down off the pedestal and waved away the last tape measure. "I want my cloak. I'm leaving."

Jane exchanged a tolerant glance with Madame Claude, who signaled for Faris's cloak. The feather-clad mannequin left, pouting. Jane turned to Faris, eyebrows raised. "There's no need to be rude about it. You merely had to tell me you were tired."

Faris accepted her cloak from the assistant and put it on with a practiced furl and snap of fabric. "No tulle. No pink. No feathers. All you've talked about all afternoon is dinner gowns. What am I to wear to the rue du Sommerard?"

"That's all settled. A walking dress. It's going to be a midnight blue serge, nice and drab. You'll like it. It will be ready next Friday."

Faris threw up her hands in despair. "I can't wait until next Friday. I am to call on Hilarion at the earliest opportunity. This is the earliest opportunity. Are you coming with me? Or are you going to order gowns?"

"There are still one or two details to be seen to, and after that I have an errand of my own. Leave Reed here and he can see me back to the hotel."

"Very well. I'll take Tyrian with me."

"Excellent. I don't think this is precisely his milieu." Jane glanced toward the reception room at the front of the shop.

"Your escort has been occupied with refreshments," Madame Claude said, "but since they have exhausted our supply of coffee, perhaps it would be as well if they were given something useful to do. And perhaps you and I, milady, may settle a few trifling details." She smiled at Jane, who smiled sweetly back.

Faris regarded their concord with sudden misgiving. "If we're so nearly finished, perhaps I should stay."

"If you wish, of course," said Jane. Her eyes narrowed. "I wonder, now that I think of it, if that violet marocain is not a little too drab, after all. May we see it again?"

"Certainly," Madame Claude replied promptly. "One moment and I shall send someone to fetch more coffee."

Faris held up her hand, startling herself with the elegance of her new gloves. "That won't be necessary. I'll leave you to it, Jane. Only remember—just a few gowns."

"And a riding habit."

"Well, yes. I do need a new riding habit. But nothing fussy. And *no feathers.*"

"I understand perfectly."

Number 24, rue du Sommerard, behind its courtyard walls, was a great turreted house with a watchtower looming over its widespread wings. While Tyrian paid their driver, Faris stared. There was nothing of Parisian symmetry about the jumble of architecture that contributed to the house—pointed windows, deep gables, slate roof—yet there was nothing of disorder either. Nestled in its courtyard, a place of quiet within a few hundred yards of the noise of the boulevard Saint-Michel, the house achieved grace. Faris remembered the chapel at Greenlaw. There was something of that silence in the harmony of this house.

"This is an old place," said Faris softly.

"I believe Roman ruins have been found nearby," Tyrian said. "This was the heart of Paris, back in the days when they called this place Lutetia."

"No," murmured Faris, more softly still, "I mean *old.*"

Inside, Faris presented the Dean's card and her own to a servant who led them into a sparsely furnished room paneled with linen-fold oak. The servant withdrew to tender the cards to Monsieur Hilarion. Faris paced while Tyrian stood at the doorway.

"What's taking so long?" she asked, when she was tired of the pattern of the parquet floor.

Tyrian consulted his pocket watch. "We have only been here twenty minutes. That's not very long to find our host in a house of this size. Then there is the time it takes for the servant to return to us."

"Perhaps he's forgotten where he put us." Faris started to pace again. "Or perhaps Monsieur Hilarion doesn't receive callers from the Dean of Greenlaw after all."

"Or perhaps you are nervous." Tyrian closed the watch and put it away. "No need to be."

Faris halted and gave him a haughty glance. "I'll be nervous if I please."

"Certainly, your grace."

Faris regarded his gravity with deep suspicion. "If you're mocking me, stop it at once."

Tyrian looked extremely mournful. "Very good, your grace."

Faris began to laugh. Tyrian looked reproachfully at her. "If you are mocking me, your grace—" he began.

The servant returned to lead Faris to Monsieur Hilarion. As if his presence were merely a matter of course, Tyrian accompanied them.

Even more than its facade, the interior of the house told of the splendor of the centuries that had visited it. Faris followed the servant along corridors with vaulted ceilings painted royal blue and powdered with golden stars, through halls hung with tapestries like clearings in an enchanted wood, and down a staircase of white stone, its spiral as tightly furled as a unicorn's horn.

Despite its age, the house seemed fresh, as though its atmosphere had but lately come from a real forest. As she descended the white stair, Faris caught the vivid scent of pine needles and damp earth and felt her eyes prickle with homesickness. At the foot of the staircase, the servant held open a door so low that Faris had to bow her head to enter. Tyrian followed. When they were through, the servant closed the door and left them.

The room was dark. Faris put her back to the arch of the door and took comfort from Tyrian's presence, so close his sleeve brushed hers. The scent of pine had gone as suddenly as the door had closed. Instead she smelled moist stone, her new gloves, and an unfamiliar aroma, a compound of coffee, smoke, and a spice she didn't recognize. With a small jolt of surprise, she realized it was Tyrian's scent. She took a step away. Underfoot the floor was smooth but not quite flat, like the well-worn steps of Greenlaw. The gloom shifted as her eyes grew used to the dimness. Now she could make out an arch across the room. Beyond, a light was burning.

"Faris Nallaneen," said a voice like the wind, as she crossed the dark room, "I have been waiting for you."

Tyrian was close beside her as she reached the arch. She paused at the top of another flight of stairs, this one slanting down the wall of a great vaulted chamber. Below them on a dais of carved stone stood two chairs and a lacquered table with a branch of lighted candles. One chair was simple and straight-backed. The other was a deep wing chair upholstered in brocade as rich as a tapestry forest. Both chairs were empty.

From the dais, the voice came again. "Don't stop there. Come down."

The sense of silence was still with her, the peace of the house reigned unchanged, but Faris found the voice unsettling. The shadows the candlelight cast might hold any terror, any wonder. She obeyed the voice, grateful for Tyrian at her back.

When she stood beside the table, the airy voice spoke again, from the depths of the wing chair. "You've been long in coming."

Faris looked at the empty chair. For a moment, in the candlelight, she thought she saw brocade leaves stirring in a tapestry forest. Then, indistinctly at first, but with greater clarity the longer she looked, she saw the man seated in the chair.

He was old, that was plain in the knotted delicacy of the hands that lay along the arms of the chair and in the hunched curve of his posture, but his eyes were young and full of merriment. Faris spent a long moment looking into those eyes, as light as her own, then said, "Hilarion."

Hilarion lifted a hand to gesture her to the other chair. It was hard to see his fingers. "Sit. I'm afraid Tyrian must stand."

Faris glanced at Tyrian. He had taken his place near her chair, one pace to the right and one pace back, and stood at ease. Though he seemed relaxed, Faris noticed that he pointedly kept his eyes away from the wing chair. "Thank you, but I think I prefer to stand, too." Belatedly, the meaning behind Hilarion's words came to her. She turned sharply back to him. "That is a name you were not given."

"Tyrian and I have met before." Hilarion's eyes glinted with amusement at the intensity of Faris's stare. "I sent him to your uncle."

Faris thought hard, so hard that she took the chair Hilarion had offered without realizing she did so, sinking into it with preoccupied grace that would have impressed even Dame Brachet. "Does my uncle know that?"

Hilarion folded his hands. "Who can say? I doubt it. Tyrian was the best qualified candidate for the task of guarding you through Greenlaw. I wished you guarded, too. It seemed simple enough to arrange. Your uncle loves complexity but he is not immune to the charm of simplicity. Neither am I."

Faris leaned forward slightly. "I think I know why my uncle wished to guard me. Tell me why you wished to guard me. Tell me who you are and why the Dean sent me to you. Tell me why I am of the slightest interest to anyone."

"Very well." Hilarion cupped one hand around the topmost candle flame. The light was scarcely dimmed, the flower of the flame plainly visible behind his fingers. "It has not escaped your notice that I am not entirely substantial."

Unwillingly, Faris smiled. "I had noticed."

"Nor am I entirely insubstantial. Had you observed that?"

Faris nodded.

Hilarion looked pleased. "That is one reason why you are of interest to me. I do not conceal myself willingly but to others I am not visible. Tyrian, for example, has never seen me, although we have spoken many times."

Faris glanced back at Tyrian. He was still standing at ease, gazing calmly into the shadows. "Is that true?"

Tyrian met her eyes. His look was as steady as it had been in the infirmary. Faris tried to remember exactly how long it had been since that awkward conversation and caught her breath in surprise. The day before. That entire dreadful interview had taken place only the day before. She felt as though she had known Tyrian longer than Reed, longer than Gavren, even.

"Indeed it is." Into the shadows, Tyrian added, "I must inform you that I have left your employment, Master Hilarion. Yesterday I promised to serve Faris Nallaneen. I owe her a great debt."

"Then of course you must pay your debt. If you work for

her as you have worked for me, she will be well served, indeed."

"Thank you, sir."

Hilarion continued, "You have skills you have not guessed, Faris. Take up the light."

Faris lifted the branch of candles. The shadows in the room shifted. The candle flames burned flawlessly. Faris realized that they gave off no heat, no melted wax, no hint of smoke, only clear golden light. Her grip on the candlestick tightened but she held it steady.

"You may put it back."

Willingly, Faris obeyed.

"You perceive the nature of that light?"

"I perceive it is not natural candlelight."

"Put out that light."

Faris looked sharply at him. "Why?"

Hilarion smiled gently. "To see if you can."

Faris shook her head.

"Why not? Are you afraid to fail?"

"Certainly not. But what if I can't light them again?"

"A sensible question. There are four people in the world who could move that light. You are one. I am another. I could not put it out. Perhaps you could. I am glad you had the wit not to try. I know of no one and nothing that can restore that light once it has been extinguished." Hilarion's hands were very still on the arms of his chair. "To answer your first question, I wished to guard you because I hope you are the warden of the north, come again after many years."

Faris stared at him.

"To answer your second question, I am Hilarion, warden of the west. Your Dean sent you here to learn what the world requires of you."

Faris continued to stare at him for another long moment, then she sprang to her feet and turned fiercely to Tyrian. "Pick up this candlestick."

Tyrian looked apologetic. "I don't think I can."

"*Try.*"

Tyrian put his hand through the candlestick. "I'm sorry." He rubbed his hands together after the attempt as if his fingers had gone numb with cold.

Faris clenched her teeth and picked up the candlestick again. Hilarion laughed. She put the candlestick down with a bang and turned on him. "Laugh if you like. But hear me. I *know* what the world requires of me. I was born to rule Galazon and that is precisely what I am going to do. You can't stop me."

"Certainly not. Your love for Galazon does you credit. Yet Galazon is not the world. Let me remind you, if the world is neglected, Galazon must surely be neglected, too." Hilarion studied Faris for a moment, then continued thoughtfully. "You may have observed that the world is a dreadful place. You are very young. If you haven't yet had the opportunity to study the matter, allow me to assure you that it is. That is one of the least satisfactory aspects of the balance of the world. Nothing in it, be it never so fair, can ever be wholly good. Fortunately, the other side of the coin is that things cannot be wholly bad, either. Unless the balance fails."

Faris turned to Tyrian again. "You honestly can't see him?"

He regarded her with concern. "I can't. If you don't care to listen, we will go whenever you wish."

Faris hesitated, then took her chair again. "No. I'll listen." Reluctantly, she met Hilarion's gaze. "Unless the balance fails. That sounds so portentous. *Does* it fail?"

"I am proof that it does." Hilarion looked at his hands. "I am old, and such is my situation that I cannot die. Nor can the warden of the east or of the south. We must remain at our posts, with what patience we can muster, until the warden of the north comes again."

"Tell me why."

"The last warden of the north attempted to gratify a whim. She tried to create something wholly good. A vain endeavor, perhaps, yet not as deplorable as the alternative. Still, her efforts destroyed her and tore a rift between this world and the next. Ever since, we three have worked to slow the progress of the rift. While we maintain what we can of this world's essence, we are stranded here. Daily, we grow closer to the next world, until we become invisible to those we defend."

Faris thought of the bubbles rising in Jane's champagne. Was Hilarion one of the bubbles lurking in the bottom of the glass? "Then stop. What would happen if you let the rift do its work?"

"Ignorant child, were you never taught the structure of the world?"

"Every morning for the past year and more. If the soap bubble that we live in mingles with the next soap bubble outward, what matter? If you speak of being stranded in this world, that implies you want to go onward to the next. Well, we'll all go."

"Mingles," repeated Hilarion, as though the word had a taste and he didn't care for it. "Mingles. If this world mingles with the next, what befalls? From the point of the rift outward, the balance of the world distorts. From the rest of the world toward the rift, what magic we have worked so hard to balance drifts into the rift and away. As the magic departs, the balance alters, and the ordinary chaos and unpleasantness of the world outdoes itself. When the rift is wide enough, when disorder encompasses all, what life is left will slip away. In its place will be order at last. But it will be the order of emptiness. All magic, all growth, all life will be gone. And the next world will receive it, like a blow to the balance it struggles to achieve. And so outward."

There was a long silence. Into it, at last, Faris spoke. "Mend the rift."

"We have tried and failed. The warden of the north made it and the warden of the north must mend it. And until now, we have had to do without a warden of the north."

"Tell me how to mend it."

Hilarion shook his head. "I cannot."

"How was it made?"

"The last warden of the north tried to combine her wardship of the world with dominion over her realm. In her pursuit of mere political power, she ignored the demands of the wardship. Then, to protect her wardency, she attempted to extend her power outward until it met itself where it began. Instead, it created the rift. She was consumed, her faction deposed, and her heir eventually exiled to die at sea."

Faris parted her lips but did not speak.

"There might have been a kind of justice in it, if she who caused the rift had been doomed to haunt the world. Instead, those she left behind must haunt it, working to mend her mistake."

"Her name—" Faris scarcely formed the words but Hilarion caught the whisper.

"Oh, you know her name."

Faris regarded him in silence for a long time. When she spoke, her voice was a husk of itself. "My grandmother was called Prosperian."

Hilarion nodded.

"My father died at sea."

"I know."

Faris closed her eyes and felt the silence of the house fold around her. A curious sense of peace made it easy to consider her father and her grandmother as abstractions. Even Hilarion's insubstantiality made sense in the calmness of the place. "I can't do it," she said finally, sorrowfully. "I'll try, of course, but I can't do magic."

Hilarion made a scornful sound. "So much for modern methods of education. You have done magic on three occasions. Nothing ostentatious, yet all three bode well for your ability."

Faris stared at Hilarion. "When? And how do you know about it?"

"I am the warden of the west, am I not? Greenlaw is in the west, is it not? I may dwell here where it is quiet, but I am not utterly out of the world."

"Greenlaw maintains its own wards."

"So it does. And those wards may cloud your vision for years. In time, however, you should find it otherwise." He glanced at Tyrian. "Yesterday you perceived Tyrian within a different form. You exerted your will to change him back to his proper guise. That was the third time you displayed your aptitude for magic."

"My third? What did I do? How did I set Menary's hair on fire?"

"Ah, now, the witch's hair. That wasn't you, that was the witch. She intended to set your hair afire. You balanced her magic. The force she used turned back to consume her." He frowned. "Indeed, the force she used was sufficient to burn you to a cinder. It puzzles me that she took no greater harm than she did. She must have formidable powers."

"The Dean said Menary did not use the magic of Greenlaw."

"No? Then she must have resources of her own."

"What are they?"

"I can't identify them. They are nothing that belongs to my wardency. They do not come from the west."

"If changing Tyrian back was the third occasion, what were the first two?"

"Weather magic does not usually go unnoticed. A year ago you made it snow in the cloister garden. Perception and will. You perceived that it should snow. Behold. Snow. That was the second occasion."

Faris thought back carefully. "I was homesick. I was thinking of Galazon." She frowned at Hilarion. "And the first?"

Hilarion smiled. "It would not surprise me if you refused to acknowledge the first occasion. It was appropriately modest for a beginner. You sneezed."

"I beg your pardon?"

"Carelessly, one of your fellow students accepted a gift. Coal, I believe. I suppose it might have been more obvious, though short of a poisoned apple, I don't see how. The coal caused an accident, as it was intended to. Even such a crude stratagem might have resulted in severe injury. Fortunately, you sneezed."

"I sneezed. But that's all I did. How could a sneeze have accomplished anything?"

"It wouldn't accomplish anything, now that both you and the young woman from Aravis have progressed. But you were both beginners. I can only suppose you balanced each other out."

Faris frowned. "Tell me how you know all this—names, deeds, intentions—"

"No imbalance in my wardship escapes me. The sooner you take up your rightful place as warden of the north, the sooner you will attain such perception."

Faris looked around her a little desperately. "Must I sit in the dark to do it?"

"Darkness suits me." Hilarion looked into the shadows. "In direct sunlight, even you couldn't see me, Faris. This place likes me well. Time runs more restfully here. Outside, the days rush past me like a high wind. But these walls are old enough to keep the wind away. These stones were set down before this city was mere muddy Lutetia. The city has risen around this place, potsherd upon potsherd, through the centuries. Here I can be quiet. And here in the dark, it does not trouble my servants that they cannot see me."

"But doesn't it trouble you to be driven into the dark?"

"When my body has worn so thin, what matter where it lies, so long as my spirit still knows my wardship? Would you care how dark it was, if your spirit could range forth and walk in truth through the woods of Galazon?"

"Could I do that?" Faris looked worried.

Hilarion laughed. "No. Not yet. Perhaps not ever. If you mend the rift, you'll never need to, for when your hour comes, you will pass away as you should, without dwindling to a shadow like smoke in sunlight."

"When my hour comes to pass away like smoke up a chimney, must I go on to the next world?"

"Has this world been so kind to you, then, that you refuse

to leave it?" Kindness subdued Hilarion's amusement, but merriment lightened the long look he gave her. "Mend me the rift and let me go ahead to see."

"If I mend the rift, if I take up my wardship, what of Galazon then?"

"Galazon remains Galazon. With you to restore the balance, why should Galazon not flourish as the rest of the world flourishes?"

"Only that much? No more?"

"Go lightly, I caution you. Remember that nothing is wholly good. Such thinking created the rift." From around his neck he drew a gold chain, long and fine as a strand of hair. Threaded on the chain was a key made of smoky green glass, the color of sunlight in seawater. "Take this."

Faris hesitated, but put out her hand. When she held it up to the candlelight, the key glowed greenish gold, the few fine imperfections in the glass like the small bubbles of sea foam. "What is that?"

"Prosperian stood at the northern anchor to work her last magic. I know the northern anchor was in the throne room at Aravis Palatine. The rift destroyed the anchor. There may have been more damage, I do not know. I have never seen the place. If anyone there at the time had a shred of sense, the room will be securely sealed. If it is, you must find the warden's stair. That is the key to the stair—the only key. Guard it well."

Faris put the chain around her neck and slid the key inside her collar. It was warm against her skin. "Where do I find the warden's stair?"

"I'm afraid I have no idea. It's outside my wardency. Tyrian, if she fails, I rely on you to return the key to me."

Tyrian folded his arms. "I am not in your service any longer."

"I know. But we must plan for defeat as well as for success. If she doesn't succeed in mending the rift, someone else will have to try."

"If I should fail, I promise to send the key back. For now,

Tyrian, if you will guard me on the way to Aravis, I will be grateful. And if I fail, I will need you to bring this back. May I count on you?"

Tyrian blushed. "You may count on me until my last hour, and for an hour beyond."

Hilarion chuckled very softly, a sound like the wind in pines, and stirred in his chair. The tapestry forest shifted as though a silent breeze rustled silent branches. "Though time runs more restfully here, you mustn't let the world outpace you. I have no more to tell you. Go lightly, child, and remember what the world requires of you."

Faris rose. The leaves of the tapestry forest shifted again and Hilarion was gone. For a moment she stood staring at the empty chair. Tyrian left the dais. At the foot of the stair he paused, looking back at her.

Faris looked from him to the branch of candles. "I would rather leave it here untouched, but if we need the light, I could bring it."

"I think we can manage without it. Come."

Faris followed Tyrian. Silently, they made their way through the shadows to the spiral stair, up and out of Hilarion's house, into the chill of the wintery night.

"Your hat is ticking."

OUTSIDE HILARION'S HOUSE it was windy, dark, and cold. While Faris and Tyrian were indoors, it had rained. The streets were wet, striped with golden light where the puddles reflected the street lamps, and almost empty.

Faris welcomed the wind. After her interview with Hilarion her mind was racing. To be still was impossible. To return at once to the stifling luxury of the hotel was intolerable. The wind pulled at her cloak. It would be good to walk into that wind until she wearied.

As they turned the corner into the boulevard Saint Germain, a horse-drawn cab approached, the only traffic moving in the wide, well-lit street. Tyrian eyed it keenly.

Faris put her hand on his sleeve. "It's getting late, I know, and cold, but I need time to think. May we walk back to the hotel?"

"Yes, I think perhaps we should." He lengthened his stride and let the cab pass by. "That same cab was waiting outside Madame Claude's when we left. I recognized the driver by his moustache."

Faris looked at him. His usual calm indifference gone, Tyrian was fiercely cheerful, as though he enjoyed swaggering along in the chilly night. "A coincidence, no doubt," she said dryly, and walked faster.

He matched her gait easily. "No doubt. There are two men following us. They are probably a coincidence, too." Despite the raw wind, Tyrian opened his overcoat.

They walked on, past the medical school, across the Carrefour de l'Odeon. Every footstep seemed unnaturally loud to Faris. She did not need to look back to know that Tyrian was right about the men following them. She could almost feel their presence, a chill on the nape of her neck that had nothing to do with the wind.

Ahead, another cab turned into the street and came toward them. "I don't seem able to think, after all." Faris hoped her voice did not betray her relief. "Shall we take this cab?"

"I think not. What are the odds of two cab horses with the same white stocking? This is Moustache again, back to see if we're tired yet."

"Oh." With an effort, Faris kept her tone light. "I don't suppose the men behind us are tired yet?"

Tyrian checked. "Far from it. They are starting to move in." From somewhere inside his coat he produced his pistol and thumbed off the safety. "Stay behind me. Don't let them get you into the cab if you can help it. I'd hate to have to shoot the horse."

From the street behind them came the growl of a combustion engine and the angled light of automobile head lamps. The cab horse tossed its head in protest at the oncoming vehicle. Faris turned as a sleek Minerva limousine drew up beside them and paused. The rear door swung open. It was impossible to see inside.

"I don't suppose you'd care for a lift." Jane's clear voice rang out cheerfully.

Tyrian helped Faris in. With one foot on the running board, he hesitated, looking back down the street.

After the windy night, the interior of the limousine seemed warm. The seat was wide and deep and covered with leather. Managing her cloak and skirt as she settled in reminded Faris of packing a suitcase.

"Uncle Ambrose loaned me his limo for the evening," Jane explained. "Isn't it lovely? We were parked the wrong way in the rue du Sommerard. You turned right and it took a moment for Charles to circle the block to catch up with you."

Reluctantly, Tyrian got in and closed the door. "Now we won't know who sent them until they try again."

"Drive on, Charles," said Jane.

With a refined roar, the Minerva pulled smoothly away. From his seat beside Charles, Reed watched the street they left behind. "Only two on foot and one with the cab? Are you sure they know who we are?"

"*We?*" Tyrian returned the pistol to its holster and buttoned his overcoat. "More to the point, do we know who they are?"

"Local help, at a guess," Reed replied. "Do you think they noticed you notice them?"

"Short of shooting one of them, I don't know how much more obvious I could have been."

"Are we going back to the hotel?" Reed asked Jane.

"We can if you like, but wouldn't you rather circle the block, catch one, and hold him at gunpoint until he Tells All?"

"There's not the smallest chance they're still there," said Tyrian.

Reed said, "Probably not, but let's try anyway."

Jane peered anxiously at Faris. "Shall we?"

"Whatever you like," Faris replied. She watched the empty streets pass as Charles obeyed Jane's orders. Jane, Reed, and Tyrian discussed the incident, but Faris did not listen. Instead she stared abstractedly into the night, and thought about her uncle.

If she had been followed from Madame Claude's to Hilarion's, there was no chance that their pursuers were simple robbers. The only real question was whether they had been hired to abduct her or to kill her outright. At a venture, she thought the latter.

At night the streets of Paris were not truly safe for anyone. If she was the victim of a crime there, who would wonder at it? Was that why Brinker had sent for her? Traveling across Europe, even by rail, could be dangerous. If she met with some unfortunate accident en route, who would wonder at that? And if she somehow managed to come safely home to Galazon, what then? A hunting accident, perhaps?

Yet, if he wanted to kill her, why had he not done so long before? Why send her off to an expensive school, haul her out of it just before she finished, and *then* kill her? And why hire a bodyguard to make the task harder for himself?

But if not Brinker, who?

There were no cabs, no sinister men strolling the boulevard Saint Germain or its side streets.

"Well, if we've accomplished nothing else, we've shaken off anyone who might be following us," said Jane cheerfully. "Shall we go back to the hotel now, Faris? Or would you rather take a run to the Bois de Boulogne? Or even out to Fontainebleau? It's a shame to have the use of a splendid motorcar like this and to waste it driving in the city."

"Why would they need to follow us?" asked Reed. "If all Paris doesn't know the duchess of Galazon is staying at the Hotel de Crillon, it isn't your fault."

"One must maintain a certain position. What shall we do, Faris?"

Faris considered the alternatives. "I'm hungry. Among those things to do in Paris that I can't do as well anywhere else, Jane, I would like to eat dinner."

"Oh, dear, didn't you? I was certain he'd kept you to dine. It's a trifle late for dinner now."

"What time is it?"

"It's after three. Why did you think we made such an effort to come fetch you?"

"No wonder there was only one cab on the street." To Tyrian, Faris said, "Time does run restfully there." She turned to Jane. "Where is the best place to find supper at this hour?"

"Back to the hotel, Charles. I shall perform my celebrated imitation of Aunt Alice, the compleat titled Englishwoman abroad. It may make you cringe with embarrassment, but I promise you'll get your supper."

Jane sat by the fireplace in Faris's room, and watched her eat the mixed grill sent up by room service. "It is just possible that I've taken my celebrated imitation a bit far. How *can* you eat kidneys in the middle of the night?" She shuddered delicately.

Faris took a sip of wine. "Does that mean you don't want any?"

"Uncle Ambrose gave me an excellent meal, thank you."

"I didn't know you had an uncle in Paris." Faris turned her attention from the wine to the last grilled mushroom on her plate.

"Oh, yes. Uncle Ambrose has lived here for years and years. He's not like some uncles, though. Paris hasn't had much effect on him. He won't own anything but a British motorcar, he smuggles all his cigarettes and cigars into France via diplomatic pouch, and at the races he still grumbles that the horses run the wrong way. Quite a dear old boy."

"I've never been in a motorcar before." Faris put her knife and fork down with a small sigh. "It was most interesting."

"You didn't seem too interested at the time. You didn't even seem too interested in your pursuers."

"I was thinking." Faris regarded Jane seriously. "You haven't asked me about Hilarion."

Jane arched an eyebrow. "I am perishing with curiosity, can't you tell?"

"It seems I have to save the world."

"Oh, dear. Do you have the training for that?" Jane asked dryly.

Faris smiled and leaned back in her chair. "I doubt it. But it seems I am the warden of the north."

Faris spent the rest of the night discussing every detail of her visit to Hilarion's with Jane, most of the following day asleep, and half of the day after that with bankers and solicitors. She returned to the hotel at the end of the afternoon in time to witness the arrival of the first parcels from Madame Claude. Jane presided over the tea tray while Faris sat beside the fire and counted boxes.

Faris accepted her cup from Jane. "I thought these things weren't to come until Friday."

Jane offered her a plate. "Bread and butter? You seemed so disappointed, I arranged matters a bit differently with Madame Claude. Most of the order will be ready this week. Anything that isn't finished by the time you leave for Galazon will be sent after you."

Struck by a sudden suspicion, Faris looked up from her tea. "How much more will that cost me?"

"I really couldn't say. Just think of it as another little annoyance for your uncle Brinker. Try the cake, it's very nice."

"Guess, then." Faris helped herself to a slice of hazelnut gateau. "Estimate."

"It's your uncle's money. If he'd ever given you a decent clothing allowance, this wouldn't be necessary."

"It is not my uncle's money. It is Galazon's money. I hold it in trust."

Jane rolled her eyes. "Don't be so disgustingly noble.

Your people wouldn't care to see you dressed in rags, would they? You're representing them, aren't you? You've got to keep up the side."

"It's more than the year's rent roll. I can't just waste it."

Jane looked distinctly nettled. "You *aren't* wasting it. Nor am I wasting it. I have chosen you a wardrobe that will probably have to last you the rest of your ridiculous life. I have managed to get the greater part of it done in less than a week. I have worked miracles for you and all you do is order me to estimate how much it cost to hurry Madame Claude a little. Yes, blush, by all means. You jolly well should blush. You owe me an apology."

Jane left the tea table and stalked to the heap of parcels. "You'll be happy enough about all this when your uncle gets his first look at you. Has he *ever* seen you dressed decently? I doubt it. Well, when he sees you with these clothes and Dame Brachet's manners, he'll rue the day he ever sent you off to Greenlaw, I can promise you that." She bent closer to inspect one of the parcels. "A few frocks, a riding habit—it's not a crime to be well dressed in Galazon, is it?"

"I apologize," said Faris stiffly. "I appreciate your help. I certainly didn't mean to be ungrateful—"

"Be still!" Jane was still bending over one of the parcels, a gray hat-box tied with silver ribbon. She cocked her head, listening. "Fetch Tyrian and Reed at once."

The urgency in her voice brought Faris out of her chair and across the room without hesitation. When she returned, with Reed and Tyrian at her heels, Jane was still listening intently.

"Do you hear that?" she demanded.

Obediently, Faris, Reed, and Tyrian listened too.

After a moment Reed looked up at Faris with great interest. "Your hat is ticking."

"It's not a hat," said Jane. "I haven't ordered Faris any hats yet."

"Is it a bomb?" Faris asked.

"Oh, probably," said Reed.

Calmly, Tyrian studied the box. "You'll have to clear the building. They may well be counting on that, so be on your guard when you leave."

"What about you?" Reed demanded.

"I'll have to try to disarm it."

Reed regarded Tyrian with disbelief. "Disarm it? We have no way of knowing what it's made out of, how it's constructed, what happens if we move it, when it's meant to go off—just untying the ribbon might set it off."

"I must try."

"With *what?* I don't carry the tools with me. Do you?"

In the silence that followed Reed's question, the ticking seemed very loud. After sixty seconds had passed, Jane drew a deep breath. "Faris, you'd better leave. I'm not perfectly certain I can do this. I discussed the theory once with Eve-Marie. A pity we can't send for her, since she's working right here in Paris these days. But we simply can't risk the time."

She held out her hands over the hat box as though she were warming them at a fire.

"Are you quite mad?" Reed demanded. "Keep away from it."

Faris seized his elbow and pulled him away. "Do you think she went to school just to read three-volume novels? She's a witch of Greenlaw. Be quiet and let her work."

Tyrian took two quick steps away from Jane. "What are you doing?"

Although her open hands were trembling, Jane's voice was steady. "One never knows. Perhaps it *is* a hat."

The air between her palms was shimmering, as the air shimmers over a fire. The silver ribbon writhed. The box grew slightly larger, as though it had drawn a breath. A smell of scorched feathers filled the room. The ticking stopped. Very slowly, as Jane brought her open hands together, the silver ribbon turned to gray and the gray hat box turned black. Jane clasped her hands. The box remained the same.

With a long sigh of relief, Jane lowered her hands. "That's

done it." She frowned and rubbed her forehead. "Thank you, Eve-Marie."

"Done what?" asked Reed plaintively. "What's that smell?"

Jane ignored him as she undid the ribbon and pulled the lid off the box. Within, nestled in gray tissue paper, lay a lady's hat. Constructed of velvet and tulle and sequins and feathers, it was a hat like a bonfire in winter, a hat of many colors, most of them variants of crimson and gold. Reverently, Jane lifted the hat free of its drab tissue nest and held it up to admire.

Tyrian cleared his throat. "Was that quite safe?"

Reed regarded first the hat and then Jane with great respect. "Is it really a hat?"

Faris stared at the hat with undisguised loathing. "I won't wear that."

Jane stroked the brim. "It's a hat as long as I say it's a hat." She looked up at Faris. "Of course you won't wear it. On you it would make you look like Menary in the Dean's garden. And it has feathers. I'll keep it." She tucked it gently back into its tissue and closed the box. She took a deep breath and closed her eyes, frowning. "I think I've given myself a headache."

Faris poured Jane a cup of tea. "I think all this makes one thing very clear. It's time I left Paris."

On Friday, Faris settled her hotel bill and accompanied her luggage, which was somehow far more extensive than she had expected, to the gare de Strasbourg. There she waited with Jane while Tyrian and Reed satisfied themselves about the safety of the compartment reserved for her.

Jane had her Baedeker open. "Strasbourg, Vienna, Budapest—you won't have to change trains until, er, Porta Orientalis? Yes? From there it's only a few hours until you reach Szedesvar. Is that how one pronounces it?"

Faris nodded. "I must thank you for all you've done." She spoke stiffly. Jane would detest any show of sentiment. Faris found it was hard for her to put her gratitude into words. She struggled to achieve flippancy. "Uncle Brinker certainly won't."

Hardly glancing up from her guidebook, Jane continued. "I hate those foreign names with mystery letters in them. Tyrian has wired ahead to arrange a coach and four in Szedesvar. Then you'll cross the border at Tura-Nerva. You'll have another day on the road from there to Galazon Ducis, and after that, there you are, home safe and dry."

Faris steered Jane out of the path of an oncoming baggage cart. "You make it sound simple."

"You'll have Reed and Tyrian to manage all the tedious bits for you. It will be simple." Jane closed the guidebook. "You *will* let me know how it all turns out?" She inspected the binding of the fat little guidebook with keen interest.

"Of course." Faris hesitated. "Back at Greenlaw, you'll remember me, won't you?"

"Oh, I expect we will. The Dean and Dame Villette particularly."

In the awkward silence that followed, Faris examined the small stack of baggage slips she held without really seeing them. "One day you must come to visit me."

Jane beamed. "Very well. Since you ask me so nicely, I'll come. I've often thought it would be jolly good fun to help save the world one day. This is probably the best opportunity I will ever have to do it."

"What? Do you mean it?" Faris blinked at Jane in astonished glee. "Come on." She turned toward the ticket kiosks. "Let's go see about it at once."

Jane stopped her. "I've already booked the compartment next to yours."

Faris turned back. Glee in abeyance, she tried to glare at Jane. "Oh, you have, have you? Did the Dean order you to keep an eye on me? I suppose she told you the Orient-Express is full of distractions, particularly for the well-to-do."

"I don't need orders from the Dean or anyone else. I decided to go with you the night you saw Hilarion. And I must

say," Jane added reproachfully, "I'm rather hurt that you
didn't invite me any sooner."

"You're supposed to be teaching at Greenlaw. It never occurred to me that you would be willing to drop everything
and come."

"You might at least have asked."

Faris looked sheepish. "I'm not much in the habit of asking for things."

Jane nodded in sympathy. "I know. It is seldom of the
least use. But I think it's wise to try it now and then, if only to
keep in practice."

Faris could not sleep that night. She tried. Compartment window open, compartment window closed, nothing seemed to
make any difference. Too many late nights and later mornings
might have thrown her internal pendulum off. Or perhaps the
flurry of activity required to leave Paris was to blame. That
included the effort to leave with all business conducted and all
luggage packed, not omitting the current newspapers and
magazines most likely to yield news from Aravill and Galazon, and a neatly docketed portfolio of reports, loaned to Jane
by someone she refused to identify. There would be plenty of
time to read it en route, Jane had said airily, "Not like comps."
And all the while, Faris knew that as anxious as she was to
leave France, she might never be able to come back.

No matter which way she twisted and turned in her
berth, Faris could not let go and allow the steady rhythm of
the train to lull her to sleep. Instead of soothing her, the
rhythm ran incessantly along under her thoughts: *Never come
back, never come back . . .*

Faris gave up and climbed out of her berth. Fumbling in
the dark, she found her new kidskin slippers by their scent
and her new dressing gown of quilted silk by touch. With the
dressing gown done up securely to conceal her old nightdress,
frayed by the college laundry, she opened her compartment
door.

The narrow corridor was empty. Evidently the first-class

passengers had been tucked in for the night. In the dim light, Faris saw the compartment door opposite hers was open. Reed was there, on watch, according to plan.

He came close enough for her to hear his murmur. "Need anything? I can ring for the attendant."

Faris shook her head. "I can't sleep."

"Glass of warm milk? Deck of cards? Patience is very boring, I'm told."

"No, thanks. I'm just restless, I suppose." She looked up and down the empty corridor. "I didn't mean to disturb you."

"You didn't." Reed closed her compartment door and beckoned her into his own. "Come smoke a cigarette or something."

Faris sat by the window. Reed kept his place by the door. When she refused the cigarette he offered, he put the case back in his pocket without lighting one for himself. She expected him to keep up a murmured stream of inconsequential remarks but he surprised her with his vigilant silence.

The silence lasted a long time. Finally Faris broke it. "What do you think Brinker wants?" she asked softly, surprising herself.

Even silhouetted against the dimly lit corridor, Reed's shrug was eloquent. "You're about to reach your majority. Perhaps he has finally come to terms with that, and decided to bring you back home where you belong."

"Perhaps." Faris was certain Reed was being foolishly optimistic, but since he was probably doing it to make her feel better, she kept her doubts to herself. "If that is it, I wish he'd waited until I managed to graduate."

Reed shrugged again. "Perhaps he has his eyes on something new. He married King Julian's heir presumptive. The king can't live forever. Perhaps there's some reason he needs you secure in Galazon before he can pursue his interests in Aravis."

Faris laughed under her breath. "You know, I just had the most ghastly thought. It hadn't occurred to me until now, but this means Menary and I are really related. Exactly how, I wonder?"

"Does it? Let's see, if your uncle married her sister, that makes you wicked stepmothers to each other, doesn't it? What *is* the matter with that girl, anyway? She's a beauty, and at least eighteen, if I'm any judge, but when she opens her mouth, she sounds about twelve."

"She's used to having her own way."

"Well, that would be a great beauty aid. But she ought to try to sound a little less like my baby sister."

"If I see her in Aravis, I'll tell her so."

"You mean it, don't you? You really are going on to Aravis?"

"I must."

"We need you more at home in Galazon, you know."

Misery and sentiment made Faris's throat tighten. "I hope so."

"Those bloody-minded aristos in Aravill are none of our affair. You'd be better off staying in Galazon. There's plenty to do."

"I'm a bloody-minded aristo, too, Reed."

"But you're *our* bloody-minded aristo. It makes a difference."

"Thank you." She was just able to keep the quaver of homesickness out of her voice.

Reed started to add something, then broke off and shook his head, disgusted with himself.

"What's the matter?"

"Oh, nothing. I just realized why I'm never going to match Tyrian at ingratiating myself with the upper classes, that's all."

"What are you talking about?"

"You know perfectly well. Can you imagine the conversation you'd be having if Tyrian was on watch instead of me? If he didn't send you straight back to your compartment, with a handy dose of warm milk he happened to have up his sleeve for just such an emergency, he'd have kept it all high-minded and impersonal. He's so good, he's almost inhuman. It's like he hatched from an egg." Reed shook his head again. "I just can't help putting my oar in."

Faris found her voice was back within her control. "You called me a carrot-haired gawk once, remember?"

There was a pause before he replied. "Well, yes. I do remember saying that. You've changed a bit since then, though."

"Will you side with me now? Against the wiliest man in Galazon?"

A longer pause. "Why ask me that? You know the answer. You knew it that night at the White Fleece."

"Tell me anyway."

"You said, those with the same ailment recognize the symptoms. You were right. Your uncle pays me. But I'll side with you."

"I'll pay you."

"Good. But I'd side with you anyway. You *are* our bloody-minded aristo, after all."

"Thank you, Reed." She rose. "I'd better make myself get some sleep, or I really will be bloody-minded tomorrow."

"Make yourself sleep? Oh, don't think of it that way." Reed let her pass him. "It's an indulgence, not a duty. 'Nature requires five, custom gives seven, laziness takes nine, and wickedness eleven.' Try to be wicked."

The following morning, Jane persuaded Faris and Tyrian to join her in the dining car for the first breakfast seating. "If Reed would rather catch up on his sleep, that's his choice. But Uncle Ambrose recommends the pastry particularly. He says the schedule is designed to bring the Express into Vienna just as the first strudel of the day comes out of the bakers' ovens."

Coffee and strudel sounded fine to Faris. Even if she had been less hungry, she recognized the note of brisk decision in Jane's voice and knew it would be useless to resist. She stifled a yawn. "Very convenient."

"Yes, and since it's so early, there won't be a crush."

The dining car, elegant with inlaid wood, cut glass chandeliers, and arched ceilings, provided enough space between the elaborately laid tables to prevent it ever being called a crush. But very few of the tables were in use when a relay of waiters led Jane and her companions to their places. Jane ordered and they were left alone.

Tyrian inspected the other diners as he shook out his napkin. "No one here we know, unless someone has taken the trouble to shape-shift."

Jane, wearing her elderly appearance, though not her veil, closed her eyes and drew a deep breath. After a moment, she let it out and opened her eyes. "Not here. Not now."

Coffee and pastry arrived. When they were served and the waiters had withdrawn, Jane helped herself to a lavish amount of whipped cream and fixed Tyrian with a steady, interested gaze. "I've asked you once before," she said, "who *are* you?"

Faris glanced warily at her but did not intervene. The pastry was still warm from the ovens of Vienna, now dwindling in the distance behind them. She concentrated on the crumbs she was scattering across the starched linen tablecloth.

Serenely, Tyrian sipped his coffee. "You asked. As I recall, I answered."

"You said you worked for dear old Uncle Brinker," Jane replied. "But now we know you worked for Hilarion first. You have no notion how hard it is to resist a figure of mystery. Tell all, do."

"If I did, I wouldn't be a figure of mystery any longer." Tyrian took a neat bite of pastry. Hardly a crumb fell.

"How do you do that?" Faris asked.

Tyrian looked blank. "Do what?"

Jane took Faris's meaning and spoke before she could explain. "Everything. You're good at everything. How do you do it? Where did you study?"

"Nowhere. I have only the education my poor teachers struggled to cram into me when I was a boy."

"Go on," Jane prompted. "What did you do when you left your poor teachers?"

"I married." Tyrian's voice was without expression. He looked composed, perhaps a little bored.

Faris studied her coffee cup. It had a pleasing shape and a delicate gold band around the rim. It was not interesting enough to hold her interest during the remainder of the conversation, but she intended to look as if it did.

Jane was not the least discomfited. "Dear me, wouldn't you have been rather young?"

Tyrian looked directly at Jane for a moment. Beneath his civil exterior, something that might have been impatience or annoyance gleamed and was gone. "I was fifteen. She was older. I married her for her money."

"Go on."

Tyrian drank his coffee.

Faris regarded Jane reproachfully. "Paris is full of sensational literature. If you thought the journey would bore you, why didn't you bring along a novel or something?"

"If it's sensational, it isn't literature," said Jane. "I'm tired of looking at the newspapers. They never get anything right. Do you know, I found a reference to our beloved schoolmate Menary? *Figaro* says she's registered for the next term at the Sorbonne—'after the culmination of her studies at Greenlaw.' That's one way to put it, I suppose. This is far more interesting. What happened then?"

Tyrian looked resigned. "If I manage to shock you, will you let me change the subject? I put all her money into my family's green-grocery business, which was what my family had in mind when they arranged the marriage. When the money was all gone, she left me."

"How long did that take?"

"I was eighteen."

Jane shook her head slightly. "Where did she go, with no money?"

Tyrian's smile was slightly twisted. "Where could she go? She took up with a young aristocrat. He treated her well. His father got a look at her, and he treated her even better. Before a month was out, she was the toast of the town."

"That must have been rather awkward for you."

"I was never very interested in the green-grocery business. I decided to go far away and find something else to do."

"And what was that?"

"My first job was as butler, valet, and general factotum to a fortune-teller who flattered the socially ambitious. I made up for my lack of experience with initiative and enthusiasm."

"What sort of fortune-telling?" Jane inquired. "Crystal-gazing? Tarot cards? Or communication with The Spirits Beyond?"

"The props varied. For the fortunes, we relied largely on gossip and guesswork. If the pigeon was skeptical, and rich enough to make the effort worthwhile, I did a little research. It's the details that are so convincing in that line of work."

"Did you use any magic?"

"Genuine magic would have been far too expensive for the likes of us. Anyway, my employer liked to keep her clients coming back for more. True magic seems to contain an uncomfortable amount of truth. Hard to develop much return custom when you dispense the entire unvarnished truth."

Jane studied him closely. "*Her* clients. And you were butler, valet, and general factotum." She laid a little extra stress on the word valet.

Tyrian finished his pastry as he returned her regard with unimpaired calm. "I made up for my lack of experience with initiative and enthusiasm."

"So that's where you learned to be cynical. Some people never manage it."

"Oh, I mastered cynicism early. But that's where I learned that I liked surprising people. That's where I learned that people who want to be fooled are easy to fool. But I learned a few practical skills as well. The basics, no more. And I learned two important principles. First, very few people do things properly. I learned there will always be a need for someone who does things right the first time. There's no teaching that. Either one has the flair or one doesn't."

"And you do."

"I believe I do." Tyrian glanced at Faris. "The second principle I learned is that the first art of being a good henchman is choosing the right employer."

Faris looked up. "Am I the right employer?"

"Do you wish this interrogation to continue? Would you like to hear more tales of my misspent adulthood?"

"Certainly not. Unless you think I should. Is there something I ought to know?"

Tyrian shook his head. "No. And that explains why you are the right employer." He turned back to Jane. "I won't bore you with any more tales. Eventually, I became the jack-of-all-trades and figure of mystery that you see before you today. Are you quite satisfied?"

"What became of your wife?"

"She endowed a school for orphaned girls three years ago, so I believe she is doing well."

Jane looked puzzled. "Don't you mind?"

Tyrian smiled at her with honest amusement. "When I was eighteen, I minded desperately. Now, when I remember to think of her at all, I can only feel grateful that I avoided spending my life as a green-grocer."

Jane's eyes narrowed. "Wait a moment." She paused, head bent as if she was studying her strudel crumbs. "Someone just came in the door behind me."

Faris looked over Jane's shoulder. "A waiter. Not ours, though."

"He certainly looks like ours," said Tyrian.

Jane tilted her butter knife and studied the reflection. "It looks like him, but it isn't."

Faris looked at her askance. "Ours is stocky and dark, this one is fair and his cheeks are wind-burnt."

The waiter arrived at their table, offered them coffee, and when Faris, at a glance from Tyrian, nodded her acceptance, refilled her cup with a flourish. Without troubling to visit any of the other tables, the waiter continued along the dining car and vanished through the doorway at the far end.

Tyrian picked up Faris's cup, sniffed at the contents, and offered it to Jane. "Unless they've changed the blend from Viennese roast to almond in the past few minutes, I think it's been laced with hydrogen cyanide."

"Poison?" asked Faris.

Jane took the cup and sniffed delicately. "Yes, indeed. Nasty stuff."

Tyrian rose. "Stay here," he told them. Hand slipping inside his coat, he left the dining car through the far doorway.

Jane put the cup down and folded her hands. "Well, I suppose if one troubles to employ an expert, one must allow him to do his job."

Faris eyed her poisoned cup warily. "Why did he look like our waiter to you and Tyrian, but not to me?"

Jane arched her brows. "That's interesting, isn't it? Tell me, how old do I look today?"

"At least eighty."

"You're exaggerating. Even so, you can't see through my magic. But you can see through his magic—always supposing it *is* his own and not something he borrowed from his auntie."

"Or uncle," said Faris darkly.

Jane studied her, ancient eyebrows raised. "Sits the wind in that quarter?"

Tyrian reappeared. He paused at their table long enough to hand Jane a peaked cap of the kind the dining car waiters wore. "I've left him in the baggage car for the moment. Study that while I fetch Reed. I think he was reluctant to lose it."

"You've left him unguarded?" Jane asked.

Tyrian looked pleased with himself. "I think he'll still be waiting for us when we return to interview him." To Faris, he added, "Don't let them clear away your coffee. It might prove useful."

Jane scrutinized the cap, then picked it up and stroked the dark fabric gently. "There's something here." She ran a fingertip inside the band. "Oh, yes." She drew forth a single strand of black horsehair nearly a yard long. "This is it." She put the cap aside and smoothed the strand on the tablecloth before her. "Foreign, definitely. Turkish, possibly." She paused and inspected the fingertips of her left hand, rubbing them with her thumb as if they had touched something hot.

"Well?" Faris bent close to examine the strand. "What is it?"

"Perhaps Russian. There's something about it I don't recognize at all." Jane sniffed her fingers. "It's only a guess, of course, but I've a notion what it's for. It helps that I saw it working. I think it's a charm to help the owner resemble whoever wore the cap last. It probably works in any article of clothing. I can't be sure without taking it apart. Perhaps not even then."

Faris picked up the cap. "This certainly looks like the genuine article. Do you suppose it belonged to our real waiter?"

Tyrian and Reed joined them. Reed paid for their meal while Tyrian took charge of the peaked cap. "Someone knocked our waiter down and locked him in a cupboard. He didn't get a look at the youthful prankster who did it. He assumes there must have been one, though, because all the prankster took was his cap." He glanced toward the baggage car and added, "Our prankster isn't going to want to talk to us, is he?"

Tyrian looked stern. "He isn't going to have any choice in the matter."

"Can you force him to talk to us?" Faris asked Jane.

Jane shook her head. "Not against his will. But if he can be distracted enough for me to work on him, and if he can be made to concentrate on what we want to know, I *may* be able to make him think out loud. I've never tried it, but I know the theory. That is, if he's what he appears to be. If he designed this charm, he's too good for me. I'll never be able to get near his mind."

"Don't worry." Faris picked up her cup and followed the others. "I'll distract him for you."

In the baggage car, Tyrian led them between piles of

trunks and valises to the far corner. There, he paused before a stack of wicker laundry crates, where the railway packed its soiled linens in readiness for the laundry at the end of the line. The bottom crate, once its buckled straps were undone, opened to reveal the neatly trussed figure of Faris's assailant. Reed trained his pistol on the helpless prisoner.

He was the young man Faris had seen with the coffeepot, compactly built, with broad shoulders and closely set blue eyes. His complexion was naturally ruddy, and, above the white linen hand towel Tyrian had used for a gag, his face was scarlet, a striking contrast to his fair hair.

When Tyrian loosened the gag, he spat it out immediately. "This is an outrage. I wish to speak to the *chef de train* immediately." He struggled against his bonds until the wicker creaked.

Tyrian's sneer was a sinister masterpiece.

The red-faced man looked beyond Tyrian to Faris and Jane. "Madame, Mademoiselle, I implore you! This man is mad. He attacked me, stole my papers, and concealed me in this place. Now they hold me at gunpoint. Help me, I beg of you."

Tyrian produced a packet of official-looking documents. "According to these papers, we see before us James Haverford, British subject, who is traveling across the continent on behalf of a firm with its headquarters in Amsterdam. They deal in spices, and he's come to bid on paprika for them." He crumpled the papers and let them fall. "Faked, of course."

The young man switched from French to English. Volubly, he protested at the treatment to which he had been subjected. He promised to lodge a complaint with the authorities, to take this to the highest circles, to write a letter to the *Times*—

"Hush." Faris dropped to one knee beside him. "You must calm yourself, Mr. Haverford. It will do you no good at all to worry yourself into a fit. I assure you, these people know their duty."

"You don't understand, young lady. I tell you that man is

a dangerous lunatic—" Despite his indignation, Haverford's color had faded to something more nearly normal.

Faris interrupted him again, this time by holding out her cup. "Calm yourself, sir. Here, have some coffee. It's gone rather cold, I'm afraid, but it will do you good."

Haverford grew pale. His eyes met hers over the rim of the cup. As she looked into his face, Faris could almost see his thoughts move behind those blue eyes. *Did she know?*

Faris smiled grimly. "No? Not thirsty just now?"

That answered the question. He pursed his lips and shook his head.

Faris rose and handed the cup to Tyrian. "Hold this for me, won't you? And be good enough to loan me your knife. I need it."

Jane joined Faris beside the crate. "Now, Faris, be a good girl and let Tyrian handle this. You know you aren't allowed to handle anything with sharp edges. It excites you so. I'm sure it's bad for you."

Tyrian took the cup and handed Faris his knife. He avoided meeting her gaze.

Haverford's eyes widened and he wriggled back into the crumpled sheets that lined his wicker crate, a slight movement, but as much as his bonds allowed.

Faris bent down to murmur in his ear. "You've misjudged the situation, you see. You tried to poison me." She touched his cheek, moved his chin so that he had to meet her eyes. "Having failed, you tried to brazen out the situation, sure that you could convince the authorities to let you go. Now you think we want to find out who sent you." She held the knife so that he could see it from the corner of his eye. "You think you're safe, so long as you have information we need." Very softly, very coldly, she murmured, "You're wrong."

Haverford pressed himself back against the wadded linen, wide eyes showing too much white. Faris dropped down beside him. "I know who hired you to kill me. Trust me. He'll answer to me for it. So I don't need you after all, do I?"

Faris shook her head slightly and raised the knife. She enjoyed the ring of perfect sincerity in her voice and could not resist adding, "You were even wrong about who was a dangerous lunatic."

Haverford's eyes rolled right back and closed as he went limp against the linen.

"I have him." Jane's voice was triumphant. "*Speak!*"

Haverford's eyes stayed shut as he began to murmur. "I'm for it. Dead meat. I'll never see a penny of my money. Bloody witch, I should have known. Curse that Copenhagen, he lied to me. A soft job, he says, with every convenience, he says. First class passage and a special bit of equipment provided by the client. A soft job! Too bloody right! A soft job for a soft head!"

"A bit of equipment provided by the client," Jane prompted very gently.

"First class passage to the middle of nowhere, and all for what? For some wog who doesn't know any better than to trust that f------ Copenhagen. He'll cheat his own staff out of the pennies on our eyes."

"That f------ Copenhagen," whispered Jane.

Tyrian and Reed looked scandalized. Faris looked down and bit her lip to keep from smiling.

"F------ Copenhagen, he said this was going to be a soft job. That's all he knows. He'll find out different when he meets the train. Hope the witch does for him, too, the beggar. Why couldn't she just *drink* the bloody coffee? Women like that should be put down, like mad dogs." Haverford's voice trailed off.

"When Copenhagen meets the train," Jane coaxed.

"Copenhagen meets the train." Haverford's mouth twitched. He took a deep breath and nestled comfortably in the laundry, like a sleeper in search of a cool bit of pillow.

"Meets the train where?" Jane's soft voice was strained with effort.

"Port-a-bloody-Orientalis . . ." Haverford's words turned

into a snore. His mouth went slack and his head dropped forward. He was profoundly asleep.

For a moment, they watched him in silence. Then Faris handed the knife back to Tyrian. Reed put his pistol away. And Jane put her head in her hands and leaned against the wicker crate. "Oh, dear," she said.

Faris touched her shoulder. "What's the matter?"

"My head is *splitting*. There's nothing about this in the theory. I can scarcely see—"

"I'll finish up here. As soon as I'm done, I'll stop at your compartment and we can discuss this." Tyrian gagged Haverford and began to buckle the straps on the wicker crate.

"What are you going to do with him?" Reed asked.

"I'm going to make sure he doesn't disturb anyone until he reaches the laundry in Constantinople."

9

Shieling

JANE'S BERTH HAD already been made up for the day. While Faris sat with her in her own compartment, Reed folded the sofa back into a bed. He retired to his compartment across the corridor while Jane was settled in with a tisane for her headache and the damask-covered blinds drawn.

By the time Faris joined him, Tyrian was waiting with Reed. "She's asleep," she told them, accepting the *fauteuil* Reed had left empty for her. "She said she's certain she can still keep the, er—hat—stable, but she is exhausted. At the moment, she isn't able to alter her appearance, either."

"If she does lose her grip on that, er, hat," said Reed cheerfully, "the bang from the baggage car will let us know."

"How long will it take for her to recover?" Tyrian asked.

"She doesn't know. She says she's never tried this technique before."

"How long can we let her rest?" Reed asked. "We're going to have to leave the train before we get to Porta Orientalis, aren't we?"

Faris looked thoughtful. "Unless we go farther and double back to Galazon somehow?"

"I think we should stay as far away from Porta Orientalis as we can," said Tyrian. "I have no idea if it's the same one, but six years ago I encountered a man calling himself Copenhagen. I have no desire to meet him again unless it can't be avoided."

"Is he familiar with this part of the world? Will he know the routes open to us if we leave the train early?" Faris asked.

Reed looked disgusted. "Why does it matter? He must know our destination. If we don't leave the train at Porta Orientalis, he can just go ahead to Galazon Ducis and wait for us to arrive."

"If we leave the train at Pavlova, we can take the next steamer up the White River, and cross the border that way," suggested Faris.

"When might that be?" Reed countered. "They never used to run more than once a week. We can get off at Islet, instead, and take the Haydock road."

Faris frowned. "How far will we get before we're set upon by a band of Haydocker cutthroats? We'd never get a carriage through the high pass anyway. We might try Epona. If we can take passage on a barge down the Lida, we'll end up in Galazon eventually."

"Eventually is the word. Why give Copenhagen the chance to reach Galazon Ducis before we do?"

"There might be others, as well," said Tyrian. "Copenhagen was never one to work alone. Although he usually has a better eye for help than Haverford suggests."

"So we may well be walking into a trap," said Reed. "That's a happy thought."

"And we can't rule out the possibility that Haverford was planted on us," Tyrian added.

Faris put her chin in her hand. "Now *I'm* getting a head-ache."

"So am I. What's your suggestion, then?" Reed asked Tyrian.

"I don't have one. You know the terrain. I agree that we must make all speed to Galazon Ducis."

Reed looked thoughtful. "The swiftest way is to cross the Haydocks from Islet to Puckrin and take the Alewash road into Galazon Ducis. Then we don't have to attempt the high pass, either. We can cross at the Ela, almost at once."

"If Copenhagen took the most direct route from Porta Orientalis to Galazon Ducis, he'd be coming from the other way. We'd run no danger of crossing paths with him," Faris added.

"Of course, it depends on what kind of transport we find at Islet," Reed continued. "If the diligence isn't available, we'll have to try to rent a coach."

"What about the Haydockers?" Faris asked.

Reed and Tyrian traded speculative glances. "I think," said Tyrian slowly, "that you can leave them to us."

"If we can't manage them," Reed added, "we'll let you offer them coffee."

Jane did not care for the change in plan. But by the time she had recovered from her headache enough to take an interest in what was going on around her, there was little time left to re-monstrate. Instead, she followed Faris's lead, packing the min-imum of clothing into a small bag, and preparing to let the rest of her luggage go on without her.

"My new brocade dressing gown—I can't possibly leave that."

Faris, who had finished her repacking long since, said, not for the first time, "Pack it in your big case, lock it up, make sure the label is firmly affixed, and leave it. They'll ship it on with the rest of our things. It will be *fine.*"

"My linen walking dress—I might need that—" Jane

managed to fold the dress and fit it, with the rest of her necessities, into her smallest valise. "Now it won't shut."

"Pack it with the rest."

"Now it won't come out."

Faris extricated the crumpled walking dress from the jaws of the valise. "Are you quite sure that your hat will be safe if you leave it on the train? I mean, it won't go off or anything, will it?"

Jane clutched her forehead. "My hat! Oh, *must* I leave my hat as well?"

"Won't you have enough to carry as it is?" While Jane was distracted, Faris closed the bulging valise and locked it. "Unless your spell needs you near?"

"It's a hat as long as I say it's a hat," Jane said grimly. "It will be perfectly safe without me. How am I ever going to fit all the rest of this back into my cases before we reach Islet?"

"Why don't you wait in my compartment while I finish for you? It won't take me long."

"You know you can't fold things properly. Everything will be crushed."

"When you eventually unpack, won't you have it all pressed anyway?"

"Oh, dear. I suppose so." Distressed, Jane surveyed the untidy compartment. "It's too ghastly. I can't let you finish for me. I'll have to do it myself."

Faris steered her out of the compartment. "Here's Reed. Make him give you a cigarette or something. I'll finish."

Reed craned to see the disarray. "Are you *still* at it?"

For answer, Faris shut the compartment door.

At daybreak on Sunday, half an hour before it reached Hatzfeld, the train made a brief halt at Islet, a prosperous little town at the foot of the Ela Pass. With speed, stealth, and the very minimum of baggage, Faris and her party left the train. They waited for an hour at the chilly inn near the railway station. Then, under Tyrian's direction, they took seats on the local diligence, a light coach of sturdy, primitive design. By the time the sun was well up, they were lurching along the road to Puckrin.

After the Orient-Express, Faris found the diligence excruciatingly slow. There were two other passengers, a paunchy older man who gazed nervously out the window at all times, and a stern-looking matron who knitted with mechanical precision, staring disapprovingly all the while at Faris and Jane. Jane, veil down, back straight, and gloved hands demurely folded, stared back, apparently determined neither to speak nor blink for the duration of the journey.

Faris spent some time trying to decide what the matron was knitting, some time gazing out the window at the passing countryside (steep and rocky, very poor cropland by any measure), and some time staring at the sky, trying to guess if it was going to clear or not. (Probably not.) Then, inevitably, she went back to her principal concern. Brinker.

What Copenhagen chose to do when the train arrived in Porta Orientalis without them, she left to Reed and Tyrian to worry about. Copenhagen was, after all, a matter of professional interest to them. If he wished to pursue them to Galazon, he would. They would lay their plans accordingly.

Brinker, on the other hand, was Faris's responsibility. Even if he were not involved with Copenhagen and Haverford (and Faris had to concede that there was no certainty that he was Copenhagen's client, oh, no, nothing so simple as *that*), he was still Faris's worry.

What would she tell him about Aravis? *Hello, Uncle, I'm off to Aravis on urgent business. Oh, didn't I say? I'm the warden of the north.* He'd love that. She could almost see the bemused expression he would put on, as if she had suddenly begun to speak in Persian and he was a little too polite to bring it to her attention. Just the expression he'd have if she were to ask, *Did you pay someone to kill me, Uncle?*

He would tilt his head a little at that, as if to marvel at how imaginative the young could be. How that little tilt of the head infuriated her. She would lose her temper then, as she always did, and add, as nastily as she could, *Did it cost very much?*

And anyone who happened to be in the room at the time would look shocked at her impertinence. Then Brinker would be able to send her away and carry on with his plans unimpeded, as he always did. As he always would do. What would be so different, after all, the day Faris came of age? Would he suddenly listen to her when she spoke to him? Would he magically agree with her, after all the years of looking bored when she spoke?

Brinker held Galazon in the hollow of his hand. He wouldn't give up his influence willingly. The only groups who had ever rivaled his importance had been the assembly of landowners called the Curia Ducis, and the advisers Faris's mother had consulted, men and women drawn not just from the land-owning class, but from all across Galazon. The seeds of reform were there, Faris thought. The ancient Curia Ducis might be revived, a ramshackle house of lords, and the new-fangled advisers might someday provide Galazon with something resembling a house of commons. It would be difficult, certainly, even without interference from Brinker. The key, she thought, would lie in the past. If she could present these changes as revivals of ancient tradition, it was just possible they might be accepted. How easy Brinker would find it, though, to frame these ideas as the socialist notions of a student who had been away too long.

In a way, Brinker had already agreed with her about the potential power of the Curia and the advisers. The Curia had been so troublesome to him, he had dissolved it. The advisers had been ignored for years. Were any of them left? Would any of them trust her as they had trusted her mother? And what would Brinker do if they did?

What would Brinker do, it suddenly occurred to Faris to wonder, if Copenhagen *did* pursue her to Galazon? If Haverford's account could be trusted, and Faris had enough faith in Jane's skill to believe it could, Copenhagen knew who his client was. Suppose Copenhagen fell into her hands. She had enough faith in Tyrian and Reed to consider it possible. With testimony from Copenhagen, with a threat of exposure to use against Brinker, what could Faris do? What would Brinker do? What did she want him to do?

Lost in happier speculation, Faris relaxed. The heavy sway of the coach lulled her. *Never come back* faded for good, banished by the slower tempo of their progress. Faris slept.

At half past five that afternoon, Faris woke from a fitful doze to find Jane frowning at her. Since Oratz, they had been the only passengers inside. Reed and Tyrian had seats on the box. Despite the relative privacy, Jane still wore her veil down and it only made her frown more alarming. Faris looked around, blinking. "Is there something the matter? Is your headache back again?"

"Yes. And is it any wonder? This road is a disgrace. Any moment now, my neck will be snapped from my shoulders. How can you possibly sleep?"

Faris stifled a yawn. "I was just resting my eyes." She looked out the window. "Dark already? At least the sky cleared. What time is it? Where are we?"

Jane handed Faris her Baedeker. "I neither know nor care. One pine forest looks very like another. Did you know the roads would be like this?"

"You want your tea, don't you?" Faris folded her arms tightly, wishing for a little more warmth.

"There's no chance of tea until we reach Ruger—and don't say anything bracing about a hearty meal and a good night's sleep, because I won't be braced. I am miserable and if you weren't so bucked about going home, you'd be miserable, too."

"It's really not much worse than the private coach from Szedesvar would have been. And it doesn't look as if it's going to rain. That's very lucky. Just think what the roads would be like then."

"And while we wander through Ruritania with comb and handkerchief and *very* little more, all our luggage is in Porta

Orientalis, mouldering in some foul hole for unclaimed baggage."

"It's labeled. The train people will send it all on to Galazon Chase. We may reach Ruger in time for supper. As soon as we arrive, I'll order another tisane for your headache."

"A tisane?" Jane was indignant. "Brandy, at least. Cognac would be better."

The diligence gave a violent lurch, followed by a crash. After a stunned moment, Faris untangled herself from Jane. The coach had stopped. As Faris put her hand on the door, it opened with an edge of chill air.

Just visible in the starlight, Tyrian, hatless and holding his elegant pistol, asked, "Are you hurt?"

"Not I," said Faris. "Jane?"

"Cognac would be far better." Jane sounded very cross. "I'm fine." She picked herself up carefully off the floor. Indignantly, she added, "I'm covered in *straw*."

"What happened?" asked Faris.

"There's a tree down across our track. The coachman was thrown off the box. I think we've broken a trace. Reed is holding the horses. Stay where you are."

Faris started to clamber out the door. "We'll help. I can hold the horses."

Tyrian didn't move. "It isn't necessary."

Slowly, eyes straining to read Tyrian's expression in the dimness, Faris took her seat.

"Thank you, your grace." The door closed and Tyrian was gone.

Surprised, Jane stopped brushing at her skirts. "What's the matter with you two? Of course we ought to help. We may be here all night as it is."

"Haydock can be rather uncivilized." Faris frowned. "These forests are renowned for the cutthroats who live here."

"Oh."

It was a still evening. Overhead, the stars seemed huge, burning ice-cold and blue-white in the faultless sky. There was no wind to trouble the pines. The coachman, calling loudly for plum brandy, was helped to his feet. The horses were quieted. The carriage lamps were lit. They hardly flickered as Tyrian set to work mending the broken harness by their light.

"That's a very large pine tree," Jane observed, her voice touched with gloom. "They haven't even tried to move it."

"I doubt they can. How is your headache now? Could you transform the tree, do you think?

Jane sounded dubious. "Perhaps I can."

"If you can't, we'll have to turn the coach and go back."

"Oh, dear. Back *where?*"

"Wherever we changed horses last."

"That was a cow byre with six horses in it. We can't possibly sleep there."

"I don't recommend sleeping anywhere but the coach, to tell you the truth. Insects."

Jane clutched Faris's sleeve. "Hush. Look!"

Faris looked. Tyrian and Reed and the coachman were already looking. From the darkness near the fallen pine, a light shone, small and golden as a firefly.

"Hello," a man's voice called out of the darkness. "Having a little trouble?" The light moved in a quick arc and returned to its place. The speaker came closer. He was a slender man with a pair of ammunition belts slung across his chest. The brim of his slouch hat concealed his face. The light was his cigarette. He exhaled slowly as he regarded the driver, Reed, and Tyrian. "Looks as if you could use some help."

"We'll manage, thanks all the same," said Reed cheerfully.

"Oh?" The man studied the fallen pine. "It appears to me you need to move that tree." His voice sounded young and thoughtful. "If you give me five hundred dinaras, I'll clear the road for you."

"All alone?" Tyrian asked.

The man dropped his cigarette and ground out the little light. In the next few seconds, thirty matches flared as thirty men lit cigarettes in the darkness around the coach. "Not at all. Better make that one thousand dinaras."

Reed and Tyrian made no answer. The driver groaned.

In the coach, Jane put back her veil. "I've still got the headache, but it shouldn't take much to frighten off a few bandits."

"No, wait a moment—" In Faris's memories, the recollection of summers long past was stirring.

"Fifteen hundred dinaras," the man said.

Faris listened intently. "I know that voice."

"While we wait, the price is going up. Who knows what Reed and Tyrian will decide to do?"

"Two thousand dinaras is less than a hundred pounds sterling. And Reed and Tyrian are just what I'm worried about. I know that young man." Faris climbed out of the coach.

Jane rolled her eyes, put her veil back, and followed.

"Two thousand dinaras."

"Done," called Faris.

Reed and Tyrian turned identically aggrieved faces to her as she joined them in the circle of light. "That's torn it," snarled Reed. Tyrian said nothing but his disgusted expression was eloquent.

"Who is that?" asked the young man, after a startled pause.

"I'll pay you two thousand dinaras to help us on our way," Faris continued, "but first tell me what brings Warin Woodrowel down from Shieling and over the border to rob honest travelers."

"Who dares to call me a robber?" The young man took a step forward and stared at her. "Speak."

"I do," said Faris, just as Reed muttered, "I can think of a few other things I'd like to call you."

Tyrian glanced at Reed, who subsided.

"Have you given up your father's cigars, then?" added Faris.

The young man squinted at her in disbelief. "That's never *Faris?*"

"Well met, Warin."

Warin Woodrowel advanced three steps to meet her before Tyrian barred his way. Woodrowel stopped and held up his hand to steady his watchful men. "Your pardon, Faris. I never dreamed we would trouble you."

Faris came to Tyrian's side. "Granted, if you explain these amateur theatricals."

Woodrowel regarded her with wonder. "How long has it been? You're decked out in such finery, it's a miracle I even recognized that long nose of yours. Have you come home to stay?"

"First tell me about your charade here."

He cleared his throat. "Yes. Well." He fidgeted for a moment, then met Faris's gaze squarely. "It's the taxes. We haven't much hope of paying them, the way things are nowadays, and since your uncle levied the penalty for late payment, well." He lit another cigarette in thoughtful silence and added, "Well, here we are."

Faris frowned. "You seem well practiced. Am I to take it that these are not amateur theatricals after all? You do this often?"

"Not at all. The coach only runs three times a week. And we don't stop it every time. Then it might not run at all. But this quarter we've been a bit behind, with bringing in the harvest and such. And the tree still looks fairly fresh, so we thought we'd press our luck."

"This quarter? Shieling pays taxes when the lambing's done, not at midwinter."

Woodrowel scowled. "This past year, Shieling pays every quarter—and so does all of Galazon."

Faris stiffened. "On whose authority?"

Just behind her, Jane's murmur was quick and calm. "Steady on."

"Lord Brinker's orders," Woodrowel replied. At her expression, he grinned broadly. "You've not changed as much as I thought."

Faris drew a deep breath. "Reed. Give Warin his money. If you don't have enough dinaras, give him marks or francs or florins, what you will. I have urgent business with my uncle. Warin, shift that pine and let my coach be on its way."

"Hold up, boys. Don't move it just yet." Woodrowel shook his head. "I can't recommend that, Faris." As she bristled, he held up his hand. "Now, don't blaze away at me. We aren't the first people in Haydock to raise a little capital, remember."

"So? Has all Galazon turned to thievery?"

"Not at all. But this has always been good bandit country. In that coach on this road, if you go another ten miles, you may well encounter professional thieves. You won't like them. They aren't as well brought up as we are." With great care and infinite smugness, Woodrowel made three perfect smoke rings.

"Is there a better road?" Faris demanded.

Woodrowel admired the last smoke ring. When it was gone, he said thoughtfully, "Not for a coach. But for riders in a hurry—"

"I'm in a hurry."

"But can you ride?" Woodrowel eyed her companions. "Can the—older lady?"

"We can ride," Jane replied.

Surprised by the youthful timbre of her voice, Woodrowel gave her a searching look. "In such a costume?" he asked politely.

"We need four horses," said Faris. "My chaperone and I require riding clothes—nothing elaborate. Can you provide these things? And a guide?"

Woodrowel looked pleased. "I think I can supply you with what you ask. Of course, the use of the horses, the clothing, the guide, and the armed escort—for I could not in honor allow you to risk meeting any of the local hedge-robbers—I think these things may command a small fee."

Faris smiled. "Then shall we say two thousand dinaras, Warin?"

"Done." Woodrowel spat into his palm and held out his hand.

Faris stripped off her glove, spat into her palm, and grasped his hand firmly. They remained hand-clasped for a long moment, regarding each other with great satisfaction.

"For two thousand dinaras," Tyrian said dryly, "will it be too much for you and your merry men to see that the coach and driver come safely to Ruger?"

Woodrowel gestured with his cigarette and his men set to work clearing the road. "Not at all." He smiled and made another smoke ring.

Jane was fairly happy with Faris's bargain until she saw the riding clothes spread out across the seat of the coach. She choked. "What's this?" she asked, when she could speak.

Faris eyed her with concern. "It is a shirt and vest and trousers. I wish Warin could let us have caps, too, but they haven't any to spare."

"Baggy trousers," Jane said indistinctly. "Shouldn't they be Lincoln green, at least?"

"Very baggy trousers, I admit. Are you laughing at our national costume?"

"No, certainly not." Jane steadied her voice. "I knew I should have packed my riding habit."

"It would be no use tonight. No sidesaddles."

"But I can't wear these things."

"They're nearly clean."

"Faris, these clothes are for a man. I can't wear them. Neither can you."

"Jane, these clothes are for working. Riding across the border at night with Warin and his crew is *working*."

"I can't."

"Why not?"

"Oh, dear—well, for one thing, I'm English."

"Rosalind was English, she dressed like a man. Viola was English, *she* dressed like a man—"

"Viola was *not* English, and dressing like a man is *not* proper and these clothes are ridiculous."

"Then get out of this coach and let me change in peace."

A short time later, Faris and Jane, both wearing the voluminous national costume of Galazon, rejoined the others. Woodrowel had detailed four men to escort the diligent driver on his way. Their horses had been appropriated for Faris and her companions. The horses were sturdy animals, gone very shaggy for the winter, unshod and only roughly groomed. The saddles were small and flat, each with a fleece strapped over it as padding, and the make-shift bridles were hackamores, little more than a few loops of rope.

At first sight of their steeds, Jane stopped in her tracks and shook her head. She was wearing her own cloak over the borrowed clothes and its hood concealed her expression.

"Do you think you can manage?" Faris asked.

"When I was four, I learned to ride on something very similar. Just show me which end is the front."

Faris woke in the best guest chamber at Shieling. It took no time to remember where she was and why she was there, because every muscle in her body conspired to remind her. Scholastic life, she reflected, was as harmful to the body as it was beneficial to the mind. She felt, after only a night and a morning in the saddle, as though she had been beaten with sticks for a thousand years. Well, five hundred, perhaps. Plainly, she had been away from Galazon too long. She stretched, groaned softly, and, with some foreboding, remembered Jane.

Jane had been cross about wearing the poor clothing that was all Warin and his men could provide. Jane had been testy before she was cross, before the pine tree, indeed, ever since they had left the train. After a long slow ride at night, a long fast ride in the morning, and an afternoon and a night spent in Shieling's drafty halls, surely Jane would be beyond cross, beyond testy, beyond reason. Faris winced. This was not the hospitality she had meant to offer Jane in Galazon.

Faris closed her eyes. The ride through the pine forest had been terrible. The darkness, the need for silence, and the necessity of speed, lest the local brigands find them, made the journey seem endless. Faris had found her discomfort compounded by a private, irrational fear that she still had pursuers. Yet if her uncle wished her harm, there was no pursuit, for Copenhagen and his theoretical minions would be content to lose her on the train, knowing very well what her destination had to be. And if there had somehow been pursuers in that black forest, they must be following her on some other enemy's behalf. Mustn't they? There was comfort in that somewhere, she had thought, if she only had the art to reason it through. In the dark, on horseback, in a hurry, logic was beyond her.

At dawn, when the clouds across the eastern sky were brindled with rose, they had come to a river, as brown as oatmeal stout in the early light. As they urged their horses into the ford, Warin had said softly to Faris, "One foot on that bank and you're back home, Faris. This is the Alewash."

The water was icy and soaked her trousers to the knee. Faris noticed no discomfort. When her horse clambered out on the other side of the river, she was seized by an impulse about equally mixed of weariness and joy. Reining up within a few yards of the ford, she dismounted and fell to one knee on the crisp brown turf. She wanted to lie full length on the ground and breathe in the scent of the soil of Galazon. Cold and stiffness and the knowledge of her own absurd appearance prevented her. Instead she bent her head for a moment as if lost in prayer. In fact, she had no thought for devotion. Her whole heart was taken up with gratitude that she was home in Galazon again.

"Are you all right, your grace?" Tyrian had drawn rein beside her and looked down at her anxiously.

Faris nodded. She started to rise. It took longer than she thought it would.

Warin drew up and dismounted. He tossed his reins to Tyrian and did not wait to see if he caught them. As Faris straightened, he halted before her and dropped to his knees, his slouch hat in his hand. "You have been too long away, my liege," he said softly. "Welcome home to Galazon."

Speechless, Faris stared down at his dark untidy head. *My liege?* Had Warin been reading three-volume novels too? Her mother had been *my liege* to the men and women who remembered the days of her exile. She had never thought to hear the words herself, least of all from her old playmate.

Reed dismounted, handing his reins to Jane. He dropped to one knee beside Warin, bowed his head before Faris. When he stood up, he looked sheepish. The early light made it hard to be sure, but Faris thought he was blushing.

One or two at a time, as they splashed across the ford, Woodrowel's men dismounted before Faris. Most contented themselves with an awkward bow. A few went to their knees before her. All remounted immediately and sat at ease, watching their leader from the safety of their saddles.

Well aware of their interest and amused at Faris's obvious discomfiture, Woodrowel made a lengthy ceremony of rising and resuming his hat.

Grateful for the chance to compose herself, Faris struggled to muster an appropriate word or two. By the time he had put his slouch hat back on at the proper rakish angle, she was able to smile at Woodrowel and say lightly, "Exiled from friends is exiled indeed. Thank you, Warin." She looked around at his men. "Thank you all for your welcome." She turned to Reed. "Thank you. It has been a long journey. May I have a leg up?" Reed put her in the saddle. As she gathered her reins, Faris looked defiantly at Jane and Tyrian.

Tyrian was looking as calm and uncommunicative as ever. Jane was paler than usual but showed no other sign of her fatigue. Hood back and hair only a little disheveled despite her exertions, she regarded Faris steadily for a long moment. Then, without a trace of mockery, she gave Faris a slight respectful nod.

Speechless again, Faris nodded stiffly back.

"Come," said Warin. "We'll be late for breakfast."

Despite wet clothes and weary horses, the ride across the hills to Shieling had been wonderful. The weather was mild for the season. The sun even shone from time to time. Faris found it impossible to worry about brigands or advisers or uncles. Weariness left her little leisure to think of anything but the ground before her and the horse beneath her. All her attention was taken up by the effort it took to stay close on Warin's heels as he rode home across his wide holding.

The hills were just as she remembered from her youth, closely grazed pastures rising into heights patched with heather, broom, and bracken. From time to time their route took them across brooks stained brown with peat, running steeply down from the heights like narrow flights of stairs. Rarely, they came to patches of bog and had to pick their way around on turf that gave like a mattress. With every brook, every bog, every patch of broom, Faris felt her spirits rising higher. It was all still here. It was all still safe.

Shieling stopped everything to welcome them home. Dogs barked, chickens scattered, the midmorning routine shattered at their arrival. Stableboys and housemaids converged on the open yard in front of the old, low manor house. A blonde girl in a brown dress, her cheeks pink with relief and excitement, ran out of the house shouting Warin's name. Woodrowel swung down from the saddle and gathered the girl into his arms. A stableboy took his horse away. Heedless of the racket all around them, Woodrowel and the girl embraced.

Faris watched a little wistfully. She dismounted as the others did and never noticed when one of the stableboys took her horse.

"Here, Flavia," Woodrowel said to the blonde girl as he turned, his arm around her shoulders, "I've brought you company for breakfast." He grinned at Faris. "Your grace, may I present my wife, Flavia." His arm tightened very gently. "The duchess of Galazon has come home again."

Flavia regarded Faris with wide brown eyes. "I beg your pardon, your grace," she said, after a moment's hesitation. "I bid you welcome to Shieling." She glanced uncertainly into her husband's smiling face, then back up at Faris. "Will you join us for breakfast? It's only pancakes, though," she added apologetically.

For a moment, afraid to speak lest her voice crack, Faris stared at Flavia. She blinked hard to vanquish the tears that suddenly filled her eyes.

Puzzled by her guest's silence, perhaps suspecting rudeness, Flavia's color rose. She glanced at her husband, who was still smiling.

"Thank you," said Faris, at last, in a voice that trembled, "I would rather eat pancakes in Galazon than truffles in Paris."

Flavia beamed and stepped out of the circle of her husband's arm to beckon Faris indoors. "There's barberry syrup, too."

Faris presented her companions. When the introductions were finished, they crossed the threshold into the house. As they entered, Faris heard Jane's soft reproachful voice at her elbow. "Easy for you to forswear them. You've never eaten truffles in Paris. I have."

Wincing at the thought of Jane's probable opinion of Galazon so far, Faris got up, washed, and dressed. In addition to the clothes he'd sold her in the forest, Warin had rummaged industriously for Faris at Shieling. He had loaned her a pair of boots only a little too big for her, gloves so long they were almost gauntlets, a few rounds of ammunition, an old but serviceable revolver, and a sash to tuck it in. She left the gloves and loaded revolver in her room but put on everything else and opened the door.

Outside the best guest bedchamber, the corridor was empty. Literally. Though almost as wide and fully as long as the gallery in Galazon Chase, the gallery at Shieling held no portraits, no carpets, and no furniture. It served only to connect Shieling's many rooms. Indeed, its best guest bedchamber was nearly its only guest bedchamber, for though blessed with dozens of chambers, Shieling had only a few proper beds.

More than the pale light of morning, the silence of the house told Faris how early it was. Moving as softly as she could in borrowed boots, she crossed the corridor and listened at the door directly opposite. She could just hear Jane humming. It was difficult to be certain through oak. She thought it might have been Gilbert and Sullivan. Faris scratched at the door.

Jane, flawlessly groomed in her borrowed clothing, resplendent in well worn boots that reached her knees and folded rakishly down again, let Faris into the second-best guest bedchamber. "I was so hoping you were the early morning tea."

"As a rule we don't do early morning tea in Galazon," Faris said regretfully. "If you like, I'll send for a tray. How is your headache?"

"Quite gone, thanks to Flavia's home remedies. No need to send for tea. I'll wait for breakfast. Will it be pancakes again, do you think?"

"Probably. Those are nice boots." Faris took a chair near the window and looked out into the yard. Below, housemaids and stableboys were starting to emerge. The day's work was just beginning.

Jane regarded her feet with great satisfaction. "They are, aren't they? Flavia is letting me borrow them. We wear the same size, isn't that fortunate? Why didn't you tell me that all your gentry dress this way? I would have felt much less absurd."

"Well, Warin and Flavia aren't precisely what you British think of as gentry," Faris replied. "They're farmers." She crossed her ankles and stared glumly at her toes. "I just came in to apologize."

Jane looked astonished. "Whatever for?"

"For the diligence," Faris answered, eyes still lowered.

"For making you leave your luggage. For the pine tree. For making you ride across the border in the dark—"

"In fancy dress," Jane added cheerfully. "For soaking my feet in the icy river. For pancakes at breakfast, galettes at dinner, and crepes at supper. For letting Flavia Woodrowel cure my headache with barberry tea—your point is taken. Very well. I accept your apology. Now, Tell All. Warin Woodrowel was your youthful beau, I take it?"

Faris regarded Jane with wonder. "What happened to you? In the diligence you were as cross as two sticks. Two *hundred* sticks."

"Don't try to change the subject. What did you do with the pocket knife he gave you? Do you still have it somewhere, tied up with a ribbon? Or perhaps a pressed flower? 'The last rose of summer, left blooming alone . . .' "

"Was your headache that bad?" Faris demanded. "Perhaps Flavia knows some home remedy that will bring it back. At least while you had it, you spared me this—interest in my childhood."

"Oh, very well. My turn to apologize. I was a bit cross in the diligence, I admit. Traveling light doesn't agree with me. Why doesn't the Baedeker mention that everyone in Galazon eats pancakes at every meal?"

"I accept your apology," Faris replied. "You have my uncle to thank for the pancakes. When I last spent a night here, Shieling was as prosperous as any place in Galazon."

Jane said dryly, "I do look forward to meeting your uncle."

After breakfast, which was, indeed, pancakes, the Woodrowels offered Faris and her party some of their men as escort.

"It would do them a world of good to go with you," Flavia said. "They get so bored when they have to stay home and behave, and it is much too soon to send them across the border again."

"Only think how an armed escort would add to your consequence," Jane murmured.

"I already have one," Faris replied quietly.

"You know the terrain," Tyrian said to Warin. "Is a larger escort necessary?"

"If you are referring to our neighbors, the Haydockers, not at all. They leave us alone." Warin replied. "But if you'd like a guide, you're welcome to one."

Faris said, "If there is one place in the world where I don't need a guide, this is it. How many times did we ride the drove-road when we were children, Warin?"

Warin smiled crookedly. "Half as many times as we fell out of trees, and twice as many times as we sprained our ankles."

"Even when I was most happy to return to Galazon Chase, I was always sorry to leave Shieling. Thank you for everything you've done for us, all of you."

Warin looked nearly solemn. "You are welcome, Faris." Flavia nodded her agreement. "Welcome home again."

Faris and her companions took their leave. Under a heavy gray sky, they set forth eastward from Shieling along a narrow road. There was thin black ice on the puddles in the ruts, and the mud was touched with stars of frost. On either side of the road, the brown pastures held nothing but occasional patches of low, bare-branched shrubbery.

"The herds graze here all summer," Faris told Jane. She gestured out across the hilltops stretched before them. "In the autumn, we drive the stock back down to the valleys. This road is for carts. If we stay on it, we'll be two days on our way to Galazon Chase."

Jane took a careful look at the hilltops. Some of the higher hills were pale, as though they had been powdered with sugar. "And if we don't?" she asked. Her voice was neutral. "I distrust shortcuts."

"The drove-road is quicker. But if you'd rather stay on this road, by all means, let us stay on it."

"How far to Galazon Chase by the drove-road?" Jane asked.

"Thirty-five miles," said Faris. "We can be there in time for supper."

"And will there be pancakes?" Jane asked.

"If my uncle is in residence, I think I can promise he will not permit pancakes for supper."

"And if he is not in residence?"

"Then I will be shocked."

The drove-road was Faris's favorite way home because it came down so swiftly from the heights to the forest. Ten miles from Shieling, while the cart track still followed the line of the ridge south and east, the drove-road turned straight east and dropped off the shoulder of the ridge into a valley filled with pine. It followed a narrow path through the pine to a shallow stream that ran in and out of ice.

For five miles, Faris and her companions followed the stream eastward. When it led them around the foot of a hill and bent northward, she left it and rode east along another valley, this one filled with oak and chestnut. From that point, the drove-road took on substance and became a wide lane through the forest. The path was well trodden, cushioned with loam and fallen leaves. The lacework of bare branches nearly concealed the gray sky overhead. On either side, briars and brambles grew among the trees so closely that no traveler would willingly have left the road.

Faris felt the calm and silence of the forest sink into her as she rode. The discomfort she'd felt in the saddle for the first few miles was gone, her stiffness melted into her mount's motion. Even without a guide, Jane had no need to fear a shortcut, Faris thought. On this road, one could not go astray.

Tyrian and Reed, always vigilant, rode beside her in the lane and Faris did not worry about what they might see or hear. She felt no twig could stir in the wood today and she not know it. Every step she took toward Galazon Chase was a little more quiet than the step before. She felt as if everything about her was softening, growing muted to match the trees. The only effort the journey required was that she keep a slow and even pace. It was tempting to urge her horse on, faster and faster, until Galazon Chase came into view. But Faris held her horse to a walk and when she was not busy wondering at the beauty of the woods, she wondered at her own reasonable behavior.

At midday, at the spot where the lane dropped over a bank and became a ford across a small river, they halted to rest the horses, and to eat the food that the Woodrowels had sent with them.

When she unfolded her cloth-wrapped packet to find only bread and cheese, Jane looked disappointed. "No pancakes?"

Tyrian was watering the horses. Arms folded behind her head, Faris was watching the patterns the branches made against the overcast sky. Reed stretched his legs out before him, and opened his own packet. "That's one thing I will miss about this job. The food. I'm not so fond of pancakes, myself, but the food on this trip was very good."

"What will you do when this job is over?" Jane asked.

Reed looked thoughtful. "Take another. And another after that. And so on, until Lord Brinker pays me enough money to buy back the title."

Jane stared and swallowed her crust hastily. "You have a title?" she asked, when she could speak again.

Reed smiled and passed the wine flask. "The title to our farm. We're perhaps not the best of farmers, we Reeds, but we make up for it with stubbornness." He tore his bread into pieces as he chose his words. "My parents lost the title when I was fourteen. Lord Brinker bought their note and let them rent the place from him. I went into his service when I was sixteen. I thought it would be appropriate to buy our farm back with money I earned from him."

"What do you think of him? Faris makes him sound like a complete ogre."

Reed rearranged his pieces of bread on the cloth. "My grandmother planted a quince tree in the garden behind our house. Quince are hard to grow in Galazon. But my grand-mother had a gift for such matters and ours grew. The spring we lost the farm, the blossoms were something wonderful to see. My grandmother was very proud. It was going to be the finest crop she ever had. Then Lord Brinker came to see if our place was worth bothering about." Reed moved a piece of bread as carefully as a chessman from one side of the cloth to the other. "He came himself and walked through the place, house and byre and all. When he left the garden, I heard him say to the bailiff, 'I'll keep it. The place is worth the money for the garden alone. Oh, and send that quince blossom home with me. It's beautiful.' So the bailiff picked every single blossom off the tree. They were wilting as he packed them up."

Jane's eyes widened. "Surely that was the bailiff's mistake, picking every blossom."

"Oh, I think the bailiff understood the order perfectly well," said Faris. She sat up and took the wine flask from Jane. "Be glad my uncle settled for the blossoms. He might easily have had the tree cut down." She took a swallow and handed the flask back, opened her packet of bread and cheese, and began to eat with fierce concentration.

"But why?" Jane demanded.

"It's his way," said Reed.

Faris looked at Reed. "At a guess, it was a reminder. He wanted to be sure your family remembered that the place was his."

Reed's face twisted. "Small danger we'd forget."

Tyrian brought the horses back and tethered them with help from Reed. When he had finished his meal, and what little wine the others had left him, he put his elbows on his knees and said, "This wood is too empty."

"I like it," said Jane. "It makes a nice change from the other night."

"No brigands here," Reed said.

"No," Tyrian agreed. "No hunters. No game. Nothing, in fact, but trees. Is it always this quiet here?"

"It's the time of year," said Reed.

"You know, he's right," said Jane. "I haven't seen or heard so much as a crow all day."

"There's no danger. We're alone, that's all." Faris sounded apologetic. She went back to looking at the branches overhead. The conversation went on without her while she stared up into the lowering sky. The silence of the forest was still with her as an abiding calmness. Even Reed's reminder of her uncle's nature could do little to disturb her. She had a growing conviction that the stillness that Tyrian had noted was responsible for her own sense of quiet. She could not explain how, even to herself. Impossible to say aloud, 'Oh, yes. The wood is calm today, isn't it? That's just Galazon welcoming me home.' Well, impossible to say it before Jane and Reed. Tyrian would probably accept that statement with aplomb. He was sane and competent himself, and he seemed to assume sanity and competence in others. A restful attitude.

The north wind rose. Overhead the branches swayed. The wind in the trees soughed like breakers on a distant shore.

It was late afternoon when Faris led her companions out of the woods of Galazon Chase. There was the home valley, its wide fallow fields running down to the river. There across the stone bridge, the road curved up and out of sight behind the hill. There was the gate, complete with carefully restored portcullis, and the gracious new wings of the house, built for comfort and not for security. But that was not the house that she had longed to see. The chess rook looming over the valley, the stout tower that had been the bulwark of her family for hundreds of years before they could afford the luxuries of grace and comfort, this was Galazon to Faris.

Faris admired the view so long that Jane sidled her horse close and asked, with great innocence, "Are we lost?"

"No, we're home," Faris said, her expression so blissfully happy that Jane made no further remark.

As they rode across the bridge, sedate with weariness, the north wind strengthened and it began to snow.

* * *

In the courtyard, Faris and her companions handed their horses over to servants who displayed little sign of interest in their arrival. Faris looked hard but saw no familiar faces among them. For their part, none of the servants seemed to recognize her.

"Where is Lord Brinker?" she asked the servant nearest to the door.

The man gave her his full attention for as long as it took to bring his eyes up from her muddy boots, past the pistol in her sash, to her disheveled hair. "I do not know if Lord Brinker is at home," he said very politely. "I will inquire."

"Please do," said Faris with equal courtesy. "If he is, ask him to attend me in the library. If there isn't a fire there already, please arrange one. And see that someone sends us tea."

As if he did not trust his own ears, the man watched motionless as Faris swept past him indoors. Without hesitation Jane and Tyrian followed her, neither sparing a glance at him.

Reed was not so hasty. He paused on the threshold, looked back at him and the rest of the speechless servants, and smiled broadly. "If anyone remembers where it is packed away, you'd better find the ducal banner and send someone to run it up," he advised. "The duchess of Galazon is in residence."

10

"We regret Bonnie Prince Charlie."

FARIS LED HER companions through the great hall, where the armory of weapons that lined the walls was enduring an inventory, and incidental dusting, under the supervision of a stoop-shouldered, scholarly looking man. High time the collection was catalogued. She ducked into the passage that led to the picture gallery. After Shieling, it seemed almost cluttered, with chairs and tables spaced at intervals along the walls, beneath the gilt-framed family portraits.

Faris was halfway down the long gallery before she could believe she was really home. It all seemed alien at first—the ceilings were high, but not as high as the ceilings she remembered. The light was different, and slanted through smaller windows than she recalled. Even the picture gallery did not seem as long, after the corridors of Greenlaw.

She had longed for this moment, and now she found her serene happiness at coming home obscured the fierce possessiveness she'd expected. It was her house, after all. Not her uncle's, nor even her mother's—her own house. Yet, even though it was something to be prized, she felt only the pride of ownership she'd felt for number five study. Like that well-beloved room, this house was hers to put to good use and then hand carefully on to the next who came.

And who would come next? Jane's teasing came back to her. In her heart, Faris knew she'd spoken truly that summer day at Greenlaw, when she'd told Jane she'd never been the sort to marry. From her study of three-volume novels, she had gleaned the abstract idea that she might have a mate in the world, the way a glove had a mate. The idea was vaguely pleasing. The thought of marriage was disagreeably concrete in comparison. Marriage with whom? There were millions of people in the world. What were the odds of even *finding* one's mate among the throng? And then to create conditions that would allow one to marry? All that effort just to make sure the house was taken care of for the foreseeable future? It was a gamble at best, and not a wager she favored.

Flavia Woodrowel, in her gladness at Warin's return, had caused Faris a moment's wistful pang. Yet her friendship for Warin Woodrowel bore no resemblance to anything she'd ever found in one of Jane's novels. She couldn't imagine herself in Flavia's place, wringing her hands at home while he went haring off across the border.

More likely, she reminded herself, she'd be the one to go

a'roving and a'reiving, and her theoretical husband would be left at home to deal with the tax assessors.

Faris reached the staircase and heard loud voices coming near. Someone caught her arm.

"Hold hard, there," Gavren bellowed in her ear.

Astonished, Faris looked up from his hand on her sleeve and met his eyes.

Gavren released her, horrified. "Your grace! They told me an intruder came stalking in, inquiring for Lord Brinker. Forgive me— They said it was some ruffian with muddy boots."

At first glance, Gavren seemed to have shrunk. Then Faris realized that he was almost the same as ever. She had grown, so he seemed smaller. His hair had gone from brindle to silver gray. His eyes were just as she remembered.

He added, "I see your boots *are* muddy." He put his hands on his hips and surveyed her disapprovingly. "You look like you lost your way to the cow byre. What happened?"

The familiar tone of censure was so welcome that Faris could hardly keep from laughing. To conceal her amusement, she shrugged and gestured vaguely. "Oh, nothing. It's snowing."

Gavren shook his head, disgusted. "Was it for this I nursed you across half the world to Greenlaw? So you could come back a worse hoyden than you left? The food must have agreed with you, I see. You've grown enormous."

Faris grinned at him. Under her interested gaze, he blushed to the roots of his hair. "Forgive me, your grace. Your return made me forget myself. I beg your pardon."

"Bilge. Listen, Gavren." Faris leaned close and murmured, "I think we may be visited by a sinister stranger quite soon. Come to think of it, he might even have beaten us here. Get the description from Reed and Tyrian. Well, from Tyrian."

"We've had no sinister strangers here. Who is he? What makes him sinister?"

"He's called Copenhagen and someone's hired him to kill me. I think he'll have a try, if he troubles to come here after me. Put the word out, will you? I want to catch him, but I want

him alive and unable to hurt anyone. Particularly me. Clear?''
Gavren nodded, eyes wide. Faris patted his arm reassuringly and left him gazing after her. It was very good to be home after all.

There was a new old carpet in the library. Faris paused just inside the door to stare at the unfamiliar oriental rug. It was magnificently large and of a quality that made everything else in the room look slightly shabby. Faded by time into a subtle trellis of scarlet and indigo, the intricate pattern of the rug diminished its apparent size. Faris felt grateful that only her companions, crowded into the door behind her, were going to witness the spectacle of her taking off her boots so she could cross the rug to the fireplace. As she bent to begin, a blonde woman rose from the armchair closest to the fire.

"Must I endure a draft in here too?" she began, then demanded, "Who do you think you are, bursting in without leave?"

Faris straightened. "Who are you?"

The woman drew herself up to her full moderate height with such indignation that her carefully arranged corona of golden hair seemed to crackle with energy. She swept to the bell rope and pulled it before she spoke, gray eyes flashing. "Get out. And be sure to close the door firmly as you go."

"I've already sent for my uncle. It would be rude to leave before he joins us. I think you must be Agnes Paganell. You remind me amazingly of your sister."

The woman stared in hostile silence at Faris. Behind Jane and Tyrian and Reed, a servant appeared at the open door. Faris's companions gave way as he entered the room behind a heavily laden tea cart.

"Excellent." Faris eyed the carpet. "Now all I need is a bootjack. Will you bring me one?"

The servant was gone before the woman released the bell rope and spoke. Her color was still high but her voice was calm. "You might have given us some notice that you were coming home."

"Why, when Brinker sent for me?" Faris asked. "Where did this carpet come from?"

Her gray eyes were icy. "It's mine. Why?"

"I just wondered. It's beautiful."

Faris and Agnes regarded each other warily. Brinker Nallaneen joined them as they were choosing their next questions. He was slim and dark, with a neatly pointed black beard, and wore English tweeds. With his hair windblown and his cheeks rosy from the cold, he did not seem much older than Faris. "I scarcely believed my ears when they told me." His voice was smooth and very deep, as though it belonged to a much larger man. "Welcome home, Faris."

Faris turned to face him and realized with delight that she was now two inches taller than he. "Hello, Uncle. The tea is getting cold."

Brinker took no notice of her impertinence. He greeted her and introduced his wife with great cordiality. Faris used the bootjack and introduced her companions with equal lack of finesse.

Brinker made Jane welcome and said to Reed, "Many thanks for your patience with these reunions. If you will attend me in the Russian room, I will join you in a moment to settle your account." To Tyrian, he said, "Has there been some misunderstanding? I sent a letter of credit to your address at Greenlaw." His dark gaze flickered, as if taking in Tyrian's appearance for the first time, and his brows rose. "Why are you here?"

Faris looked hard at her uncle, then glanced at Tyrian, who was even more impassive than usual. The journey on horseback had been hard on Tyrian's somber clothes. He had circles under his eyes and a good start on a beard. His hat had long since gone and his fair hair was uncombed. "I am now in the service of the duchess herself," he explained. "I had already resigned my duty on your behalf when I agreed to serve as escort to her grace. I don't consider myself of any further concern to you, my lord." He hesitated, then added, "I was never really needed in Greenlaw, anyway. Her grace is very capable."

After a pause which made it amply clear that he still did not understand what Tyrian was doing there, and that it had never occurred to him that Faris was capable of anything at all, Brinker tilted his head a little and said, blankly, "Yes, of course." He studied Tyrian a moment longer, then turned back to Faris. "You will want your old room, I imagine. We could put Jane in the Chinese room, if you like." He smiled at Jane. "You would be just down the hall from Faris. There is a very pleasing prospect from the windows there. Shall I have your luggage sent up?"

Jane gave him a brilliant smile in return. "Not just yet, I think. Perhaps in a few days."

While Brinker and Agnes blinked at Jane, Faris drew an armchair closer to the fire and settled into it. "The tea really is getting cold. Will you pour out for us, Aunt? Tyrian, if you and Reed will be so good as to join us, we can be quite informal. As for rooms, I will have Queen Matilda's. When we are finished here, please arrange it." She stretched her stockinged feet toward the fire and added, "My uncle Brinker is right about the view but you should be warned, Jane. That room could more accurately be called the Chinese red room."

"Oh, dear." Jane accepted the cup of tea Agnes offered her. "Is it anywhere near Queen Matilda's room?"

Agnes served all four companions with rigid courtesy. Brinker nodded approvingly at her. She stared back, eyes wide with sheer unblinking irritation.

"No, not really." Faris ate a macaroon and stared dreamily into the fire. Some of the silence of the woods was still with her. It made it easy to ignore the other people in the room, their words, their looks, the palpable undercurrent all around her. Instead she concentrated on the room itself, which gave Faris a sense of tranquil welcome as comforting as the warmth of the fire or the flavor of her tea.

"Queen Matilda's room," Brinker told Jane, after a long, faintly bewildered look at Faris, "is in the keep. It has neither heating nor plumbing. It is not at all suitable." Puzzled, he turned back to Faris. "I should think you would prefer your old room."

Faris studied the carpet absently. From her chair the pattern seemed less like a trellis and more like a forest of foliage. "My old room," she replied, looking up at her uncle, "is occupied." At Brinker's blank expression she added, "by your daughter."

"We weren't suggesting you return to the nursery." Agnes refilled Jane's tea cup. "Though it might be a very good idea at that," she added softly, as if to herself.

"By no means," Brinker said. "I was referring to the rose room."

"I will have Queen Matilda's room." Faris selected another macaroon. "Or, if they are available, I will have my mother's rooms."

"I'm sorry, those rooms are occupied," said Brinker. "I wish you would consider other people for once. You have a whim to sleep in Queen Matilda's room, very well. Yet think of the work that means for the servants."

"Who has my mother's rooms?"

"We do, of course," Agnes replied crisply. Her air of irritation became unmistakable. "Are you going to eat *all* the macaroons?"

"Probably. If I do, let me just remind you that they are *my* macaroons," Faris said, far more gently than she had intended. Certainly there was some calming influence on her today. Between the comforts of the tea cart and the solid luxury of the library, she felt positively mellow.

Agnes put the teapot down. "Did you learn to behave this way at Greenlaw?"

"Yes." Faris glanced apologetically at Jane. "Once I might have behaved badly in this situation. I might have reminded everyone of everything that is mine." Faris knew perfectly well that she *was* behaving badly, but she also knew she was enjoying herself far too much to stop. The novelty of being in the same room with Brinker without losing her temper was exhilarating.

"Not yet," said Agnes. "It is not yours yet."

"If it is not mine, it is not yours either."

"Except for the carpet," murmured Jane into her teacup.

"In a few months it will be yours," Brinker told Faris. "I hope you will find that I have been a wise steward."

"Oh, Uncle, I hope so, too. I hope so, too."

When Agnes had taken Jane off to show her where to wash her face and comb her hair, and when Tyrian had taken Reed off to see about preparing Queen Matilda's room for human habitation, and when the ravaged tea cart had been removed, Faris turned to Brinker. "And now perhaps we should discuss why you sent for me."

Brinker rose and began to pace, hands clasped behind his back. "Belatedly, it occurs to me that in summoning you, you might claim I have prevented you from completing your last term at school. I trust you won't try to persuade yourself that I commanded you to interrupt your education."

"Me, leave Greenlaw for a little thing like an urgent summons home? Don't be silly."

Brinker stopped pacing and studied her with disfavor. "I wonder now how wise I was to send for you. I have evolved a plan which may quite possibly win our independence from Aravill once and for all. Now that you are here, however, and I see how little effect your schooling has had upon your demeanor, I doubt that you are the proper person to employ. I may have summoned you in vain."

"I suspected as much." Faris smiled grimly. "You had a plan. It simply didn't encompass my return."

Brinker gave her another long, faintly bewildered look. "I don't know what you mean."

"Of course you don't." Faris drew the revolver from her belt and inspected it fondly. "Have you ever considered more direct methods? I have." Brinker started to speak but she held up her free hand to stop him. "No, no. Don't bother to say it again. You don't know what I mean." Very carefully she leveled the revolver at him. "I was taught never to point a gun unless I intend to use it."

"Is this what you learned at Greenlaw? I am surprised at you," Brinker said crossly.

Faris regarded him with something so close to affection that she was shocked at herself. "I hoped you would be. Now, let's try it again. Why have you sent for me? If you don't tell me this time, I'll be forced to jump to conclusions."

"I dislike your tone. Still, you have had a long journey and I suppose allowances must be made. Travel often makes me peevish, too. Very well. To put it bluntly, relations between Galazon and Aravill have changed since my marriage."

Faris grinned. Before she could speak, Brinker added, "I think you should refrain from making any of the doubtless vulgar remarks that have just occurred to you."

Faris stopped grinning.

"Relations have improved so much that Aravis has consented to receive a diplomatic mission from Galazon."

Faris stared.

Brinker looked extremely pleased. "Precisely. A country doesn't receive an ambassador from one of its own provinces. The bare existence of such an embassy would be tacit admission that Galazon is a sovereign nation." He paused. Faris was still staring at him. He took advantage of her silence to add primly, "I thought you were the obvious candidate for the post. It is plain that I was mistaken."

Faris frowned. "If Galazon is a sovereign nation, I'm its sovereign. Why would I be the obvious candidate?"

"Who else should I send? Some farmer? You have the training." Brinker caught himself. "That is, you should have the training. If you don't, simply say so. You certainly don't seem to have benefited much from your time at school, riding in dressed like a brigand and waving a pistol to get your way."

"Why don't you go?"

Her question surprised him into smiling. "Would you trust me enough to send me?"

Faris smiled back. "Of course not."

"Just as I thought. Now, will you put that thing away? It's making me extremely nervous."

"I doubt that. Anyway, it's supposed to make you nervous. *If* I were to visit Aravis, and *if* I managed to pass myself off as the ambassador from Galazon, what then?"

Brinker lifted his hands. "Who can say? I must leave some of this to your wit and discretion. A treaty? A trade agreement? Subsidies, perhaps?"

"Delicious thoughts, one and all." Eyes narrowed thoughtfully, Faris regarded Brinker in silence for a moment. "What is the money for?"

Brinker looked baffled. "Money?"

"The tax money." Faris brandished her revolver very carefully. "Tell me about the tax increase."

"Don't be absurd. I think I've been very tolerant of your flights of fancy. Now I begin to find this rather wearisome." Brinker turned toward the door. "You obviously need to rest and recover from the hardships of your journey. We'll discuss this again more sensibly when you've had time to think the situation over."

"Tell me."

Brinker paused with his hand on the knob. "You don't seriously expect me to believe you will fire at me, do you?" He wore his bemused look.

Faris rose, revolver steady. "I do, in fact."

"Indoors?" Brinker looked disapproving. "Things have certainly changed a great deal since I was sent away to school. Well, if you're going to shoot your own uncle in your own library, perhaps you'd better get on with it."

Faris leveled her weapon at the spot between the toe of her uncle's left boot and the edge of the carpet. It was at least as wide as a playing card.

"Perhaps your mother is to blame for insisting you be

sent to an educational institution in France. Vienna was always good enough for the rest of us."

Faris squeezed the trigger. The shot reverberated in the closed room. Brinker neither moved nor spoke as he regarded the scar of white wood gouged in the floor before him. The smell of cordite filled the room. Faris aimed at the doorknob. "Now," she said, perhaps too loudly, but her ears were ringing and she couldn't be sure, "I suggest you take your hand off that knob before I fire again. Or simply tell me now, why do you need the money?"

Before Brinker answered, the knob turned and Tyrian came through the door, pistol first. Reed was behind him, Jane hard on their heels. At the expression on Faris's face, all three halted abruptly.

The door had knocked Brinker back as far as the center of the carpet but he had not lost his balance. He turned to face Faris as the newcomers stared at them both. "If you're quite finished, I have some business to see to before it's time to change for dinner. You do change for dinner in France, don't you?" His low opinion of Faris's costume was evident as Brinker walked past her companions and out the door.

Faris put the safety on and slid the pistol back into her sash, then turned to Jane. "I apologize for that. I miscalculated."

"I'm sure you had your reasons."

"In fact, I did." Faris regarded her companions gravely. "Brinker says he called me home because he wishes me to go to Aravill on Galazon's behalf. 'Relations have improved so much that Aravis has consented to receive a diplomatic mission from Galazon.' I quote."

"How interesting," said Jane, "and how convenient."

Reed was perplexed. "Is that why you wanted to shoot him?"

"I wanted more information. I didn't get it." Faris shook her head. "I can't believe that's all Brinker has in mind. I'll have to try him again after dinner." She glanced down at herself. "Any chance of a quick scrub and brush in Queen Matilda's room before then?"

"Your room is not yet ready," Tyrian said. "I think it would be wise for you to stay here until it is."

"Gavren's had them light a fire and the flue must be clear because it's drawing all right," said Reed. "There's a chest there now, and a couple of chairs on the way. He's got a few of his boys moving a bed up the stair in pieces. It's like watching ants at a picnic."

Jane looked at the bullet hole in the floor. "Go ginger them up a little. Faris can show me over the house until the room is ready, but don't let them take all night about it."

Reed departed. When Faris and Jane left the library, Tyrian accompanied them. Faris didn't ask why. She knew he would stay with her until she reached her defensible bedroom. Efficient and unobtrusive, he considered it his duty to guard her, even in her own house.

Faris made a vague gesture that took in the ranked golden frames. "Picture gallery. Ancestors. Very dull." She walked toward the stairs. "I'll introduce you some other time."

"Goodness," said Jane. "What eyes. Who is that?"

"Oh, that's many-times-great-Uncle Ludovic. He was all right. His two-handed sword is downstairs in the great hall armory. See the hilt over his shoulder in the portrait? Blade and all, the sword had to have been at least his height. His armor used to be here, too. They must have moved it."

"Did he live very long? He's got that duelist's look about the chin."

"Died in bed at an advanced age. They say he killed a hundred men before he turned thirty, so perhaps you're right about the jaw. He was a soldier, though, and most of his victims were, too."

"Not in the same army, I hope."

"Luckily not. He was flourishing back when the kingdom of Lidia had its last gasp. The old king died, there was a feeble attempt to put a Haydocker on the throne, which failed, mercifully, and Lidia split apart into the four duchies: Galazon, Aravill, Haydock, and Cenedwine. Ludovic ended up running Galazon. That settled him down nicely."

As they walked along the gallery, Jane examined the portraits. She did not ask for any further identifications. She merely eyed the paintings closely and remarked from time to time, "There's your uncle's beard. There's his nose. There's his beard again." Faris nodded abstractedly but did not speak until they reached a small canvas at the foot of the staircase, an oil painting of a severely dressed woman with wide brown eyes and a formidable chin. "That's my mother."

Jane regarded the painting in silence for several moments, then turned to Faris. "So that's why your uncle wears a beard. He didn't get the chin."

Faris led the way up the stone stair. "You've seen your bedroom? Right, I'll take you the other direction. This is called the Florentine room, for the spinach-colored carpet, I've always suspected."

The tour lasted until Reed found them at the door of the great hall armory. "Queen Matilda's room awaits you," he told Faris. "Gavren couldn't decide on a straw mattress or a featherbed, so he gave you both. I'm supposed to find a pea to tuck under it, to finish up the job."

"Too kind of you," said Jane, "but we're almost finished here. I've been hearing about Lidia, Cenedwine, all these places I can't find in my Baedeker—you have no notion how confused I am. Faris tells me there's a map painted on the west wall of the armory. I have to see it, or I'll never get it all straight in my head."

"Simple," said Reed, as he held the door for them. "Lidia looked like a hand pulling a cork out of a bottle. Aravill's the bottom of the bottle, Cenedwine's the neck, Haydock's the hand, and Galazon's the cork."

"That's absurd," said Faris.

"Not if Italy looks like a boot, it's not," said Reed. He led them past the cataloguer, whose troops had dwindled to one housemaid with a feather duster, to the map frescoed on the plaster wall. "There. What did I tell you?"

At the far end of the hall, Brinker entered. "If you are quite finished amusing your friends," he called, "we would like to know what time you wish dinner to be served."

Faris turned back from the map. "What time would it be served if I hadn't been summoned home from Greenlaw?" she countered. It was, strictly speaking, Agnes's responsibility to determine such things, as it had certainly been before Faris's return. Yet if Agnes chose this method to register her indignation, Faris was glad to oblige. She could make sure the household staff was treated as they used to be treated in her mother's time. Who knew what Agnes considered proper?

Jane and Reed studied the map, and Tyrian turned to watch Brinker cross the great hall toward Faris. The housemaid took the scabbard the cataloguer handed her, duster at the ready.

And the cataloguer raised the sword, a two-handed sword nearly as tall as he was.

Faris saw the blade start to swing, had just time to think, *why, that's Uncle Ludovic's sword*—and then—*Copenhagen*—as the blade swung down toward her.

Someone shoved her. *Tyrian?* She fell forward. Her eyes were on the bright steel, and she knew she was in its path. She put out her hands to break her fall. Before she touched the floor, a shot deafened her. *Tyrian?* She hit the floor, rolled, and glimpsed Tyrian, just bringing out his pistol.

Ears singing, Faris looked up. Across the great hall, Brinker was putting away a pistol. Between them, the stoop-shouldered man sprawled on the floor. Part of his forehead was gone. Faris glimpsed that much, then the scarlet that had spattered everywhere. The two-handed sword was on the floor nearby, still vibrating with its fall. It had probably made a noise hitting the stone flags, but her ears were too stunned to hear it. She stared at the sword, afraid to look at anything else. The polished steel blade was the only clean thing she could see.

* * *

Faris's hearing came back while she was still on the floor, braced on her hands and knees. It was faint at first, and she would have been glad to do without it. The housemaid was screaming. Jane and Reed, who had made sure that Faris was unhurt, were trying to calm her.

"Are you quite well, my dear?" Brinker asked her. He picked up the two-handed sword, inspected it carefully, and slid it back into its scabbard. His voice was as calm as if he were inquiring about the weather.

Slowly Faris looked up into his face. He looked intently back. Faris thought, *If you hired Copenhagen, you're safe from him now.* Aloud, she said, "I'm all right." She started to push herself up, saw the fine spatter of red on her hands and stopped, staring.

"Is it your custom to carry a gun in your own house?" Tyrian asked. Faris hardly recognized his cold voice.

"It is since my dear niece made it a custom of hers to shoot at me." There was a little pause, just enough time for him to tilt his head, then Brinker added, "I see you carry a weapon, too. Curious. This was a peaceful house, until today."

"Until this man arrived," Tyrian countered. "How long has he been here?"

"Oh, a day or two. I needed someone to inventory the collection. He seemed qualified." Brinker's voice trailed off. "My dear, are you certain you're all right?"

Faris was certain she wasn't. Her palms were clammy, colder than the floor beneath her knees. Her stomach was bucking. With chill resignation, she knew it was not a question of if she would be sick, but when. Soon, she thought. She cursed herself for every macaroon. Very soon. Almost at once.

Tyrian was beside her then, his unshaven face filled with concern. She met his eyes, had an instant to marvel at the bags beneath them, like bruises, and realized that he was offering her a helmet.

"Oh, thank you." She took it from him and saw her own

hands, blood-spattered and trembling. There, crouching at her uncle's feet, while Tyrian held her head, Faris was ignominiously sick.

Tyrian took her to Queen Matilda's room, that was all Faris knew. She sat in the chair he had drawn up near Gavren's roaring fire and shuddered. The serene part of her mind, the part that had helped her through the entire day, reminded her that she ought be busy soothing housemaids, seeing the dead man was properly dealt with, making sure that Jane was fed and lodged as befit her station.

Instead, Faris huddled beside the fire, head in her hands, elbows on her knees. She was just aware of Tyrian in the room with her, moving with purpose and decision. Her empty stomach jerked. She put her head a little closer to her knees and mumbled, "Don't leave me."

"No. Of course I won't." Tyrian's voice was so changed from the cold one he had used to Brinker, it seemed impossible it could be the same man. He came to her, holding a basin of water, a linen towel over his arm. "Here. Let me wash your hands."

The water was warm. The linen was limp with age, as soft as his voice. "Gavren is on guard at the foot of the stair. Reed will relieve him. Your door will be watched every moment. If Copenhagen has left anyone here to harm you, we will stop them."

Faris let him dry her hands, but when he tried to fold the towel away, she held it so that he couldn't. Tyrian bent close. "It's all right." His blue eyes were calm. His voice was gentle. He dabbed her forehead with the damp cloth. "No, hold still. There. That does it."

Faris touched her forehead with cold fingers. "Is there blood on my face too?" Her hands began to shake again.

"No." He put the cloth away. "You're safe now."

Faris hated the way her voice quavered. "Are you sure?"

Tyrian nodded. He looked exhausted. "You're quite safe."

Faris wished she were tired of hearing those words, but she wasn't. Every time she closed her eyes, she saw that glimpse she'd had of the dead man, his forehead gone, and all the blood in its place. She still felt ill. Her throat hurt and her mouth tasted foul. She wanted to throw her arms around Tyrian and sob. No one was there to see her do it. There was nothing to stop her. Except Tyrian. And herself. "Sorry." She laughed weakly and rubbed her forehead. "I'll be better in a minute."

Tyrian was still watching her intently. "You're safe now," he repeated.

Faris realized he was saying it as much to persuade himself as to convince her. "Yes. I am safe now. You're here and I'm all right."

Tyrian frowned. "I made a mistake. If your uncle hadn't had his gun, Copenhagen would have killed you." He shivered, slightly, but he was so near Faris shivered herself without realizing it. "Forgive me."

"Of course," Faris whispered, hardly knowing she spoke. "I saw him when I came in, and I didn't give it another thought. I should have asked Gavren when he came—"

"That was my responsibility." Tyrian shivered again. Slowly, he drew away from her, as if he had just realized how close they had become. He shook himself a little and sat back on his heels. "I'm sorry. It must seem strange to you. I have not quite recovered from my brush with Menary, I think."

"Didn't the Dean do something—" Faris let her words trail off. She didn't feel up to diplomacy and she dreaded offending him.

"Oh, yes. But you—" Tyrian caught himself and started again. "My recollection is not clear. I have the impression that I owe you my life. My manhood. Everything." He paused. In the silence, only the fire spoke, a muted hiss and crackle. "I owe you—a great deal. When I saw what was happening—I had a desperate moment." He broke off and laughed very softly. "How bad I am at this. Words don't serve me." He rose and began to fold the linen towel with obsessive care. "If you call, Gavren will hear you. When his watch is over, he will knock at your door, to let you know that Reed is on duty in his place. You must let one of us fetch you in the morning. Don't come down to breakfast until we do."

Faris nodded. "I'm quite safe now."

Tyrian shivered again and crumpled the blood-stained towel. "You are. I promise."

Queen Matilda's room was large. It had a single window, consisting of a narrow slit in the thick stone wall, which provided a view out across the treetops if one put one's head into the slit and craned one's neck. Even on the sunniest day, the room was dim. Early the following morning, when Jane arrived with a procession of dependable servants, it was dark, lit only by the embers dying on the hearth.

Jane lifted her lamp and surveyed the barren expanse of the room. The curved stone walls of the keep were ornamented so sparsely that the glass in the window seemed luxurious. The only furnishings were a battered oak clothes chest, heavily carved with swags of wheat, acorns, and apples, and the bed, stacked mattresses in a frame of polished rosewood with curves as simple and neat as a sleigh.

"As I suspected," Jane said darkly.

Faris pulled the coverlet up to her chin. "What do you mean?" She felt utterly defenseless. Yesterday's discarded clothing lay in a heap on the floor nearby. She had nothing else to wear, since she had no idea what had become of her valise. The thought of putting on her blood-stained, dirty riding clothes again made her feel ill. "What are you doing?"

Jane directed the servants as they brought in furniture, and more lamps, and what looked like a breakfast tray. "Reed didn't say anything about a washstand, or a writing desk, or a proper light. You didn't get any dinner, not too surprisingly. Your valise was sent to my room by mistake. I'll be astonished if you've so much as combed your hair."

Faris cowered under her blankets while Jane ordered the servants about. By the time she had finished, the room no longer looked sparsely furnished. The fire had been poked into new life, and beside it was set a small, sturdy table bearing a breakfast tray. There was a writing table by the narrow window, and a matching chair with a white-work cushion. There were lamps, enough to read by. There was a washstand, with basin, soap, towels, and a ewer of steaming water. There were extra pillows for the bed. There was a dark dressing gown folded at the foot of the bed, and slippers on the floor beside a small rug. There was her valise. Faris began to feel she might get out of bed someday after all.

Jane closed the door after the last servant, and turned to Faris. "It's your uncle's dressing gown. I hope you don't mind. I nipped in and took it while Tyrian and Brinker were lecturing each other on security. The servants were all scuttling about trying to watch without being so obvious that they had to be shouted at. I would have asked Lady Brinker for permission, but she's shut herself in her boudoir and won't come out." She touched the dark silk. "He doesn't deny himself much, does he? There was one for every day of the week." Jane tossed Faris a pillow. "Sit up so I can pin you beneath the breakfast tray. The tea is probably stone cold by now, but it will do you good."

Faris drank her lukewarm tea gratefully. She thought she managed to get the cup back on the saucer without rattling it noticeably, but Jane gave her a keen look and poured her another cup without waiting to be asked. When Faris had finished it, she cradled the empty cup, and said quietly, "Thank you for everything."

"I enjoyed it." Jane's gray eyes gleamed. "You've no notion how much. And it helped take my mind off the late Copenhagen. Consider it amends for making you finish my packing on the train."

"I suppose it really was Copenhagen?" asked Faris. "Not some innocent scholar who just wanted to show me the sword?"

"What a ghastly thought. No, it was Copenhagen. Tyrian identified the body, by the shape of the ears, for some peculiar reason. He's questioning the rest of the staff, to find out if any of them are Copenhagen's minions. Even if they are, they won't have much chance at you here. Reed tells me there's a cistern for rainwater which Gavren has thoughtfully had filled. The garderobe works as well as it ever did, and there are reliable people guarding the stair in shifts. Still, the questioning gives Tyrian something to do. Other than glare at your uncle, I mean. He'll fall over with fatigue in a few more hours. Reed and Gavren have a wager on it. Gavren says he won't last until eleven, Reed says noon."

"They'll fall over before he does, I expect." Faris investigated the breakfast tray, found a covered dish, and lifted the lid. "What's this?"

"Eggs *au beurre noir*. Somehow I didn't think you'd fancy pancakes."

After a first cautious taste, Faris was surprised to discover that she was hungry. "This is very good. What's Uncle Brinker doing?"

Jane said dryly, "Just what you'd expect, given that his wife has locked herself in her boudoir, and his servants are being questioned about their complicity in an attempted murder. He's gone hunting."

Faris gaped. "What? Fox hunting? He can't have done. There's a hard frost and snow on the ground."

"Not fox hunting. Woodcock. He went off on foot hours ago, with just the gamekeeper and a small boy to carry his guns for him. Perhaps he merely wants to kill something in order to relieve his feelings."

"I'll have to ask Gavren about it. Listen, if you get a free moment sometime later today, will you take a look at the carpet in the library for me? There's something strange about it. I can't put it into words. I had too much else to think about when we were there yesterday. I couldn't examine it properly. It reminds me of something, that's all."

Jane's eyebrows lifted. "I'm glad you reminded me. Yes, I agree. There is something rather curious about that carpet.

Not magic. At least, I don't think so. But I'd like a closer look. I'll go now."

Faris finished her eggs. "Shall I meet you there? I'm afraid it's going to take me a while to clean up." She lifted a lock of her tangled hair and inspected it without enthusiasm. "Perhaps I'll have to cut it off instead of combing it."

Jane took the tray. "Take your time. I'll ask Tyrian to send you an escort. Shall we agree on a secret knock? Or perhaps a password? How's this? *O my prophetic soul! My uncle!*"

Jane had put Faris's traveling suit firmly in the grasp of Gavren's daughter, a notable hand with stains. She brought it, still damp but perfectly wearable, just as Faris finished pinning up her hair. Faris put it on, grateful not to have to touch her riding clothes again.

It was Tyrian who came to fetch her to the library. He did not use Jane's password. He merely said her name. When Faris opened the door, she was shocked at the weariness in his face, a gray pallor that surprised her into exclaiming, "What's happened?"

Tyrian looked faintly amused. "Nothing. We've been making certain that nothing will happen. I think I can assure you that you will be safe walking in your own house. At least as far as the library."

Faris put her hand on his sleeve. "That will do for now."

Jane was still inspecting the carpet when Faris and Tyrian reached the library. At the door, Faris touched his sleeve again as he turned to leave her. "Get some rest," she told him.

Tyrian was impassive. "I think there are one or two things of greater importance to be seen to first."

Faris did not release him. "I disagree. You're not much good to me half dead with exhaustion. Do you realize that Reed and Gavren have wagered on how much longer you can keep this up?"

Something glinted behind the tired blue eyes. Although he did not smile, Tyrian's amusement was plain to see. "I do realize it. Jane put a bet down on my behalf, and I intend to collect."

Faris shook her head and let him go. "Idiot. Don't kill yourself with overwork. I can't spare you."

For the first time since their arrival at Galazon Chase, Tyrian looked smug. "I know."

Jane had finished with her first examination of the carpet, and turned to the rest of the room. She was quick but methodical enough to make the inspection a lengthy one.

"There's something here," she told Faris, "but it's so faint I can't be certain it's the carpet. It could easily be something else."

As Faris watched Jane work, the household returned slowly to normal. At nine o'clock, Brinker came in from shooting at small birds. At ten, Agnes emerged from her boudoir and troubled to send a message to the library. Luncheon would be served on the dot of one. At eleven o'clock, Gavren lost his bet and took himself off to bed, pausing on the way to look in and tell Faris that he had instructed a workman to repair the bullet hole in the floor the next day.

Faris sat beside the fire and watched Jane in silence. Any tranquility the room might have held the day before eluded her now. Even the pattern of the carpet looked different than she remembered, far less like foliage and far more like geometry.

Jane finished with the rest of the room and returned to the carpet. She lay face down in the center of it and ran her palms across the pile. After another moment or two, she sat up, rubbing her palms together. "There's nothing magical about this thing now, nothing that I can detect. At most, it has a kind of bouquet, as though it has been around magic, perhaps long ago." She inspected the tips of her fingers, rubbing them with her thumbs. "I can't test anything more here. Should I send a piece of it back to Greenlaw?"

Faris grinned. "Will you explain it to dear Aunt Agnes?"

"Certainly not. I know my limits."

"So we leave it alone—unless I can remember what it reminded me of."

The library door opened and Reed peered cautiously in.
"The luggage has arrived, your grace. We've looked for assassins and infernal devices. There aren't any. Would you like to
inspect it yourself, or should we have it taken to your rooms?"

Jane's face was transfigured with relief. "Luggage! Is it all
right?"

"It seems to be. And it's all there."

"It's a miracle," said Jane.

Faris and Jane accompanied Reed. The miracle was
stacked at the foot of the stone staircase, amid traces of melt-
ing snow. Jane scrutinized the luggage and agreed with Reed
and Tyrian that it seemed to be perfectly safe.

"Have it taken up, then," said Faris. "Don't unpack too
thoroughly."

Somewhere, a clock struck twelve. Reed looked at Tyrian
despairingly. Tyrian regarded him with calm interest.

Jane eyed Reed and lifted an eyebrow. To Faris, she said,
"One is either packed or unpacked. There is no middle
ground." She held out her hand and Reed reluctantly surrendered a small stack of coins. Jane accepted the money and
Reed took himself off, yawning convulsively.

Faris said, "Well, there's quite a lot of middle ground between Galazon and Aravis and we may be on it very soon."

Jane and Tyrian watched Reed go. When he was out of
sight, Tyrian held out his hand to Jane. Jane dropped the coins
into his palm and they smiled at each other with evil satisfaction.

Faris took her time about changing clothes. More even than
the quantity, the quality of the garments stunned her. She
spent many minutes sitting on the hearth, staring into the fire,
and considering the alternatives Jane's taste and industry had
provided. Then, with great deliberation, she chose a dress of
moss green merino, with a single row of tortoise-shell buttons
running from nape to hem. When she pulled it over her head,

the soft fabric slid effortlessly into place. Faris straightened, and took a few experimental steps. Cuffs, hem, neckline, all fell into perfect order. As she began the long struggle to fasten the buttons, even those between her shoulder blades, she realized Jane's guess had been right. Never before in her life had she worn clothing that truly fit her.

When Faris joined the others in the east drawing room, it was evident they had been waiting for her some time. Jane, in a dress Faris had never seen before, of violet washed silk as delicate as a butterfly's wing, was chatting animatedly to Brinker. Brinker's attention seemed to be divided equally between Jane's conversation and a nurse, who was showing Agnes a well-wrapped bundle of flannel. The bundle moved and Faris realized she was about to meet her cousin Prosperian.

Brinker looked up as she entered and his dark eyes grew wide. After a moment, he murmured, "You don't feel the need to carry a gun any longer?"

"Do you think I can't defend myself against a baby?" Faris countered, almost absently. She approached the nurse with caution. Nestled within the bundle was a large round baby with large round brown eyes. Faris was surprised and slightly irritated to see that the fuzz on the infant's head was orange—not much different from her own hair color. While she looked at the baby, the baby looked at her. Faris studied the infant's moist features until it turned scarlet and burst into furious howls. Agnes made a small gesture and the nurse withdrew with it, headed back to the nursery. When the door shut, the drawing room seemed strangely silent. "Splendid baby." To her private astonishment, Faris found she meant it.

Agnes merely gazed at Faris with dislike but Brinker nodded. "She has the family temper." He smiled at Faris, rare warmth in his expression.

Faris glanced at Agnes. "Whose family?"

Agnes ignored her and pulled the bell rope. "I think luncheon is served."

* * *

At the table, Agnes did not seem inclined to say anything to anyone. Brinker seemed interested only in watching Faris. With the most animation she had shown since Paris, Jane applied herself to sustaining the general conversation. She steadfastly addressed Lord and Lady Brinker by their first names, as they had addressed her since her arrival. She confided to the table at large that she did not find the Chinese room intolerably red. She made observations on the weather, the architecture of Galazon Chase, and the novels of Marie Corelli.

Faris listened, slightly awed by so much enthusiasm. She knew Jane did not truly believe the novels of Marie Corelli to be satirical social documents. She wondered how genuine the rest of her opinions were. In any case, it seemed certain that furnishing Queen Matilda's room and the recovery of her luggage had done wonders for Jane's spirits.

When he had finished his cutlet, Brinker joined Jane in conversation. Having consulted his copy of Burke's *Peerage*, he knew all about Jane's family. Now he wanted to know all about Jane. Jane humored him briefly, then turned the conversation to the Nallaneens.

"Faris has tried to explain it to me, but I just don't seem able to follow. The immediate family is so small, yet whenever she refers to the Nallaneens, it sounds as though she is referring to a tribe. Like Scythians."

"Say rather a clan. There is a sense in which everyone born in Galazon is a member of our family. Put quite simply, we are the head of the clan, and all other families merely septs."

"Rather like the Scottish tribes of your own country," said Agnes languidly. "Those who have only a cow or a goat look to those who own many cows and goats as their nobility."

Faris tried and failed to muster yesterday's sense of tranquility. Her usual annoyance with her uncle had returned full strength, with plenty to spare for her aunt. "Not at all like the Scots, for we know our duty. In Scotland, when times were troubled, those who had only a cow or a goat looked to the lords they rented from and their lords turned them out to starve. We must follow a better example than that."

"That was a matter of simple economics," Brinker corrected her gently. "There is no room for a cottage with a single cow where the sheep need to graze."

"It was a matter of simple greed." Faris glared at her uncle.

"Perhaps it wasn't a very good analogy," Jane ventured. "The clans of Scotland are various and quarrelsome. There seems to be only one clan here."

Agnes looked bored. "You know best, of course. I am not familiar with either place."

"How long has it been since you came here from Aravill?" Jane asked politely.

"It seems an eternity," Agnes replied. "Brinker came to Aravis to meet me before my father would consent to the marriage. I often think I ought to have come to Galazon Chase instead. Far more important than beholding one's suitor is beholding one's suitor's home."

Faris stared at Agnes, eyes narrowed with annoyance. It was *her* house, not Brinker's. Well, it would be a pleasure to send Agnes back to Aravis. She wished Brinker joy of his father-in-law.

Jane glanced from the silver on the sideboard to the chandeliers overhead, then to the diamond-paned windows and the view of the snowy gardens beyond. "It is a splendid house."

Agnes followed Jane's gaze. "It is a ridiculous climate." She sighed. "My father meant well. He fancied it was his duty to summon Brinker to me."

Jane nodded sympathetically. "I have a father myself. He sometimes has curious ideas about his duty to the family. What is worse, he sometimes has curious ideas about mine."

"Ah, yes," said Brinker, as if he had just remembered something he'd been straining after for a long time, "your duty. Surely this is not a propitious time of year for you to leave your duties at Greenlaw. I understand what brings Faris and her menial here. But what brings you?"

This rudeness made even Agnes stare. Faris's jaw dropped slightly. Jane returned Brinker's challenging gaze with unruffled good humor. "To be perfectly honest?"

"By all means."

Jane lowered her voice. "Bonnie Prince Charlie." She enjoyed the long moment of baffled silence that followed, then confided, "Once upon a time, we English mustered the common sense to resist putting Bonnie Prince Charlie on the throne. A triumph of logic, but at what cost? We have been sensible ever since." Brinker attempted to speak but Jane beamed and fluttered her hand to silence him. "I will be honest. We regret Bonnie Prince Charlie. We regret him extremely. And we wish to expiate our common sense. So we look for thrones and people to put on them. Playing kingmaker in obscure corners of the world has become an English sport. When the duchess invited me to visit her here, how could I resist? I felt it was my patriotic duty to accept."

Brinker looked amused. "You do not expect to do any kingmaking here, I trust?"

Jane laughed with him. "I have scarcely unpacked. You must allow me more time to study the ground before I surrender my ambition."

Plainly troubled, Agnes studied Brinker while she spoke to Jane. "I must remind you that the only available king is my father. He already has a throne. The only available throne."

"Then I must find our guest some other diversion."

"That shouldn't be hard," said Faris. "You're good at games, aren't you, Uncle Brinker?"

"And I'm so easily diverted," said Jane cheerfully. "I knew I should enjoy myself here."

11

Snow in Season

🌺 "AN INTERESTING ITEM," said Jane, "and so simple, I cannot tell how the dickens it works."

It was long after dinner. Jane and Faris were alone in the library. Faris was trying to discover, through study of her mother's papers, which of her advisers might still be a) interested in advising a duchess of Galazon and b) alive. Jane was examining the horsehair cantrip she had removed from Haverford's disguise. Both were tired, yet neither was willing to retire for the evening. The blaze in the fireplace was too good to leave.

"It's interesting, isn't it, that you could see Haverford as he really was, while to Tyrian and me, he portrayed the waiter so convincingly. Why, I wonder."

Faris put her work aside. "May I see it?"

Jane handed the cantrip over. While Faris held it up to inspect it by the firelight, Jane stretched out on the carpet before the hearth, chin propped on the heels of her hands. "It's a charming little bagatelle. Let's keep it handy in case we need to disguise Agnes as a human being."

"Do you think it might be anything like your veil?"

"My veil is just a veil. I do the hard part. This is something different. It's simplicity itself, I think. Only it's *so* simple, I can't make head or tail of it."

Faris ran the gleaming black strand through her fingers. "Your veil works on me." She held the strand up and inspected it minutely. The glossy surface caught the firelight and reflected it subtly, like the colors on a starling's black feather. "This doesn't."

"Greenlaw magic. You saw a bird when I changed that

champagne cork. You saw a hat when I changed the bomb. You saw my old face when I put down my veil."

"So this isn't Greenlaw magic."

Jane shook her head.

Faris handed the strand back to Jane, who put it carefully away. Diffidently, she said, "I was a little tired. And I wasn't thinking very clearly. But that morning in the Dean's garden, Tyrian looked like a cat to me. So was that Greenlaw magic?"

"With Menary, who knows? But after all, it wasn't a matter of what he looked like. He *was* a cat."

"Yes." Faris stared into the fire.

There was a long silence.

"If he looked like a cat to you, how did you know he was Tyrian?" Jane asked.

"I knew when I saw his eyes."

Jane picked herself up off the carpet and took the wing chair opposite Faris's. Looking warily down at the oriental rug, she asked, "How did you know there was something curious about this carpet?"

Faris followed her gaze. "I'm not sure."

"You just knew?"

Faris shook her head. "It changes. Sometimes the pattern looks geometric. Sometimes it looks like a garden or a forest."

"How does it look now?"

"Stair steps. Neat rows of those lozenges that are supposed to look like elephant footprints, only the lozenges are bordered with stair steps."

Jane looked relieved. "That's how it looks to me. Do you see it change? Does it move?"

"No. I look away, and sometimes when I look back, it's changed. That's all."

"Well, if you notice that it changes again, tell me, will you?"

"Of course. It looked like a trellis yesterday."

"A trellis. Marvelous."

The two of them went back to staring glumly into the fire.

* * *

It snowed all that night and went on snowing all the next day. The day after that, when Brinker persuaded Faris to accompany him the next morning on a long-scheduled visit to the almshouse at Holle, there was enough snow on the ground to require the sleigh. There was room for only two in the sleigh, a fact that Faris found oddly reassuring. She informed her companions of the plan over tea in the library.

"Bilge," she said, when they protested. "He's planned this visit to show the entire countryside that I'm alive and well. He'd hardly plot to kill me during a demonstration of our mutual goodwill."

Reed regarded Faris with mild suspicion. "Very well. Suppose that's why he planned the visit. Why did you have to agree to his plan?"

"Same reason. To prove that I haven't killed him. Not so far, anyway."

"I think an escort would be a reasonable precaution," said Tyrian.

Faris laughed. "To an almshouse and home again? It's hardly an hour's drive to Holle."

"You believe your security lies in your uncle's willingness to travel with you alone," Tyrian stated.

"As long as there's no one else around to blame things on, I'm sure Uncle Brinker will be circumspect."

"Ah, but what if someone joins you unexpectedly?" Jane inquired. "Suppose he hands you over to some henchman of his—a woodcutter, say, who leads you deep into the forest . . ."

"I'll leave a trail of crumbs."

"You generally do," Jane murmured.

"Quiet, you. I'm going. I have a few questions to ask Brinker and this will be an opportunity to do it without interruption."

Jane began to tick off the questions on her fingers. "Did he hire Copenhagen and the others? Why did he really call you home from Galazon? Are you going to Aravis as an ambassador, or as part of some deeper scheme? Where did this peculiar yet handsome carpet come from? Why has he been taxing the life out of the citizens of Galazon?" She switched hands. "What possessed him to consider marrying Agnes—"

"I think that's obvious enough," Faris replied. "Agnes is first in line for the throne and Prosperian is second, poor little devil."

"Ambition is all very well. Imagine spending your life with Agnes. It would be like having Menary for a tutor." Jane's brows shot up. "I have just had the most *ghastly* thought. Imagine if Menary had been better at dissembling her wretched self. What if she'd stayed at Greenlaw to teach? What if she'd become a proctor?" Jane shuddered. "Think of her poor students."

"What if she'd become warden of the north?" Faris countered.

All four of them shuddered, even Tyrian.

After a thoughtful silence, Jane poured tea. "Upon reflection, I think we were in no danger of that. That isn't something you become. It's something you are."

"Born to the purple?" Faris inquired bitterly. "It's something I could have done without." She sipped her tea and added, "Imagine the next wardens of the west and east and south. Do you suppose they're waiting impatiently for me to mend the rift so they can get on with replacing the old ones?"

Jane cleared her throat. "The Dean told me something about that. I gather they have no notion of their impending responsibility. No one knows who they are—unless perhaps Hilarion and the other two wardens do. I have the impression that it will be a bit of a shock to them when the old wardens cross over."

"Poor devils," said Faris, with great feeling.

"An epiphany," said Tyrian. "If a responsibility well discharged brings new strength for new duties, surely the wardency must bring responsibility enough to earn a new life. A rebirth."

Faris regarded him gravely. "Is that what you believe? Is

that why you are so notably devoted to your duties and responsibilities?"

"A slave of duty," murmured Jane.

"Well, no," Tyrian admitted. "I think in my case it's mere vanity."

The next morning dawned clear and cold. Faris wore her merino dress and enough assorted coats and shawls to stuff a mattress. She carried a fur muff to keep her hands warm and had wrapped a white-work scarf into a turban to protect her head, but Brinker made her take it off.

"You may have all the carriage rugs you please," he informed her, tucking one neatly over her knees, "but you must not cover your head. How is anyone to recognize you without seeing your red hair?"

Faris unwrapped the scarf and tied it around her neck. "Fair enough. Let's go."

With a flourish of Brinker's whip, the sleigh set off, drawn by a matched pair of bays. They left the gatehouse behind and set off at a swift trot along the Alewash road. Brinker drove well, though the pace he set was a trifle fast for the condition of the track. Faris leaned back comfortably in the deep seat.

The sky was a light steely blue. It was still early enough that the sun cast long shadows, slanting pale blue on white. The sleigh's runners made a faint singing sound across the snow, and the bays' harness jangled incessantly. The wind of their passage was chill and clean. Faris smiled, and began to unpin her hair.

Brinker glanced at her, a little alarmed. "What are you doing?"

Faris slid the pins in her pocket as her hair came down in an unruly coil. She shook her head and felt the wind lift her hair like a banner. "My ears got cold," she said.

Brinker handed her his top hat. "Here, put this on."

Faris laughed and shook her head. "Thank you, no. I prefer it this way. And so will anyone trying to identify me at a distance." She considered adding, *Anyone with a loaded gun, for example,* but held her peace. Plenty of time for interrogations and accusations later.

The first houses of Galazon Ducis appeared ahead. To an unpracticed eye, their passage attracted no attention. The few people they saw as they drove through the village carried on with their business without interruption. The only sign of recognition came from the blacksmith, who looked up from his forge just long enough to lift a hand in casual greeting.

Faris smiled and waved. The blacksmith grinned back and returned to his work. Faris clasped her hands inside the muff. The sleigh swept on. Brinker cracked his whip in the air and brought the tip of the lash expertly back.

"That went rather well, I thought," said Brinker, when the last cottage of Galazon Ducis was out of sight.

"Very well," agreed Faris. For theirs were not unpracticed eyes. They had seen the curtains that stirred as they passed, the heads that turned, the necks that craned. That lifted hand had been the equivalent of an ovation.

The rest of the villages they passed were the same. The almshouse was more so. The folk Faris spoke to, as she took the midday meal with them, seemed more concerned to point out to Faris her poor taste in leaving Galazon, even for a few years, than to suggest any good deeds she might do for them.

"It's the climate," one told her. "We all live long and healthy lives in Galazon, and it's the climate that does it. You won't do as well anywhere else."

"She was born here, same as us," another observed, "so stands to reason she ought to stay here, if she wishes to live as long as we do."

"I did miss Galazon," Faris said. "I'm glad I've come home. Now, isn't there anything you need here? Come, be honest. Is the food always this good? Is it warm enough at night?"

"It's the winter climate. That's a fact. You live longer where the winters are properly cold."

"Cold storage, you mean. Stands to reason, doesn't it?"

"Best stay here where you belong, young one."

And that was the longest conversation Faris had.

In the sleigh returning to Galazon Chase, Faris looked gladly around her. After days of overcast, the sky seemed wonderfully blue. After so long in Queen Matilda's dim chamber, the snow crust over the fallow meadows seemed dazzlingly bright.

Faris glanced over at Brinker and discovered something that amazed her. He, her wicked uncle, was watching the meadows and the woods as he drove with the same half smile her mother used to have. The same half smile, very likely, she herself had at moments like this. He was enjoying the weather, certainly, but that smile had something more behind it. Something that looked very like love to Faris. It seemed that even Wicked Uncle Brinker, in his own fashion, loved Galazon.

On impulse Faris asked, "What's going to happen to Galazon?"

Brinker looked bemused. He tilted his head a little as he looked at her curiously. "What do you mean?"

"Just that. What's going to happen to Galazon?"

"I don't know. I'll tell you what I think will happen, if you like." After a thoughtful pause, Brinker continued, without taking his eyes from the bays' progress. "I think, taking your age and experience into account, you will make an excellent ambassador. You will return from Aravill as soon after you reach your majority as duty permits. I cannot tell precisely how much autonomy Galazon will have from Aravill. Much depends upon what you achieve in Aravis. No matter. You will rule wisely and well. You will marry and have children and they will rule wisely and well."

"And you? Once I come of age, what of you?"

Brinker sighed gently. "I have spent many years working for Galazon on your behalf. I grudge neither the time nor the effort, don't think it. But I look forward to working on my own behalf. When Galazon is yours, I will be free to turn my attention to broader horizons."

"What do you mean?"

Brinker smiled inscrutably.

Faris regarded him with interested suspicion for a moment, then reached a conclusion. "Aravis. You've set your sights on the throne."

"The throne is not vacant."

Despite his words, Brinker's smile confirmed all Faris's suspicions. "You'll take your wife and daughter to Aravis and wait for Julian to die. Let's see. Prince Consort sounds rather imposing. Or will you demand a different title? Something more impressive?"

Brinker merely smiled.

Faris's eyes narrowed. If his ambitions stretched beyond the borders of Galazon, perhaps he did not have the obvious reasons to eliminate her after all. "Did you pay someone to kill me, Uncle?"

Brinker's reaction was as annoying as she'd assumed it would be. He regarded her quizzically, head tilted in mild inquiry. "Why would I do that?"

"For Galazon."

"You know, I wondered at your reaction the other day. You puzzled me. After some consideration, it occurred to me that you might have some idea that I was at fault. But why would I need to pay someone to kill you when I could have done it myself long ago? And if I had paid someone to kill you, why on earth would I prevent him just as he was about to succeed?"

"You still haven't said you didn't."

They were nearing a village, but Brinker took his attention off the road long enough to meet her eyes. He looked grave and reliable. "I didn't. I wouldn't. I won't. I need you, Faris. Trust that much, if you can't trust me."

Faris held his gaze. "Why are you sending me to Aravis?"

Brinker returned to his driving. "I've told you that. Tell me this. Why are you going so meekly?"

Faris surveyed the village as they passed and returned

the greetings she received. "It is my duty. Just as it was my duty to return when you summoned me from Greenlaw."

Brinker laughed softly. "Yes, of course. You are very careful to do your duty when it pleases you to do so. You weren't so conscientious about your duty when I sent you to Greenlaw."

"I didn't want to leave Galazon."

"You certainly did not."

They were clear of the village. Faris frowned. "Why did you send me? I've always wondered. If it was just to be rid of me, there are any number of boarding schools—why Greenlaw?"

"Your mother's will was quite specific."

"You wouldn't let a little thing like that stop you."

"Your trustees would have. Bankers can be so inflexible. No, perhaps you're right. Perhaps the real reason was your reaction. The prospect alarmed and angered you. I rather enjoyed that. And it pleased me to insure your admission. Though I admit I was a trifle disappointed that you didn't find some way to foil my plans and come home. I looked forward to shipping you back again."

"They made it clear that your effort 'to insure my admission' had nothing to do with my acceptance. They intended to return the money with a stinging message."

"I received neither money nor message."

"The money was set aside in case there was a delay in my tuition payments."

Something in her tone brought Brinker's attention sharply back to her. "At your suggestion?"

Faris nodded.

"How thoughtful. Let's see. As I recall, the last tuition payments were wired promptly to Greenlaw. So your account would have shown a substantial credit when you left. What became of the money?"

Faris said dreamily, "Traveling is so expensive these days." She thought of Jane and added, "You've no notion."

Brinker was all affability. "You spent it. Of course. And

you've taken that foreigner into your personal service. You'll find that sort of extravagance comes dearer than you think."

Faris wished to challenge her uncle on that provocative remark, but she had not yet finished with her questions. There was no telling if she would ever find him in such a forthcoming mood again. She preserved her dreamy tone with an effort. "You know about all sorts of extravagance, I imagine. What particular sort was it that increased the taxes so? I have yet to see a sign of where the money might have gone. Not a bridge or a road or even an almshouse that I don't remember."

"You really can't expect me to go into the technicalities with you here."

"Why not? How technical can it possibly be? Is Aunt Agnes so expensive?"

"I had hoped that Greenlaw College would train you out of that vulgar inquisitiveness of yours."

"If anything, they trained me to cultivate it. Come, Uncle. There's still time before we reach Galazon Ducis. Tell me."

"You needn't keep asking and asking."

"Oh, but I do, for you don't answer."

"There's answer enough for you. Make do with that."

"No answer? Well, that's honest at least. I'll reward you."

"You'll hold your tongue?"

"Never. But I'll ask a new question."

Brinker sighed. "If you must. I'll answer if I can—and if you answer a question of mine."

Faris thought the offer over and agreed. "Tell me then, where did the carpet in the library come from?"

The question startled Brinker into laughter. "That's simply answered. It came with the rest of my bride's things. My turn."

"Not quite yet. *Where* did it come from?"

"Why, from Aravis. From the palace. It's rather valuable, in fact. It was one of the very few things they managed to save from the throne room fire."

"What fire?"

"What fire? Why, the great fire. The fire that destroyed

the throne room and killed your grandmother. The fire that nearly consumed all Aravis. Have you had no education at all?''

Faris's silence lasted until they reached Galazon Ducis. There she was kept busy returning salutations with the proper degree of interest and recognition.

They left the village behind. Scarcely a mile from the gatehouse at Galazon Chase, Brinker asked, "Is it my turn now?"

Faris regarded him with suspicion. There was a bright edge to his voice she did not care for. "I may make use of your own answer."

"No answer? Fair enough. I'll draw my own conclusions. Riddle me this, Faris. How are you most like your mother? In your unswerving devotion to your duty? Or in your unswerving devotion to a menial paramour?"

Faris blinked. This time there was no ignoring the provocation. In some remote part of her brain she retained just enough grasp on her temper to consider the possibility that there might be some alternative to losing it. No. The question didn't merit a civil answer. And anything short of the response he expected—outrage—would leave Brinker wondering if he had chanced upon a secret of hers.

Brinker held the reins and the whip firmly. He expected her anger, that was plain from the way he slowed the pair and steadied them, ready to calm them if she screamed out her rage. It was all too evident, from his bright-eyed interest, that he expected her to scream.

Faris blinked again, and said huskily, "Why, neither. I am most like my mother in *this.*" Before he could free his hands of whip and reins, Faris cast her muff aside and hit Brinker in the eye.

When he slackened his grip, she wrenched the whip from him. It was too long to be of use at close quarters, but she managed to startle one of the bays. That tied up Brinker's hands with the reins again, so she was able to prod him hard in the ribs with the butt of the whip. Out of breath and off balance, he released the reins and the sleigh veered off the road.

Faris kicked free of the carriage rug tucked over her knees. If the sleigh tipped, she would have to jump.

Earlier in the day, the bays, well-rested and well-fed, might have bolted. Now, although alarmed by the driver's bad behavior, they were headed home along a road they knew well. The lure of the stable brought them back into the road and they picked up speed.

For thirty seconds Faris wrestled Brinker in grim silence. Brinker had the advantage of her in strength, but not in determination. He had gotten the response he was after, and he was enjoying it. Even as he struggled with her, he could not keep from laughing. At most, he wanted her indignation to subside a little, just enough to let him drive her safely home. She, on the other hand, wished only to prod him out of the sleigh, out of her sight. Rage ruled her.

A lucky blow landed, and Brinker let himself fall free into the snow. Faris gathered up the reins, but instead of soothing the horses, she urged them on. She spared a glance over her shoulder. Brinker was on his feet, still laughing as he dusted snow from his caped driving coat. As she watched, he bent to retrieve his fallen top hat.

The road curved. Brinker was left behind to trudge home alone. Faris let the bays enjoy another quarter mile at full speed, then drew them back to a respectable pace. It would never do to bring them in blown and sweating.

At the stable, Faris turned the bays over to the head groom's lad and ordered a horse to be saddled. She spared a moment's wistful thought for the riding clothes from Shieling, then altered the order to a side-saddle. The merino gown was no riding habit, but it would do well enough. She was still too furious to linger for such trifles. "And send someone along the Alewash road with a horse for my uncle."

The lads moved to obey her, trading glances. The head groom dared to ask, "Has there been an accident? The bays don't seem to be upset."

Faris flashed a smile that silenced him. "It is such a lovely day. My uncle said he preferred to walk, but I'm sure he's changed his mind by now."

Her mount, a neat gray mare with the hocks of a hunter, was brought forth and the head groom put Faris up. She arranged her coat and skirts as well as she could, aware that she presented an absurd appearance. "Is the track open to the Spinney Bridge road?" She handed the head groom the last of her shawls and the white-work scarf.

He accepted them with aplomb. "It is. They brought the mail that way this morning."

"Good. I'll be back in an hour, or perhaps a little longer."

For miles Faris rode, trying to calm herself. The well-trampled track led her into the hills south of the manor. A wind had risen at her back. It pushed her hair forward so it got into her eyes. The sky was still clear ahead of her, but clouds were edging in from the north. She reached the road and turned toward Spinney Bridge.

She tried to find some comfort in the emptiness of the snow-covered hills and meadows. Her pleasure in the landscape, in the sunlight, in the clarity of the sky, had vanished. She wanted to regain some of the calmness she'd had that morning. She tried to take comfort in the clear sky to the south, to gaze into blue, to think of nothing. She failed completely. Eventually her anger with Brinker burned away and left her no distraction from her anger with herself.

She had let him do it again. Despite her resolve to use the sleigh ride to question him, she had allowed him to turn the tables on her. To reveal her anger was to give him a weapon as tangible as a knife or a gun. How was she to face him again, knowing she had armed him herself?

And why had she let him do it? What had he said, to flick her on the raw? A reference to the old lies about her mother—she should be used to such slanders. A reference to Tyrian—what was there in that to anger her? Or was she angry on Tyrian's behalf? Could there be some seed of truth in Brinker's words?

Menial. Paramour. She did not know which word was more absurd. Taken together, they were so far from truth that she had to laugh. Yet the words had served Brinker's purpose. They had ended her interrogation.

Faris shook her head and laughed again. She had done her uncle good service today. She could only do better if she broke her neck riding or stayed out sulking in the cold until she caught a chill. She halted at the stone arch of Spinney Bridge and sat motionless in the saddle, listening to the wind and trying to remember the last time she'd been free to go riding alone. Certainly not since she'd left for Greenlaw. Years.

On the wind, Faris caught the sound of another rider approaching. She looked back and saw Tyrian riding toward her at a steady and sensible gait. Her hands jerked and her mare tossed its head in protest. She stifled the urge to ride on at top speed. Her freedom was gone. She was no longer alone. Fleeing Tyrian would be as impossible as fleeing her shadow. It was foolish to have started without him. She collected herself and turned the mare back.

Rational thought lasted as long as it took to cover the ground between them. When she met him, Faris demanded, "Are you going to follow me around this way for the rest of my life?"

"Probably." Tyrian betrayed neither surprise nor irritation at her rudeness. Instead, as she was about to speak again, he handed her the gauntlets she'd worn on the ride from Shieling.

Faris felt something twist in her throat. Surprise, certainly. Gratitude. And something more that she did not dare to consider closely enough to put a name to. Silenced for a moment, she accepted the gloves, pulled them on, and thanked him with a stiff nod. Her mare sidled, torn between distaste for moving into the rising wind and longing for its stable. Faris urged it forward.

Tyrian said nothing. He simply turned his horse and followed her at a respectful distance.

Faris drew rein. "Ride beside me. I want to talk to you."

Tyrian obeyed but for several minutes Faris said nothing. Finally, with great reluctance, she managed to ask, "What do they say of me?"

"Who, your grace?"

"Don't—you needn't be formal. What do the servants say?"

"Nothing."

In the north, the sky had gone solidly gray and looked low enough to touch. Riding homeward took them into the teeth of the wind. Faris felt her face growing red and could not decide if cold or embarrassment were more to blame. She asked, "Nothing at all? No rumors?"

"I am an outsider. Reed could give you better intelligence. They are at ease with him. He banters."

His light tone irritated Faris. "I would rather have intelligence from someone who listens than from someone who talks. Have you heard no gossip?"

"None worth repeating."

"I'm ordering you to repeat it."

Tyrian looked resigned. "Very well. Most recently, I have heard that you strangled your uncle and threw him from your sleigh. You then returned the sleigh and horses to the stable in good condition and went for a refreshing canter. You left without changing into riding clothes, without troubling even to ask for a pair of gloves."

When Faris said nothing, Tyrian continued. "I think it was that, more than concern for your security, that made me follow you."

Faris stared. "To bring me a pair of gloves?"

"I thought something might be wrong." He waited for her denial. When it didn't come, he smiled a little. "I think I must have been mistaken."

Faris squinted into the wind. "So they think I tried to strangle my uncle. Do they know why?"

"They don't care why. They are more concerned with why you haven't done it long since. Why *did* you try to strangle him?"

"I didn't try to strangle him. I just pushed him out of the sleigh. Let us go on to other gossip, not so dangerously fresh. What do they say of my aunt?"

"She's a fine lady, for a foreigner. She dislikes Galazon and would be happier living in Aravis. Galazon would be happier if she were living in Aravis too. She's resolved her daughter will rule Galazon one day, if she has to kill you to bring that about. She tried in the library that first night, it's said, but you sneered at her and the bullet went astray."

Her gloved hands tightened on the reins. "And what do they say of me?"

"Are we back to that? You are their ruler. Greenlaw gets the blame for the changes they see in you."

"Such as?"

"You have grown. You wear fine clothes. You behave with decorum." Tyrian cleared his throat and added, "This afternoon will ease many minds."

"And what do they say of my companions?"

"Jane is a lady and they know it. I have no idea what they make of Reed or me. Why do you ask?"

Faris felt the words would choke her, but she got them out. "You are always with me."

"I am."

Faris looked at him. *"Why?"*

Serenely, Tyrian returned her look. "You know why."

His calmness steadied Faris. "I know you promised to go with me to Aravis to repay me for restoring you to your natural shape."

Tyrian's eyes widened. "My natural shape was the least of it."

Faris watched the memories of fear and guilt and pain cross Tyrian's face, and wondered precisely what had passed on that last evening at Greenlaw. Tyrian was looking past her, looking back into that night.

After a long pause, he continued. "As soon as I gathered some of my wits, I had to thank you. I would have given you anything in return. I think I could have fallen as far under

your sway as I had under Menary's. Instead, you set me free."
He hesitated. "The Dean summoned me and she was able to
restore the rest of my scattered wits. Then I understood what I
had undertaken when I promised to accompany you." He
smiled. "So you may go to Paris or to Aravis or to the world's
end. I'll follow."

Faris laughed shakily. "Won't that cause gossip?"

"Is *that* why you're concerned? If you shot your uncle between his beady eyes, the talk below stairs would be that you
were just having your little joke. Don't waste a thought on
gossip."

"Sound advice." Faris tucked her chin into her collar and
wished for her scarf back. The wind brought tears to her eyes,
and she had trouble seeing the road before her. "I will try to
take it."

By the time they rode into the yard at Galazon Chase, the
clouds had closed in completely. The wind had strengthened
and gained an edge that promised more snow. At her order,
Tyrian left her in the stable yard. Reluctant to return to the
house despite the cold, Faris accompanied the horses to the
stables. Inside, she sat on an upturned bucket and watched the
lads work. She pulled off her gauntlets and kneaded warmth
back into her stiff fingers while the fierce color faded from her
face.

Warm and peaceful, with smells of horses and hay and
leather that were wonderfully soothing, the stables held a
sense of timeless order. The horses in their stalls mulled over
their feed tubs, shifted weight occasionally, blew into their
water buckets, and drew deep sighing breaths that sounded
like contentment. Worked together, these small sounds became no sound at all, merely the still background to a great
calm. For the first time since leaving Hilarion's house, she felt
some of the peace she had encountered there.

Faris took comfort from the silence and succeeded at last
in thinking of nothing. She remained there long after the last

horse was put away gleaming in its stall. Finally, shivering a little, she rose and left the peace of the stables behind.

It was only four in the afternoon when Faris had washed and changed and was finally ready to go down for tea, but from Queen Matilda's window it looked like nine at night.

The wind sounded as if it was trying to blow half a gale. As it raked snow this way and that around the courtyard, it murmured ominously against the windows. On the keep stairs, the great wind outside had fostered many little winds within, icy drafts that stirred Faris's skirts as she descended.

The weather matched Faris's frame of mind precisely, she decided. It would be far easier to race around the courtyard, rattling all the window panes, than to settle down for a quiet cup of tea as if nothing were troubling her.

Faris joined Jane, Agnes, and Brinker for tea in the drawing room, glad her cheeks were still scarlet from the cold. It helped to conceal her blush as she greeted Brinker. With irony veiled by courtesy, he showed her to a chair beside the fire, and asked after her health.

Faris answered politely and returned the inquiry. She looked closely at his eye but could see no sign of her handiwork. "I hope you enjoyed your stroll home this afternoon."

Brinker regarded her with genuine amusement. "I did. There is nothing like a brisk walk in the fresh air to clear one's mind." He glanced around to be sure Agnes and Jane were listening. "I've had an inspiration."

"Bread and butter?" Agnes offered a plate.

Gently, Brinker took the plate away from her. When she glanced at him inquiringly, he repeated, "An inspiration, my dear," and smiled at her. "We are going to Aravis."

Agnes did not smile back. "Don't tease me about going home, I beg you. I am so ready to leave this frozen place, I would gladly walk twice the distance."

"I am quite serious." Brinker offered Faris bread and butter. "Your credentials should be here any day now. I never felt it right to send you to Aravis unsupervised. While I was— strolling—this afternoon, it came to me that we should accompany you. Prosperian can be presented to her grandfather, too."

"Such an honor for her," murmured Jane into her teacup, as Agnes expressed her rapturous surprise and gratitude.

Faris demanded, "Who will look after Galazon if we both go?"

"Galazon will do perfectly well while you're away," Agnes said. "It's cold enough to keep nicely."

"Lord Seaforth made a very capable steward while I was in Aravis to sue for my bride's hand."

Faris frowned. "Lord Seaforth. Is he the one who enclosed three hundred acres of river bottom and turned it over to sheep?"

Brinker looked pained. "He may be. I don't know his idea of what constitutes good grazing land. But he is trustworthy. The tax money he collects will be turned over in its entirety. Which is more than could be said for most of your acquaintance. Young Woodrowel paid a call here this afternoon. It was a pity you were out."

"Warin! Here? Did he say why?"

"In fact, he did." Enjoying her impatience, Brinker finished his cup of tea before he continued. "He came to Galazon Ducis to pay his taxes. He said as long as he was so near, he thought he'd stop in on the way home—to see if you had managed to kill me yet, was the way he put it."

"I'm sorry to have missed him."

"I told him you would be. He wouldn't stay. I invited him, but he said he had to return home. No doubt he could see his visit was premature. Perhaps he'll be back."

Faris met his eyes and held them. "Perhaps. Warin has moments of rare perception."

"I would have said that he had moments of perception rarely," Agnes observed.

Before she could stop herself, Faris replied, "You'd be the judge of that, wouldn't you?" Then, alarmed at her lack of self-control, she retreated behind the barriers of etiquette. As teatime wore on, she put all her trust in civility. Faris practiced every art and grace Dame Brachet had drilled into her. When the meal was over at last, she accepted Jane's suggestion of a walk in the gallery. She even kept up a lively narrative of the portraits until they were alone at the far end of the long hall. Then Jane seized her wrist.

"We're out of earshot now. It's safe to Tell All. Just what the dickens happened this afternoon?"

Faris freed her wrist and rubbed it. "Brinker and I had a little argument, that's all."

"That's not what I heard."

"What did you hear?"

"That Brinker tried to push you out of the sleigh and you strangled him for his pains."

"Who told you that?"

"The maid who brings my hot water."

"What's her name, do you recall?" Faris inquired. "Does she have very blue eyes? That's Ismena, Gavren's niece."

"Stop that. I won't be distracted with nieces. I want to know what happened."

Faris blushed painfully. "He made me angry and I lost my temper. Then I went for a ride to recover my wits. That's all."

"You'd better tell me all about it."

Softly, Faris gave Jane an exact account of what she and Brinker had said to one another. When she finished, Jane was frowning. "I suppose you *had* to clout him one? You couldn't just stubbornly refuse to catch his meaning?"

"What meaning?"

"Yes, like that."

Faris blinked. "What are you talking about?"

Jane studied her for a moment. "I suppose we'd better go back to Queen Matilda's tomb. I have no desire to be overheard."

Faris let Jane lead her back up the drafty staircase to her room. With the door locked and the keyhole stopped, Jane steered Faris into the chair beside the writing desk. While Jane stoked the fire, Faris eyed the neatly docketed report that topped the stack of books on the desk. Apparently Jane had been unpacking. "Brinker said my credentials should be here any day. Will you be ready to leave for Aravis when they arrive? For that matter, how are we ever going to mend the rift if Brinker insists on coming along with us?"

"Don't change the subject." Jane put the poker down and stood with her back to the hearth. Her voice was crisp. "I ought to have asked you this long ago, I suppose, as I am here *in loco Decanis.* It's absolutely none of my business, of course, but you know it's important, or I wouldn't ask."

Faris nodded.

It was difficult to be certain, for with her back to the fire Jane's expression was hidden in shadow, but she seemed to be waiting expectantly. After a long pause, she added, "I won't tell a soul, you know."

Faris said, "What *are* you talking about?" but before she finished speaking, she felt her too ready blush rise up to betray her. Even by firelight, her discomfiture was plain.

Jane shook her fist at Faris. "You wretch, you knew what I meant all along and you wanted to torture me until I said it aloud. And don't dare ask *Say what aloud?* or I shall *smite* you."

"Very well. But don't try to persuade me that the Dean would ever ask me to explain my—my menial paramour."

"She wouldn't have to ask. She could tell just by looking at you. I can't."

Faris rose and began to pace. "How could you, when I have no idea myself?" She shook her head. "If you'd asked me this morning, I wouldn't have known what you were talking about. But when he brought me my gloves this afternoon, I finally realized. Oh, God, I'm so thick. And Brinker is quite right. He is my servant. He's married. Why am I even thinking about this?"

Jane sat at the writing desk and watched Faris pace restlessly before the fire. "Stop that. I don't need an answer after all. Your behavior makes it all perfectly clear." In a murmur, she added, "I wonder if that's how the Dean does it?"

"What am I going to do?" Before Jane could reply, Faris lifted her hands in despair and answered her own question. "What am I saying? I know perfectly well what I'm going to do. I'm going to pretend nothing's changed. I'm going to ignore it. Nothing's happened. I'm fine. Everything's fine."

"Just what I was going to say."

"What am I going to *do*, Jane?"

Jane shook her head. "Wait and see."

The storm lasted all through the night and well into the next day. When the snow stopped, the wind went from cold to ridiculously cold and stayed there for two days. Once the weather eased, the countryside lay silent in white, colored only with the blue shadows cast by wind-carved snow. For a day longer, the silence held. Then the wind came back, from the south this time, the snow slowly vanished into brown fields, and a richly dressed messenger arrived at the gates of Galazon Chase. The king of Aravill had sent the duchess of Galazon her diplomatic credentials, and a warmly phrased invitation to attend him in Aravis.

Volume Three

The Warden
of the
North

12

Aravis

⚜ FARIS HATED EVERYTHING about the next five days. She had
to pack, which was tedious, and then watch Jane pack, which
was worse. She was leaving Galazon, but not Brinker. She was
going to Aravis, where Hilarion had sent her, to attempt
something she had no idea how to do.

To reach Aravis, they had to travel by carriage to Wex,
then down the Lida by river steamer to Shene, and finally, by
carriage again to Aravis. The meals were poor. The beds,
when they managed to find a wayside inn that met Brinker's
high standards, were damp. Neither the meals nor the beds
mattered much to Faris, but both did to Agnes.

As they left the high meadows and deep forests of Galazon behind, the horizon dropped and the sky seemed to open
and broaden. By Wex, the land was quite flat. Faris felt a sense
of foreboding that increased as the journey went on, a mood
she could not reason herself out of. Leaving Galazon was bad
enough, but leaving it for the monotonous flats of the Lida
river valley, was somehow worse.

The signs of snow vanished as they moved south. The
bare trees regained only a little of their golden foliage, but the
grass was still green. Faris was troubled by the feeling that
they were running most unnaturally backward in time.

She had managed, with difficulty, to put her anxiety
about Tyrian away where it could trouble neither of them.
Tyrian, she told herself, had promised to go with her to Aravis
so that she could mend the rift. To concern herself with anything beyond that was folly. There was no assurance there
would *be* anything beyond that.

Tyrian's duties en route meant she seldom saw him for

more than a moment. Faris could not help but feel relieved. She had utter faith in Tyrian's sense of decorum, but she feared for her own and dreaded that Agnes—or worse, Brinker—might surprise her in some fit of bashfulness.

Brinker and Agnes were traveling together in the lead carriage. The baby and her attendants were in the second. Jane and Faris were in the third, while the rest of the entourage, including servants and baggage, with Reed and Tyrian watchful over all, brought up the rear.

Preparations for the journey had kept Faris extremely busy. Despite her best intentions, she had not yet had time to finish Jane's neatly docketed report. She packed it with her personal effects but did not take time to look at it until the journey was nearly over. Even then, it was in self defense.

Jane had pored over her Baedeker ceaselessly since entering the carriage for the final stage of the journey. The steamer voyage down the river had reduced Jane to silent misery. Despite the smooth passage they had enjoyed, unusually calm for the season, Jane suffered the violent reaction to travel over water to which most witches of Greenlaw were prone. Since their debarkation at Shene, however, Jane's spirits had recovered completely.

Faris, on the other hand, was struggling to conceal her gloom, which deepened with every mile that brought her closer to Aravis. Though the flatness of the landscape was gone, replaced by stony ridges, the sense of exposure remained. In an effort to discourage Jane, she brought forth her report and tried to pretend she could concentrate on it while the carriage swayed along. "Where did you say this report of yours came from?"

"I didn't say." Jane turned a page. "*Aravis, the capital of Aravill, and one of the most romantically beautiful cities in Europe, is finely situated on a series of ridges, separated by ravines, south of Shene Inlet, of which charming views are obtained from the higher parts of town.*"

"Riveting. *The principal political parties of Aravill are Royalist, Conservative Royalist, Monarchist, and Liberal Radical. The* king's ministers are chosen by a coalition of the first two parties. The latter two parties have formed an uneasy coalition to represent the opposition." Faris held a page of the report up to the carriage window and squinted at it. "British watermark. Yet you came by it in Paris. Odd."

"You're supposed to read it, not appraise it."

"Very well. *The Monarchist party, in particular, bears a misleading label, since part of their platform repudiates the house of Paganell and denies its right to rule. By far the newest of the parties, it has been active only in the past four years. The extremist element of the Monarchists hold that reform, by any means necessary, is vital. These extremists, who revel in elaborate passwords and countersigns, may provide a disruptive element in the future. The party anthem,* Tom o'Bedlam's Song, *has been outlawed by royal fiat.*"

"How interesting. Allow me to inform you that *the population, excluding Shene, is (1908) 350,500. Aravis is the seat of the administrative and judicial authorities of Aravill, and is renowned for its excellent university and schools.*"

"Bilge. *Members of the Monarchist party are predominantly young and uneducated. The party leader, Istvan Graelent, is a recent graduate of the University of Aravis. Reliable sources inform us that the popular songs concerned with the modern exploits of Tom o'Bedlam, obviously inspired by the party anthem, refer to this individual. Rumors associating Monarchist party fortunes with Austrian financial interests cannot be confirmed, but neither can they be discounted.*" Faris stopped reading aloud, but turned the page, absorbed.

Relentlessly, Jane continued. "*Excursions in the neighborhood of Aravis are extremely beautiful and historically interesting. The royal chateau at Sevenfold is one of the greatest attractions.*"

"Oh, Jane, put it away."

"*Perhaps no fairer or more harmonious combination of art and nature is to be found among the cities of the world, and even the buildings of little or no beauty in themselves generally blend happily with the surrounding scenery. The stranger is advised to begin his acquaintance with the 'Modern Athens' by obtaining a general view of it from the castle or from Artegal Hill.*"

"Look, I'm putting the report away. I won't read any more if you don't."

Jane was resolute. *"Near the center of the city and between the main street and the castle, there are some pretty grounds called Montleret Gardens. At the heart of the grounds lies Montleret Water, a small but picturesque natural lake which is enhanced by fountains, the water supplied by the elaborate cisterns, a triumph of engineering, which have been carved into the living stone beneath the castle rock. To the north of Montleret Gardens—* Did you say something?"* Jane looked up. "Is anything the matter? You look dreadful. Are you going to be ill?"

Faris put her head in her hands. Her governess had taught her history and geography in which Galazon and Aravill were inextricably mixed. Yet now she realized just how little she knew of Aravis. The dry facts conspired to fog her mind. Even the crowded, noisy, smelly quay side they had left behind them at Shene became ephemeral as soon as Jane read the name aloud. She groaned softly. "What am I doing? I don't know anything about protocol. I don't know anything about cisterns. I don't know anything about the Monarchists or the Conservative Royalists."

Jane studied Faris for an instant, then clapped shut her red Baedeker and rummaged in the depths of her valise. She produced a flat silver flask, pulled the stopper, and handed it to Faris. "Drink this."

Faris eyed the little flask mistrustfully. "Brandy won't solve everything."

"It's cognac and it will solve what's wrong with you. You've got stage fright, that's what. Let me just remind you that you don't have to know anything about protocol. That's what I'm for. Nor cisterns, that's what the Baedeker's for. And as for the Monarchists—" Jane snapped her fingers. "They can look out for themselves."

Faris took a cautious sip. Jane held out her hand. "That's enough. Save a little for first-night jitters."

Faris returned the flask. "Thank you. I think I'll be fine now, if I don't hear any more about the charming views."

Jane stoppered the flask and put it away. "Too late. Here comes one now." She nodded toward the window.

Faris turned to look. Their route had taken them south from Shene into gray hills, rocky and dry, then eastward along the brow of a ridge. Now from the right side of the carriage they could see the hills drop away into a vale of scattered houses, and far beyond rise again in a ridge as jagged and stark as a dragon's spine.

The line of the ridge rose and fell and rose again, as if mocking the rise and fall of a dragon's haunch and back and shoulder, a silhouette familiar to Faris from her first school books. At this distance, she could not make out the summit of the last rise. Plumes of cloud or smoke concealed it. But from those same books, she knew that the distant ridge, scaled with roof tops and scored with streets, was Aravis. The dragon's head was crowned with the castle that gave the city its older name, Aravis Palatine.

Jane and Faris watched in silence until the route turned south again and the carriage windows showed them only trees and houses and featureless garden walls. "Perfectly charming. If only it were a clearer day, we might have been able to make out the castle itself from here." Jane started to reach for her Baedeker but Faris's glance of mute entreaty stilled her hand. "I expect we'll see the castle soon enough."

"At close quarters." Faris shut her eyes. She badly wanted a cup of coffee.

The road took them down into the valley, across a bridge, and into an area closely built with houses, where it turned into a street. Gradually the houses came closer and closer together until they bumped into each other and ran in even rows, squashed shoulder to shoulder facing the street.

Faris regarded the cramped symmetry with dislike. As their route began to rise again, the street passed through a city gate and then climbed to the foot of the ridge. Here the streets were narrow and crooked. In places buildings had grown together overhead, leaving only a tunnel to let foot traffic continue.

Some of the sweating brick passages were hardly more than a flight of steps connecting two streets. Some were large enough to warrant a street sign set into the wall near the entrance. Faris savored the names: White Horse Close, Anchor Close, Hunter's Tryst.

The main street (Castle Street, the signs said) rose and fell as it followed the dragon's spine through the city. At the dragon's shoulder, broad Castle Street widened still more. It became the Esplanade and swept up the dragon's neck to the castle gates.

Faris and her party did not go so far. At a spot between the dragon's shoulder blades, their carriages drew up before the imposing facade of the Hotel Metropol.

Jane lowered her veil and gathered up her bag. Faris sat motionless, eyes shut again. "More cognac?"

"Coffee," said Faris plaintively.

"Soon, I promise. You'll have to come inside, though."

Faris sighed and opened her eyes. "You English. You're so strict."

The door of the carriage opened and Reed joined them. "Slight delay." At their inquiring looks, he explained. "Change of plans. The hotelier must reorganize the available suites to accommodate Lord and Lady Brinker, too. They'll be in your suite, Faris. Be patient. They're doing their best to make room for you somewhere."

Jane looked surprised. "Why can't they stay at the castle as they planned?"

"The official reason is that Lord Brinker has decided he cannot allow his niece to stay alone in a hotel, even a first-class hotel. He must stay and add to her consequence. The embassy is Galazon territory, even if it's only a hotel suite. He's here to help make it more so."

"And the real reason?" Faris asked.

Reed smirked. "In fact, I can give you a fairly authentic answer, since I caught a snatch of the argument. It has come to Lady Brinker that she does not wish her infant daughter to stay in the castle. She will have it brought there, when the time is right, for her father to look at. But she won't stay there herself and she won't let the child stay there under any circumstances."

"Why not?" Faris asked.

"I gather it's bad for children. I didn't catch enough of the quarrel to follow the reasoning. Something to do with her baby sister."

Jane looked concerned. "Menary's not here, is she?"

"God, no. At least, I don't think so. I'll ask, if you like."

Faris raised her eyebrows. "Ask whom?"

"Oh, I'll just ask around." Reed opened the carriage door and prepared to descend. "It's the only way to find out anything, you know. Even Tyrian stoops to it occasionally."

The suite assigned to Faris was enormous. The task of rendering it secure kept Tyrian and Reed fully occupied. Despite Agnes's arrival taking precedence, Jane humbled the hotel staff in short order. Luggage began to arrive.

Without quite realizing how it happened, Faris found herself with nothing to do but sit in a comfortable chair near a window. For a while she simply stared blankly out at the bustle of traffic on the Esplanade. Then it began to rain steadily, sleet-edged rain that would certainly have fallen as snow in Galazon.

She watched the traffic thin. It was as close to winter as Aravis ever saw, this steady rain that scrubbed the gutters of the street clean. It stained the stone buildings black, and polished the slate roofs until they gleamed like pewter. The wind blew rain against the glass and the street became mere shapeless gray beneath the lighter gray of the sky.

Faris dozed. She dreamed that she was on the landing of a staircase. The light was poor. She couldn't tell where she was. She only knew she was supposed to go down and she was afraid to. It was safe to go up, but she wasn't meant to do that. She was poised on the landing, perfectly balanced between alternatives.

"Wake up. It's only a dream, whatever it is. Wake up."

Jane released her shoulder and stepped back. "I thought for a moment you were having a heart attack. What on earth were you dreaming?"

"Nothing. It was nothing." Faris rose and looked around at the hotel suite, miraculously orderly, blessedly peaceful. "What have you done?"

The daylight was gone. Twilight made the window a dark lookingglass until Jane closed the velvet drapes.

Jane looked pleased. "Very little. It *is* nice to sit still at last, isn't it? No carriages, no boats, no trains."

Faris nodded. The suite, the second best the Hotel Metropol could offer, was very different from her rooms at the Hotel de Crillon. Larger, though not so high-ceilinged, it held less furniture. What furniture there was had none of the overbred delicacy that she remembered in Paris. This was heavy stuff, solidly made of dark oak. There were no paintings with gold encrusted frames, no chaises longues, only deep carpets and comfortable chairs. Faris felt she had gone from iced champagne to cellar-cooled ale and was a little surprised that she found the change so welcome.

"The rain's stopped. You must be feeling better."

Faris frowned a little. "What do you mean? I feel fine."

"I don't mean your health. I mean your frame of mind. I think it's been asserting itself again." At Faris's clear lack of comprehension, she prompted, "Remember Hilarion said you made it snow at Greenlaw?"

Faris nodded.

"Well, is it a coincidence that the bad weather we had at Galazon Chase started immediately after Brinker upset you? And is it a coincidence that it began to rain after you started feeling nervous today?"

"It's winter, Jane. It often snows in the winter. If it doesn't snow, it rains. You're being fanciful."

"You *are* feeling better. I knew it. Oh, don't bother to contradict. Now, I've arranged something that will cheer you up completely."

"The rift mended itself while I slept and we can go home."

"Well, perhaps not completely," Jane conceded. "There are supposed to be suitable places to dine somewhere in Aravis but I haven't had time to find out which they are. Instead, I've arranged a meal to be served here. We are to have a distinguished guest—traveling incognito, no less—who will be more comfortable speaking to us in private."

"How distinguished? It isn't the king, is it?"

"Oh, dear, *no*. No, he's firmly ensconced at his country house. Trust me. It's someone you'll be glad to see." With that, Jane crossed to the door of the outer room and opened it. Through the doorway, smiling, came Eve-Marie.

Faris sprang up to greet her. "What brings you, of all people, here, of all places? Why aren't you back in Paris, laboring ever so cannily on behalf of the government?"

Eve-Marie's clear blue eyes shone with amusement. "Because for the past fortnight, I have been laboring ever so cannily here. I finished yesterday. Now, mind, that's confidential. I start for home in the morning. Train most of the way, but first I have to catch one of those rickety little steamships to Varna. I'm dreading the journey. Water makes me so sick. What are you doing here? Last news I had, you'd finally given Menary her comeuppance and the Dean gave you both your *congé*. Was it worth it?"

"Oh, absolutely. Jane, you genius, they've already laid the table. How do you manage these things?"

Dinner conversation was merry and far-ranging. Eve-Marie had news of Odile, who had worked with her recently in Rocamadour. Four times Eve-Marie turned aside inquiries about her doings. Faris and Jane were candid about their activities, and welcomed Eve-Marie's advice. Eve-Marie grew more and more animated. Finally, over coffee and cognac, she surrendered.

"This is all completely confidential, mind."

Jane and Faris eagerly concurred.

"The government sent me here as a favor to Aravill.

They're rather entwined with the royal family over this and that, you know. When the king expressed a need for, um, a technical adviser, my employers were glad to oblige."

"What sort of advice was the king looking for from a witch of Greenlaw?" Jane asked. "Magical?"

"Something like that," Eve-Marie replied. "You've heard of the gardens at Sevenfold, I imagine?"

"Sevenfold? That's the king's country house?" Faris asked.

"You might call it a country house," Jane said dryly. "According to my Baedeker, the house is three times the size of Galazon Chase. Gardens designed by Le Nôtre and restored to their original splendor at least twice. Two rivers diverted to make the fountains splash nicely. You *could* call it a country house."

Eve-Marie looked a little disdainful. "It's no Vaux-le-Vicomte, but I suppose it is fairly grand—in a rather obvious way. Hardly Le Nôtre's best work. I was to appraise the labyrinth in particular, the rest of the grounds in general, and find out if it all still worked properly."

Jane toyed with her cognac glass. "Let me guess. Le Nôtre's efforts at Versailles and Kensington Gardens were not his only essays into our field of expertise."

Eve-Marie nodded. "How nicely you put it."

"Wait. You mean to say, Versailles and Kensington Gardens are enchanted?" Faris asked.

"Oh, yes. As if his genius for design were not enough, Le Nôtre was quite a talented magician, in a purely experimental way. He did some very interesting things with the Tuileries, too," Eve-Marie replied. "I think Vaux was his best, though I must confess he had more to work with there. Really, the perfect setting. And a good patron makes all the difference."

"How is Versailles enchanted?" Faris persisted.

Eve-Marie's brow furrowed slightly with the effort it took to find simple words for a technical explanation. "All Le Nôtre's work was variation upon the same themes: harmony of proportion, tricks of perspective, perception of time. He's particularly good at evoking a negative response to time and the perceived passage of time."

"Visitors to his gardens are reluctant to leave," Jane explained.

"Well, yes. That is putting it rather bluntly," Eve-Marie said. "He balanced his gardens so perfectly in a few places that it was theoretically possible to see through time. I've never spoken to anyone who experienced it first-hand. I have been told that the proportions were so precisely arranged that at Versailles a hundred years ago you could conceivably meet Le Nôtre himself, out for a little air, a century or so after his own death."

Faris glanced mistrustfully from Eve-Marie to Jane. "You are joking."

"I said theoretically." Eve-Marie smiled. "That's the thing about gardens. They grow. Gradually the perspectives change, the proportions alter. Now, you might see him walking ankle-deep in the turf. Or hear him, without being able to see him. And the wonderful thing is, that even if Le Nôtre himself were really there, he would not wish to leave."

"Even after a century?" Faris asked, thinking of Hilarion.

"It wouldn't seem like a century. You can walk your feet bloody in a Le Nôtre garden and never notice until you leave the grounds," said Eve-Marie. "Now, the interesting thing about Sevenfold is the labyrinth."

"A maze? Like Hampton Court?" asked Jane.

"Well, more like the Troytown mazes you find in England, built of raised turf. The pattern is very like *La Lieue*, the pattern of stones laid in the floor of Chartres Cathedral. Le Nôtre achieved some of his effects with shrubbery, that much is like Hampton Court. But it is called the labyrinth, and even though it is not Le Nôtre at his best, it is still impressive."

"So it passed your inspection?" Jane inquired.

"I had to make some minor adjustments the king wished."

Faris smirked. "Don't tell me. He brought a witch of

Greenlaw all the way from Paris to trim his topiary. How like a Paganell."

Eve-Marie looked serious. "All I did was restore the labyrinth to its original working condition. The proportions had changed, but now it is almost as Le Nôtre intended it." She hesitated. "This is not my secret to betray, you understand? Yet I will abuse the trust put in me and tell you this much. If you find yourself a guest of the king at Sevenfold, do not enter the labyrinth. For if you do, you will not leave it until the king wishes you to."

The next morning, Brinker invited Faris to breakfast. She accepted, not without a pang or two of suspicion, and after Eve-Marie's departure, she joined him in the grand suite he and Agnes shared. Agnes, indisposed, did not appear, so Faris was alone with her uncle.

"Brave of me, isn't it, to entertain without a bodyguard?" Brinker remarked, as Faris was being served. "But then, my courage has always been a byword."

"You won't get an apology out of me, so save your hints. Anyway, I'm not a bit sorry I did it. You provoked me."

"I know. Of course, it bodes rather poorly for your diplomatic career, I imagine."

"Just as well I display no aptitude. My career will come to an abrupt close once I come of age. Three weeks left."

"Twenty days."

"So you count them too. I'm touched."

"I'm looking forward to the day. Believe me. In the meantime, I am anxious for you to make the best show you can as Galazon's ambassador. Do you plan to resign the moment you come of age, no matter what negotiations are in hand?"

"Of course not. But do you honestly suppose there will be any negotiations? I can't even begin until I've presented my credentials and the king is off lurking in the countryside."

"I've received word. He returns tomorrow. You may make your curtsy to him as soon after that as I can gain you audience."

"There's a bit more to it than a curtsy."

"Of course." A sudden thought appeared to strike Brinker. "Would you feel more confident with a little coaching? Perhaps I might prevail on Agnes to recommend someone."

"Thank you, no. If I make an idiot of myself, I'd prefer it to be my own fault."

Brinker gave her a patronizing smile. "Admirable philosophy for a private person. Once you come of age, however, I think you'll find it more practical to blame as many people as you conveniently can."

Faris smiled back sardonically. "What need of that, as long as I have you to blame?"

The day of Faris's audience was sunny and, even for Aravis, unseasonably warm. By noon, Faris was too nervous to speak. She was unable even to remonstrate when Jane took away the merino gown Faris had planned to wear and made her put on a severely simple black walking suit instead. Jane pretended not to notice Faris's anxiety.

"I know you don't like to wear red." Jane fastened the scarlet sash at Faris's shoulder and hip. "The sash is terribly official looking, though. What a pity you don't have few orders to wear with it. Here, take your gloves." She stood back and admired the play of fabric as Faris moved. "Now the hat, that's right. Very nice."

Faris found a lookingglass and examined her reflection warily. Except that she seemed in imminent peril of strangulation from her high white collar, she looked very well. With difficulty, she was even able to swallow. "Are you certain this is the proper thing to wear when one must present credentials to a king?"

Jane nodded. "There's really no feminine equivalent for a cutaway, more's the pity. Still, it could have been worse. It could have been silk stockings and satin knee breeches." She handed Faris the leather portfolio containing her credentials. "National dress is considered proper, too. I can just see you striding up to the king wearing boots and baggy trousers, with a pistol stuck in your sash." She held up her hand before Faris could answer. "I know—you'd enjoy that, wouldn't you? Well, too late. You're ready."

Down in the Esplanade, a state coach and an escort of carbineers, under the stern eye of a master of ceremonies, waited to convey Faris from the Hotel Metropol to the castle. Faris let them put her in the coach and concentrated on not mislaying her portfolio as they thundered slowly up the street.

Since she was alone, there was plenty of kneeroom in the state carriage. Although the plush lining was faded and worn, and the gold-leafed trim was slightly chipped, the coach was as spotless inside as out. The narrow seat was as hard as a wooden bench, though here and there its leather upholstery had cracked slightly, enough to betray the horse-hair stuffing within. Faris wondered if all the king's coaches were in similarly worn condition. Or perhaps Galazon's ambassador was not deemed important enough for them to send one of the very best conveyances.

Back straight, head high, face pallid, and hands clammy, Faris rode in solitary threadbare splendor as they entered the grand court of the castle. The carriage drew to a halt. The guards presented arms, and a military band played a chorus of *Long Live Queen Matilda*.

It was a spectacle intended to impress. It might have, if Faris hadn't been so nervous. As it was, she was intent on her mission—to present her credentials to the king without embarrassing anyone, particularly herself. Impatiently, she waited for the attendants to open the carriage door and help her down. She wanted to have the whole thing over with. A little thing like a military band playing the old Lidian anthem could not be permitted to distract her from her duty.

Faris followed the master of ceremonies, a thick-necked man with very red ears, from the grand court into the great hall. He led her to the foot of a staircase so perfectly detailed it might have come from a confectioner, and so large it might have come from a nightmare.

At the foot of the staircase a second master of ceremonies accepted Faris from the first. He led her in awe-inspiring silence up the gleaming marble steps. The footing was slippery and Faris wondered how safe the steps were. She kept her eyes fixed on the back of the second master of ceremonies' neck, which was thick and rather bristly, and made the climb without incident.

At the head of the staircase the second master of ceremonies turned Faris over to the grand master of ceremonies. The grand master of ceremonies wore his hair in a black mane well past his collar, so she could not tell if his neck was thick and red or not. He marched her down a long gallery lined with civil and military members of the household.

At the extreme end of the gallery stood the prefect of the palace, who was quite bald, and of rather sallow complexion. He preceded Faris to the king's presence chamber and retired the moment he announced her. "Your Majesty, here is her excellency, Faris Nallaneen, the ambassador extraordinary and plenipotentiary of Galazon."

The king's response was an amiable nod. "Good afternoon." His voice was not particularly loud, but it was curiously penetrating, the kind of voice that would carry a long distance.

Faris stared unabashedly. Julian Paganell, the king of Aravill, was a man in his middle fifties, perhaps an inch shorter than Faris for all his barrel-chested bulk. His proud bearing made his stiff collar seem natural. He wore normal morning dress, save for his extraordinary jacket, a long-tailed cutaway, tailored in peacock blue velvet. Faris could only wonder what Jane would have to say about that jacket.

The peacock blue was not a flattering shade. The king's broad face showed the patchy ruddiness of one who has drunk a great deal of claret and port. His hair might have been glossy black once, but it was silvered now. His dark blue eyes regarded Faris keenly.

Under Jane's tutelage, Faris had prepared a speech, an obligatory speech, about the relations between Galazon and

Aravill. It was obscurely phrased but extremely civil. Faris drew breath to begin.

The king did not give her the opportunity to deliver it. Instead he crossed the room toward her. "Welcome to Aravis, Faris Nallaneen. We hope you'll enjoy yourself here."

Too nervous to stop herself, Faris demanded, "Why?"

The king looked surprised. "Because Aravill can be a very enjoyable place. Perhaps it isn't what you're used to, but we think you'll find it entertaining." He smiled at Faris, yet she thought she detected a watchfulness behind his eyes. He seemed preoccupied, for all his friendly informality.

Somehow Faris kept herself from saying crossly, *I didn't come here to be entertained.* Instead, she said, "I know that you, if anyone, will understand the work I left behind me at home. As long as I can be of service to Galazon, I will enjoy my stay here."

"If not our nearest neighbor, Galazon is surely our dearest. We hope that we may work together in the same way Galazon and Aravill do."

We hope we do better than that, Faris thought. "I'll work for Galazon with a will."

The king laughed at her. His lips were chapped and drooped in an unappealing way. Yet it was a charming laugh, rich and merry. "Such zeal. Yet we wish to entertain you, too. And we have the right—or at least we have the right to try."

Belatedly, Faris remembered the portfolio under her arm. "If I may?" At the king's nod, she presented her credentials.

The king accepted them without a glance. His eyes measured Faris. "You will now be entered upon the list and you may work as hard as you like, if work is what gives you pleasure. You must call upon all the other ambassadors as fast as you are able. Be finished by Twelfth Night. That's when we give our New Year's masked ball. We invite the entire diplomatic list. Even your uncle will attend, provided Agnes permits him. You'll be obliged to be entertained then."

"It seems I must make haste."

The king smiled again and summoned the grand master

of ceremonies. As she followed her escort through the icy perfection of the castle's antechambers, she remembered with chagrin that she had forgotten to deliver her speech.

Something of Faris's confusion lingered over the next five days, although she worked hard enough at paying calls and receiving compliments to forget her chagrin. Even at their worst, the other ambassadors were nothing like Dame Brachet in a temper. Faris found her social footing quickly, though she often had the feeling she had stepped where someone was already standing.

Whether through her own efforts or Brinker's, Faris found the diplomatic circles in Aravis accepted her eagerly. Almost every invitation she accepted, after the first two days, brought her another encounter with the king. At formal dinners, at musical evenings, at the opera and the theater, she saw him everywhere. He was unfailingly polite, determined to make her enjoy her stay in Aravis, and his interest did more than anything to ensure Faris's success in society.

Faris put her trust in Dame Brachet's training and Jane Brailsford's genius for clothes. Correctly as she behaved, however, she could not rid herself of the notion that there was something more to the king's attention than mere civility. It made her uncomfortable. But then, almost everything in Aravis made her uncomfortable.

Far smaller than Paris and far larger than Greenlaw, Aravis seemed very strange to her. It was not easy to get her bearings. The steep streets and high walls shut out much of the sky and made it difficult to find directions. There was noise night and day, even in the Esplanade. At times the streets grew very dirty, with a smell that was hard to bear even with the winter chill to restrain it. At other times the mysterious cisterns under the city were made to disgorge their water and the gutters ran clean in a few hours.

Faris approved of the plumbing arrangements she encountered in Aravis, grew resigned to the strange coil of streets that sprawled below the Esplanade, and became accustomed to the noise. But she could never accept the castle itself.

It rose, solid enough to all appearances, over the city like a mountain crag. Yet mountain crags do not have sash windows set into the solid rock. Mountain crags do not always wear a becoming ring of mist around their uttermost heights, no matter the weather. Mountain crags do not conceal, behind their solidity, a sense that there is less there than meets the eye.

Yet that was precisely the sense that Faris had, whenever she looked unwarily in the direction of the castle. It seemed to her that there was nothing beyond the first few levels of the castle. Any appearance of rooftops and chimneys and battlements and bartizans were only her imagination. If she looked at them out of the corner of her eye they were still there—yet they did not convince.

Faris discussed these impressions with Jane and no one else. Jane found them interesting and wondered if the rift was perhaps to blame. Faris put them down to fatigue. Never mind the noise at night, she was having dreams.

She had always dreamed. In her time at Greenlaw, Faris had dreamed of Galazon so exclusively, she'd nearly forgotten there were other sorts of dreams to have. Yet in Aravis she never dreamed of Galazon. Instead she dreamed of the castle.

Night after night she passed through the palace halls to the foot of the white icing stairs to the king's antechamber. Sometimes she walked. Sometimes she rode in the state carriage with its benchlike seat. Sometimes she rode in a tumbrel, usually with Tyrian beside her, but once unaccompanied save by a sense of impending doom.

Night after night she passed through halls hung with blue and gold and found herself in endlessly twisting passages that took her in directions she did not wish to go. She had a sense, in the dreams, that the passages followed some pattern but she could not recognize it. Despairing, she would turn and double on her tracks, pause at crossed corridors and strain after the pattern, ever just out of her reach, knowing with the certainty of any dreamer that she had seen the pattern in full not very long before. Yet she could not get anywhere, it seemed, but deeper into the muddle that she had made. She welcomed waking.

Jane found the intricacies of the diplomatic list in Aravis a welcome change from ordering around the hotel staff. She accompanied Faris on those social occasions for which a chaperone was indispensable. As Faris was twenty years younger than the youngest ambassador and forty years younger than most of the others, she found Jane's company extremely welcome. Sometimes, however, Faris had to venture out alone, as when the Spanish ambassador invited the entire list to hunt with him.

"I explained that I keep no horses here," Faris told Jane in the hotel suite, late on the evening before the hunt. "He promised me a mount from his own stable. He has the entire list coming, from all accounts. The king is to ride with us. Apparently they are great cronies. The Spanish ambassador is staying at the next manor house but one from his. Is there *any* graceful way out?"

"I thought you liked to hunt?"

"I do. But not when I have strong sympathies for the fox. I think this invitation comes out of the same drawer as the box at the opera with the Austrian legation, where the king just happened to look in, and the musical evening at the Danish embassy, where the king paid his respects to the ambassador's wife and asked her to sing ballads from Galazon. Lucky she didn't know any. There are quite a few that mention Aravill, and almost all of them are extremely rude."

"You could be indisposed. Let me see. There are a few diseases that never fail. What about a nice old-fashioned case of gout?"

"How soon could I recover? The Twelfth Night ball is less than a week away. Dare I dance so soon after claiming to have an attack of gout?"

"No gout, then." Jane considered. "Still, it's a pity not to make an appearance at least. Your riding habit came out so well. Why don't you just fall at the first fence?"

Faris slumped into the wing chair by the window. "And then?"

"Oh, dear. Heroic rescue by his majesty, I suppose." Jane frowned abstractedly into the fire. "Is he really so dreadful?"

Faris rubbed her forehead wearily. "No. Perhaps not. But his mouth is too red and his lower lip droops. And I'm half afraid he's going to hunt himself into a heart attack."

At nine the next morning, Faris rode out with the rest of the Spanish ambassador's guests. It would probably be a fine chilly day later, for the sky was clear overhead. There was still mist on the ground, and not a sign of frost. It was too foggy to see clearly and too chilly to be sociable but Faris did her best to look amiable. The prospect of hunting over strange country on a strange horse depressed Faris more than the fit of her new riding habit could cheer her.

She knew there was no flaw in her appearance, from the tilt of her high crowned topper, veiled rakishly in tulle, to the snood that confined her unruly hair, to her gloves of Russian leather, to her highly polished boots. Riding sidesaddle was about appearance, after all. If there were any work to be done, one would ride astride and be safe. But to be highly ornamental, sidesaddle was mandatory.

The Spanish ambassador had evidently decreed that she be ornamental, for he had loaned her the largest horse she'd ever ridden, a brilliant bay gelding, well up to her weight, with a neck curved like a roundabout pony's. So huge was he that Faris suspected she might even look delicate atop him. "An aesthetic triumph," she muttered, as the bay stamped and snatched at his bit.

"I beg your pardon?" The rider beside her was the Danish ambassador's American wife. "Did you speak to me?" She seemed too worried about her own mount's behavior to pay much attention to Faris's musings.

"A perfect morning, I said."

"Perfect for sleeping. Still, this is better than shooting. If we keep moving, we may keep warm."

As they spoke, they had followed the rest of the hunt from the forecourt of Crail, the ambassador's extremely ugly country house, down a lane of rhododendron. Far ahead, the hounds muddled along under the supervision of the huntsmen. Far behind, the hunt servants brought spare horses along at a sedate amble. Reed and Tyrian were among them, to Faris's secret relief.

"Do you hunt much here?" Faris asked, in hope of advice about the terrain.

The ambassador's wife shuddered elegantly. "I intend to follow the others as far as the first likely lane, where I shall detect some lameness in this poor animal. I'll be back before they've cleared the breakfast dishes."

A familiar voice spoke, deep as a bassoon but as penetrating as an oboe. "We'll tell your husband you said that." The king had ridden up behind them. He greeted the ambassador's wife and Faris and rode beside them companionably. His hunting clothes were almost unexceptionable. Almost. Instead of the customary buff waistcoat and scarlet coat, both waistcoat and coat were the same shade of bottle green. The fabric of the waistcoat reminded Faris of the interior of the state coach, as it might have looked when new.

"You won't surprise him," predicted the ambassador's wife.

"And you won't alarm him, we hope. We are here to enjoy ourselves, after all. We'll accompany you and young Faris. It never hurts to have a faithful cavalier to manage the gates for you. And to summon assistance if necessary."

Faris regarded him narrowly. *Wrap your legs up like a bolster and see how you fare,* she thought. Aloud, she said, "How is the country here about?"

"Fine high banks and lots of them. We should have excellent hunting—if this pack ever finds."

"What crops?" Faris inquired. "Are the fields fallow now, or should we keep out of the plowing?"

The king looked surprised. "We came to hunt, not farm." At the sudden change of expression on Faris's face, he added apologetically, "We should have said we are here to relish the hunt. And we know we shall, in your company. Don't worry about missing the death. We will simply do the best we can and divert ourselves together."

So, it's do the best we can, is it? Faris kept her eyes on the space between her bay's ears and tried to sustain a pleasant expression. *Fox and hound and horse willing, I shall do the best I can to leave you in a ditch, you care-for-nothing. Patronize me, will you?* Anger washed nervousness away and for the first time since her arrival in Aravill, Faris felt wholly herself, at ease and annoyed. "Do you get much hunting?" To her own vast surprise, she sounded perfectly civil.

"It's been a bit off these last few seasons, but we get out when we can. The doctors tell us the fresh air does us good."

They reached the covert and drew rein. Across the rocky patch of shrubbery the huntsmen worked the hounds with care. The other riders in the field ranged themselves around the covert. Positions were chosen partly in accordance with etiquette, for it would be very bad form to interfere with the huntsmen and their hounds, and partly in accordance with strategy, for a good start could make all the difference to a run. Protocol, for once, didn't seem at issue. Precedence meant nothing to the master of the hounds.

Faris let the king choose his spot and settled her bay at his side. She had already grown accustomed to the crutches of the borrowed sidesaddle. The bay's manners were good and she had his rhythm now, in her spine and her wrists.

"We try to get out two or three times a week in season," said the king. "It makes a good excuse to ignore those tiresome administrative briefings, for one thing. For another, it makes a good impression with the people, taking an interest in sport."

"There speaks the true king," muttered Faris. Luckily her words were lost in the squeal of the huntsman's horn. The hounds struck off at full discordant cry, an urgent babble that put Faris forcibly in mind of a flight of wild geese.

"Gone away!" shrieked the ambassador's wife.

"Stay close to us," said the king to Faris. "We'll see you come to no harm."

Eyes narrowed with disdain, Faris gave her bay his head and left them both behind. It was time, after all, to do the best she could.

Faris followed the field across a rocky pasture beside the covert and through an open gate. There were riders behind her so she left the gate as she found it. Beyond the gate lay another pasture, a stone wall, and yet another pasture. Faris waited her turn at the stone wall and the bay took her easily over. Far ahead, she could see the pack of hounds, very white against the brown grass, as they surged ahead of the huntsmen. She could not glimpse anything of the fox.

The thunder of hooves and the rush of the wind in her ears could not drown the wild cry of the pack. Faris forgot her annoyance in the exhilaration of the ride. In the chaos of the field, she was alone. In the confines of her impractical riding costume, she was free.

At the far side of the far pasture was another stone wall, a little higher than the first. The hunt spilled over it. Faris followed. Her bay let her pick the approach and sailed over the fence with perfect nonchalance. In the fifteen minute run that followed, the bay gained ground on the huntsmen with such speed that Faris drew him in a little. It would not do to go thrusting herself before the rest of the field.

The bay humored her until they reached the first fine high bank. There he took no notice of Faris's preference for a more modest approach. He simply vaulted to the top at the highest point, changed feet as easily as a stag, and scrambled down into the lane beyond, giving Faris the sense that she had just been kicked gracefully downstairs. She recovered herself and let the bay forge on in the wake of the huntsmen. A glance back showed her the rest of the field encountering the bank. She did not see the king in the melee.

The hunt led her along the lane and across a field planted to turnips and swedes. Faris's agricultural soul forbade her to follow and she persuaded the bay to flank the field and rejoin the chase at the far side. The rest of the hunt tore heedlessly through the crop. Faris sneered happily and sent the bay on at a pace that pleased him.

Twenty minutes later, Faris came down off another big bank and splashed across a muddy stream. Some of the morning mist was still hanging in the little hollow where the stream ran. Faris had to blink to see the best footing up the opposite side.

Once out of the mist, she drew rein. The hunt was out of sight but not out of earshot. She could hear them ahead and a little to her left. From the splashing, she judged not all the field had managed the stream as neatly as her bay. Faris smiled grimly.

Ahead lay a long stretch of rolling meadow, no rocky pasture, but carefully tended turf. Faris concluded that a hunt that would ride across crops would not stick at riding across a lawn. She gauged the pack's progress by their noise and sent her bay after them.

The groomed turf led her up a hill. Faris and the bay topped the rise and saw the hunt to the left. Behind the hunt and beyond them, the stream curved past a dense cluster of oak trees. To the right, the hillside swept down to the river the stream was meandering to meet. Before her, centered in gardens of mathematical precision, lay a manor house of ocher brick, roofed with slates like blue-gray scales.

Faris gazed across the gardens, and winced at the thought of the damage the hunt would do. The gardens held a harmonious network of privet hedges, an avenue of statuary, and a fountain, fed by a diverted stream. At the heart of the gardens, the network of privet hedges became a maze of walls, doubling and redoubling into a labyrinth. Eve-Marie's warning came back to Faris, for this, surely, must be Sevenfold.

The hounds had been hunting loudly along a strong scent. At the edge of the garden, they checked. The huntsmen tried valiantly to rally their pack. But from every shrub—it seemed almost from every shadow—ran foxes. Not one fox, not one dozen foxes, but thirty foxes or forty.

The hounds went mad, each after its own particular fox, and forgot they had ever heard of huntsmen. The foxes scattered and the hounds scattered with them. The huntsmen cursed and followed, hooting and tooting in vain. The rest of the field found the foxes' sudden appearance and equally sudden disappearance unsettling. Their horses scattered too. Faris held her bay firmly and watched the chaos unfold.

In a few moments, she had the garden to herself. The last huntsman was no more than a dwindling sound of hoof beats in the mist beyond the stream. It did not occur to Faris to turn and follow.

The empty garden held her motionless. There was something more than foxes here. She watched the symmetrical grounds as intently as the huntsmen had scanned the covert but saw nothing. There was a pattern to the garden, a pattern that brought back memories of her dreams. If she could walk it awake, could she not walk it in her dreams?

Minutes passed. The bay tossed his head until his bit jingled. Faris found that small noise comforting in the utter stillness of the garden. No fountain, no river, no stream could be heard. She sent the bay toward the house at a walk. Except for the slow, even beat of his hooves, there was no sound.

As she rode down into the garden, Faris felt the mist close in around her. It was chill and she thought it held a faint acrid scent, unpleasantly like that of a fox's earth. By the time she reached the labyrinth, she could hardly see the avenue of statuary, white against the mist beyond the avenue. As all sound but the bay's passage faded, so all sight but the walls of privet faded.

From the saddle, Faris could see her way through the maze but the rest of the world was lost. The bay turned and doubled as their route demanded. At the center of the maze, as the passage widened, the bay came to a halt.

With a lack of surprise she usually experienced only in her dreams, Faris recognized the girl who waited, cloaked and hooded, at the center of the maze. The girl, small and slenderly made, put her hood back and smiled mockingly up at Faris.

"So the gossips had the news right after all. I didn't think it was possible. You've come to seek your fortune in Aravill," said Menary Paganell.

Faris held the bay steady. She would not retreat. She could not go forward. Unless she trampled Menary. Part of her thoughts busy calculating the merits of trampling, Faris countered, "I see you still like gardens."

Menary studied Faris intently. A faint line appeared between her brows, as though she suspected another meaning beneath the words. "Oh, yes, better than anything. Almost anything. If you have come to pay a social call, you should dismount. We will walk together. I will show you my garden."

"No, thank you. I'll stay where I am." She looked at Menary more closely and realized that she wore a wig. It was beautifully made and simply styled. Faris, no judge of such matters, would never have guessed at the artifice had it been made in Menary's own blonde. Instead, it was a shade of red very close to her own. She wondered if it was an obscure insult and since she felt obscurely insulted, she decided it was. "Is it your garden? I rather think it belongs to your father. This is Sevenfold, isn't it?"

"It is. My father has decided I should have it. He means to make amends for summoning me home from Paris. I was having a nice time there. I conducted some business. Perhaps you met some of my hirelings? I instructed them to call on you. You must have left Paris before they could."

With an effort of will, Faris held her hands perfectly still. She wanted to make fists, but feared confusing the bay. "I don't know if I met them or not. Who are they?"

Menary's enjoyment of Faris's discomfiture was unmistakable.

"Oh, I don't know their names. I dealt with an agency. All they asked for was an accurate description and an abundance of cash. I gave them a little something I thought might prove useful, but apparently they neglected to use it properly."

Faris thought she held herself motionless but the bay shifted uneasily. "A little something like a horsehair?"

"It looked like a horsehair. I might have known I'd have to take matters into my own hands. They had better refund my money, since they've failed to execute my commission." Menary smiled up at Faris as she spoke, and put special emphasis on her final three words.

Faris laughed. The bay started slightly at the sound. Menary's eyes widened and her smile faded.

When Faris could speak, she told Menary, "One of your hirelings isn't going to execute anything, ever again. Do you know why? My uncle."

Menary's eyes were wide with annoyance. "What are you laughing for? What about your uncle?"

Faris shook her head. "Nothing. Nothing." She managed to stop chuckling.

A half-grown fox cub, orange as a tabby cat, slipped through the privet hedge and sat down at Menary's feet, panting cheerfully. Menary bent to scratch its ears. It shed a few stiff hairs on the hem of Menary's black cloak. Faris eyed it distrustfully. It *looked* like a fox cub.

Menary noticed Faris's scrutiny and curled her lip in disdainful amusement. She knelt and bent her head as if to listen to the fox cub. "All safely gone to earth and the hounds left snuffling? Excellent. I know a hen house not far from here. Ah, you've heard of it? Very good. Tell them I sent you." The cub left, grinning. Menary rose. "And who sent you here, I wonder?"

"No one."

"The Dean of Greenlaw?" Menary mused. "No, I'm done with her and she with me. We'll trouble each other no more."

"I found my own way."

Menary looked impatient. "You couldn't."

Annoyed all over again, Faris shrugged. "If you insist."

Menary looked extremely cross. "Why are you here, then?"

After a moment's consideration, in which she decided honesty could not possibly hurt, Faris replied, "Curiosity."

The instant the word was out, she knew it was a mistake. Menary's eyes widened as if she had been struck. Bristling with indignation, she drew herself up to her full height. "Go look at the lions then, if you like to peer at locked-up creatures." She took one graceful step closer to the bay, put her hand on its neck, and hissed a word at its flattened ears.

The bay went up like a startled pheasant. Faris had all she could do to keep her seat without worrying about trampling Menary. Yet somehow, when the bay came down, Menary wasn't in the way. Nothing, save for the walls of the privet maze, was in the way of the bay's spectacular bolt. Faris sat down hard, knees clenching the saddle crutches with all her might, and set about surviving Le Nôtre's labyrinth.

The bay scraped first one side of the privet corridor, then the other, all the way out. Beyond the maze the mist had lifted slightly, enough to make it possible to avoid the statuary. The bay took the fountain as easily as if it were a water jump at a church sports day, and hurdled a wrought-iron fence without apparent effort. After that, there was nothing left to do but splash across the stream, scramble up the far bank, and leave Sevenfold behind at top speed.

13

Twelfth Night

❧ WHEN FARIS RETURNED to the Metropol, Jane was out. By
the time she returned, Faris had changed from riding clothes
to her favorite merino gown, and was pacing relentlessly the
length of the suite. She had given Reed and Tyrian the news
on the way back to Aravis. While they did what they could to
find out what Menary was doing at Sevenfold, all she could do
was wait for Jane.

Jane was concentrating on unbuttoning her gloves as she
entered, followed at a few paces by one of Brinker's men, bearing an armful of oddly shaped parcels. At the sight of Faris's
expression, she halted. "What happened?"

Faris started to answer but broke off to consider Jane's escort.

"Just put those down on the table," Jane told him, "and
you may go."

As the escort turned to obey, Faris lifted her hand to stop
him. "As soon as they return, ask Reed and Tyrian to attend
me here." With a nod, the escort withdrew. When they were
alone, Faris said, "Menary's at Sevenfold. She hired Copenhagen and the others to kill me. Not Uncle Brinker. It wasn't
Uncle Brinker after all."

"*Oh, dear!*" Jane dropped her gloves. She stared at Faris
for a long moment, then recovered sufficiently to retrieve the
gloves. "Who told you so?"

"She did."

"Menary did?" Jane frowned. "And just where at Sevenfold, precisely?"

"In the labyrinth." Faris started pacing again. "I can't believe it. Do you realize what this means? He saved my life."

"What were you doing in the labyrinth at Sevenfold? You said you had to go fox hunting with the Spanish ambassador."

"Oh, him. He really is thick as thieves with the king. That's probably why he picked a country place so close to Sevenfold. Anyway, I *was* fox hunting. Menary hasn't lost her interest in animals. She conspired with about a hundred foxes and I don't think either the hounds or the huntsmen will ever be the same." Faris hesitated. "I think they were foxes."

Jane looked askance at her.

"Real foxes. Not sailors or anything."

"Stand still. Stop trying to distract me with foxes and answer me. What were you doing at Sevenfold?"

Faris stopped pacing. "That's where the hunt went. It isn't far from Crail. When the rest of the hunt, ah, dispersed, I went on."

"What possessed you? Were you lost? Don't you remember what Eve-Marie said?"

"I remembered what Eve-Marie said perfectly. The king didn't even know I was there. And even if he did know, why should he wish to keep me there?"

"Oh, Faris, use your head. What have you been telling me and telling me about that antique gallantry of his?"

Faris smiled. "He's *old*. Do you really think it would suit his majesty to catch girls in a garden the way a spider catches flies? Even if he had the inclination, what about his dignity? He's much too full of his own importance to resort to that sort of thing."

"Then why did he take such pains to have the labyrinth brought into working order?"

"To give to Menary, as if she needed any more mischief to get into." Faris made Jane sit down before she gave her a full account of her conversation with Menary.

Jane's eyes narrowed. "I don't believe it. If Menary had just been given the king's favorite country house, why wasn't she busy unpacking or having a servant thrashed? Why was she in the labyrinth, of all places, communing with a beast that might well give her fleas? And why, if she truly had come into possession of the place, was she in such an ill temper?"

"Well." Faris looked apologetic. "I was there."

"So you were. And she didn't do a thing about it, even though she'd just boasted of arranging your assassination. What restraint. Not really like Menary, is it?"

"She did say something upsetting to my horse."

"I would expect Menary to try something a trifle more direct—if she could," said Jane darkly.

"Could she? Didn't the Dean take care of that?"

"When the Dean expelled Menary, she stripped her of the magic she learned at Greenlaw. Yet think how easily Menary misbehaved, even within the wards." Jane shook her head. "Until the end of your first year, when you stayed on for the summer while Menary left, the Dean told me she believed Menary was the one Hilarion was waiting for. She had great potential, the Dean said. And what magic she brought with her, she quite probably retains." Jane paused, as though measuring out her words like medicine. "If the Dean of Greenlaw can't be sure what Menary can do with her magic, what do you imagine her father thinks of her behavior?"

"So he gave her his country place to keep her busy and out of his way."

Jane shook her head again. "I think she lied. I think he didn't give her Sevenfold at all. He gave her to Sevenfold. I think she's a prisoner there."

"Why would he try to imprison his own daughter? And if she's so powerful, how could he be sure he'd succeed?"

"If you were trying to keep the country running, would you want Menary about, turning people into animals?"

"Then why call her home from Paris?"

"Would you want her loose there either? And he took pains to be certain he'd succeed in imprisoning her. He sent for Eve-Marie."

"But did he succeed? Would the labyrinth be strong enough to hold Menary? Le Nôtre's been dead a long time."

"She's there, isn't she?"

Faris said blankly, "But why would he need to keep her there? He's her father. She'd have to do as he told her."

"Oh?" Jane looked cynical. "The way you do as Brinker tells you?" A knock at the door kept her from continuing.

Reed and Tyrian entered, each in his own manner looking pleased with himself. Reed still wore the riding clothes his duties among the hunt servants had demanded. Tyrian had changed back to his usual black.

"Lock the door. Anything useful so far? Jane may have an explanation for Menary's presence at Sevenfold. Meanwhile, I would like to find out what Menary thinks I'm doing here, if possible. I won't be any help. I have to be at the Danish ambassador's house for a dinner party, worse luck."

Faris broke off and tried not to look startled as Tyrian cleared his throat. "I have been able to make some inquiries," he began. Always reserved, since their arrival in Aravis Tyrian had become absolutely taciturn. Any speech was an event. "At the king's command, Menary was summoned back from Paris. She arrived in Aravill the same day we did. The king received her at his country residence. Unofficially, she's still under house arrest there. Officially, she is not expected to return from Greenlaw until the term ends at Whitsun, when she would be supposed to have graduated."

"House arrest?" Reed shook his head. "She must have been having far too much fun in Paris. I hear she has been wiring for money at a shocking rate."

"If she's kept out of the way until after Twelfth Night, we don't need to change the plan," Jane said.

"Do you think it safe to assume that house arrest at Sevenfold will keep her out of the way?" Tyrian asked.

"In a case of Eve-Marie and André Le Nôtre against Menary Paganell," Jane replied, "I'll back Eve-Marie and André Le Nôtre every time."

"But are we set for Twelfth Night?" Reed asked. "It's not much of a plan really, is it? A case of swap the lady: keep the other guests watching Jane when they think they're watching

Faris. I've arranged the costumes, as instructed. But are we even sure where the rift is yet?''

Jane chose a parcel from the armful on the table beside her, a cylinder as long as her arm, neatly wrapped in brown paper. "Here's a little something we might find useful." Jane undid the wrapping, pushed a lamp aside to make room on the table, and unrolled the cylinder. It was a pictorial map of Aravis, with the castle looming over all. In the decorative border were plans of each level of the castle, rendered in great detail. "I've studied the little map that folds out of my Baedeker until I gave myself a squint. This will be much more helpful."

Faris stared at the map, then at Jane. "Where did you get that?"

"This?" Jane smiled apologetically. "There's something I've been meaning to mention, Faris. When he heard I planned to visit Aravis, Uncle Ambrose asked me to look into one or two matters while I was here. To be sure things ran smoothly, he put me in touch with some people in Aravis. The map came from them. They seemed very happy to be of help."

Faris nodded slowly. "Ah, yes. The uncle who smuggles tobacco via diplomatic pouch. Uncle Ambrose wouldn't happen to have anything to do with the diplomatic corps, would he? Or the neatly docketed report on the political climate of Aravill?"

Jane looked demure.

"He's Sir Ambrose Hay, the British ambassador to France," said Tyrian. At Jane's startled expression, he added, "I made some inquiries while we were in Paris."

Faris's voice was cold. "Is that why you were so anxious to come home with me?"

"Oh, don't be cross. I would have come with you in any event. In fact, I haven't done a single thing that I wouldn't have done if Uncle Ambrose didn't exist. But it does help having friends here."

"Just what matters are you looking into for him?"

"Shene is a deep-water harbor. There isn't a better place

for a fleet to refuel on the entire coast. And since the Paganells took the throne in Aravill, they haven't been as friendly to us as they are to the Turks and the Persians."

"So you're a spy," said Reed.

Jane drew herself up indignantly. "Not at all. I am here to help Faris." Suddenly her indignation vanished, to be replaced by an expressionless face and an uninflected voice. "Although in the case of a disputed succession, I've been told the British government is prepared to be generous to the rightful heir."

"Provided the rightful heir is generous to them," Faris finished. "Oh, Jane."

Jane, still expressionless, watched Faris in silence.

Faris sighed. "You do realize, don't you, that Shene is no concern of mine? If Galazon had fifty deep-water harbors, the British fleet could sport about in any of them. But Galazon doesn't. And all I'm concerned with is Galazon."

Jane looked relieved. "Oddly enough, I have noticed that. Fond as I am of Uncle Ambrose, the harbor doesn't matter. The rift does. I'm here to help you if I can. Are you going to look at this map or aren't you?"

All four gathered to inspect the map.

"It's a copy of a late-eighteenth-century original owned by the British Museum. I wanted to be certain to find a floor plan made well before the rift was created."

"Here's the throne room," said Faris, after some consideration. "I don't see anything marked "the warden's stair." Are you sure there aren't more levels than this?"

"I would have said fewer," Jane replied, "although I assume some were lost in the rift."

"That must be just about where the lions are now," remarked Reed, tapping a forefinger on the view of the castle.

"Lions?" Faris turned to him. "There really are lions?"

"Oh, yes. Guard lions, you might say. Parts of the castle are mouldering away. People would wander off into the older bits and turn their ankles. Guards didn't do much to solve the problem of stray visitors, so a few years ago, someone had a bright idea. They sent for lion cubs and let them grow up in the dangerous area.''

"A simple method to keep people away," Faris said dryly, "yet somehow completely typical of the Paganells. And I thought the lions had to be a flight of Menary's fancy."

"It doesn't work, though," Reed continued. "People don't stay away. They come to look at the lions—from a safe distance."

Jane looked up from her scrutiny of the map with such satisfaction that she almost purred. "Your index finger is precisely on the throne room, Reed. How interesting."

Reed studied the map more closely. "So it is."

Tyrian cleared his throat again. "So Reed and I must crash a fancy dress ball, Jane must pass herself off as Faris, Reed and I must escort Faris to a room that hasn't existed for sixty years, and we must do all this while coming and going through a pride of lions."

Reed looked troubled. "It really isn't much of a plan, is it?"

"The lions may complicate things a trifle," Jane conceded. "I've already taken care of the invitations, thanks to Uncle Ambrose's friends at the British embassy here. It helped to have your authentic invitation to use as a basis for the forgeries."

"I still have to find a reason to slip away from the ball once you've attended to the lions."

Jane smiled serenely. "That should be simple. Surely you may indulge a whim to look at them—from a safe distance."

Faris pretended to examine the map. She was far from cheerful about the plan. She had suggested it the day her invitation had arrived. Nothing better had occurred to any of them since. And however faulty a plan it was, it had the merit of speed. The sixth of January was only four days away. If they were not able to carry out the plan, they would simply have to think of another.

If Jane could control the lions, she still had to pose as Faris. If Jane succeeded, and Faris was free to find her way to the throne room—or to what was left of the throne room—then Faris could worry about what to do with the rift. Jane believed that Faris, as a warden, would know intuitively how to mend the rift. Faris had no confidence in that theory. The fact remained: it was her duty to find the rift, and her duty to close it. If she failed—Faris reminded herself there was a great deal to do, as well as to worry about, before she even had to make the attempt.

When Faris looked up from her reverie over the map, Tyrian met her eyes. He had been watching her closely and he seemed concerned by what he had seen. "It would be better to find the warden's stair. That would allow us to come at the rift as Hilarion suggests. The stair may well be on the map, unlabeled."

Jane looked haughty. "Search the map for it, by all means. But I think I can manage a few lions."

"Vanity?" Faris inquired.

"Dame Brachet told us we couldn't reject vanity until we understood it fully. I've always understood it fully but I've never been able to begin to reject it."

"Dame Brachet would shake her head and say, *Vanity of vanities, all is vanity. What profit hath a man of all his labor which he taketh under the sun?*"

Jane's serene smile returned. "Now, just because I am extremely vain, I'll cap that quotation for you: *'One generation passeth away, and another generation cometh: but the earth abideth forever.'* And so, I dare say, vanity abideth too."

At the dinner party that evening, Jane's words came back to Faris. On the heels of the memory came a sudden image of Hilarion, waiting patiently through the generations in the silence that lay beneath the city of Paris. She stopped eating her caviar. If she failed in her duty, how much longer would he have to wait? Yet if she succeeded, what then?

With an effort Faris collected herself and returned to the dinner table conversation. The image of Hilarion remained with her all evening.

* * *

Faris dreamed that night, but not of the castle. She was back in
the labyrinth at Sevenfold, moving on horseback through a silence as palpable as the mist all around the garden. The privet
walls turned and doubled in a pattern that she could never
quite recognize. In the dream she knew that the pattern was
taking her into the heart of the labyrinth and that she was
afraid of what she would find there.

The last turn came. The pattern ended. Faris found herself
in the center of the maze. Menary was not there. Instead,
prone in the grass, naked, as he had lain in the Dean's garden
at Greenlaw, lay Tyrian.

Faris woke.

As she lay in the silent darkness, panting and sweating,
waiting for her heart to stop banging against her ribs, Faris
tried to explain the dream to herself. She had dreamed of the
labyrinth. That was natural, for she had been there that very
morning. She had, all unexpectedly, met Menary there. What
was more natural, then, to dream of the last time she'd met
Menary in a garden. And so, logically enough, she had
dreamed of Tyrian as he looked in that garden.

Considered rationally, it was only to be expected that she
would dream of Tyrian. Faris wiped her forehead with a corner of the sheet. She had not spoken to Tyrian alone since the
day of her sleigh ride with Brinker. Since her arrival in Aravis,
she had hardly even seen him. The conversation over Jane's
map was the most Faris had of his company since her quarrel
with Brinker made her realize how inappropriate her feeling
for Tyrian was. Of course she had dreamed of him that night.
It was only natural.

The next day, Faris invited Brinker to breakfast. Across the
table, he eyed her with interest and asked, "What fell deed are
you planning? This unexpected hospitality must have some
dark origin."

"Why? You invited me to breakfast."

"Not without some trepidation."

Faris finished her coffee and braced herself. "The truth is, I wish to offer you an apology."

Brinker's jaw dropped. "I beg your pardon. I cannot have heard you correctly. It sounded almost as if you said—"

"I thought you'd hired someone to kill me. I was wrong. I'm sorry I suspected you."

"Ah, yes. I remember. You mentioned this before. I told you that you were mistaken. I take it you finally believe me. What sort of corroborative evidence have you found?"

"I'm not at liberty to tell you."

"No? What a pity. It must have been impressive. Well, I accept your apology, my dear. I hope you won't be so quick to question my motives in the future. Though I expect you will."

"I expect so, too. It isn't easy to change the habits of a lifetime."

"No. Perhaps not. By the way, I trust that the corroborative evidence means that your life is no longer in danger?"

"Not at the moment. So far as I know."

"Good. It would be a pity if anything happened to you now, you know. That day in the armory gave me quite a start."

"You saved my life. I'm grateful."

Brinker dismissed her words with an airy wave. "Think nothing of it. In fact, I am thankful to you. It gave me an idea for the Twelfth Night fancy dress ball. I hate masquerades, but I shall be ready for this one. As soon as Agnes reminded me that we would be here for Twelfth Night, I knew just what to have packed."

Brinker would not elaborate on his choice of costume, but he made the topic last for the remainder of the meal.

Jane studied Menary's horsehair cantrip carefully but was unable to learn any more from it. For safety's sake, she insisted on destroying it.

Tyrian found not one unmarked staircase in the map of the castle but fourteen. Further inquiries showed that all were still in use for the mundane tasks of household maintenance.

Reed discovered that even before the advent of the lions, few people had ventured willingly into the area between the rift and the habitable part of the castle.

The lions, fed regularly, were as much decoration as deterrent. The desolation of broken masonry and shattered brick would have been forbidding even without their presence, but a careful climber could have passed unhindered.

Twelfth Night finally arrived. Brinker and Agnes left for the ball early, cloaked from head to heel to conceal their costumes.

When Faris emerged from her room, she found the others ready and waiting for her in the suite's outer chamber. Jane, in a red cloak over an expensively simple red gown, made a Little Red Riding Hood of a certain age, extremely soignée, despite (or perhaps because of) the bonfire-in-winter hat, which she had insisted upon wearing. Her escort, Tyrian, in impeccable evening clothes, wore a full wolf's head mask which rendered him completely unrecognizable. Reed appeared happiest of all with his costume: satin coat and knee breeches, powdered wig, black tricorne, half mask, and hooded cloak, a perfect replica of an eighteenth-century gentleman incognito, down to the slender rapier that hung at his hip.

Faris was wearing her Parisian evening gown. It was slenderly cut in the latest mode, of satin that was either black or midnight blue or both at once. Embroidery of gray and white and silver thread meandered up from the hem in a design that might have been peonies and tree branches, or might have been puffs and whorls of smoke. The bodice was simple. The sleeves were full and made of some diaphanous black material which fluttered in an extremely pleasing way.

With her great height, Faris could not dare any sort of headdress. Instead, her hair was braided and pinned into a coronet beneath a fine black veil that shrouded her from the crown of her head to the heels of her slippers. Despite her finery (or perhaps because of it) Faris was cross.

"I look as though I've wandered in from a touring production of *The Magic Flute*," she observed gloomily, scowling into the mirror.

"You don't." Jane's voice was crisp. She was trying to see past Faris's shoulder. Her bonfire-in-winter hat was perhaps a trifle crooked. She adjusted hatpins deftly. "You look just as you should."

"There will be at least a dozen ladies who will come as Night," predicted Faris. "Everyone will think I'm one of them. I should wear your hat and go as Sunset instead."

"If every lady present came as Night," said Jane patiently, "you would still be wearing the best gown by far. You are going as Smoke. If your gown doesn't make that clear enough to satisfy the other guests, you have my permission to light a cigar."

"The Queen of Swords." Reed drew his rapier and offered her the hilt. "Would you care to borrow mine for the evening?"

Faris smiled at him.

"Don't tempt her." Jane put her basket over her arm. "She'd only find a use for it."

"I know. Oh, I know." Reed smiled back and put the rapier away.

Tyrian said nothing.

At the castle, footmen were hard at work managing carriage steps, opening the doors into the forecourt, and handing guests in to the attentions of the masters of ceremonies. Faris and her companions presented their invitations, one genuine and the others forged, and entered. After the perilous climb to the top of the white icing staircase, they were relayed to the grand master of ceremonies, who announced their assumed identities with such calm dignity that his bored indifference was nearly audible. "Smoke. *Le Marquis de Carabas. Le Petit Chaperon Rouge.* The Wolf."

The ballroom, with its chessboard floor of black and white marble, was vast and nearly half full. On the far side of the room, against the hangings of sky blue velvet, an orchestra played. On the right, a few of the gilt chairs were taken already, by guests who obviously believed they needed to husband their strength to last out the ball. On the left, champagne was being dispensed. In the center of the room, fifty couples were waltzing, and still the room was not yet overly warm. At the edges, waiters roamed, offering inexhaustible trays of crab puffs and lobster patties, refreshment to the weary.

Glad of Reed's satin sleeve to rest her fingertips upon, Faris took her first steps into the ballroom. Jane and Tyrian came after her. Behind them, the grand master of ceremonies continued. "Mary, Queen of Scots. Father Time. Columbine. Harlequin. Night. Lohengrin."

Despite the great number of guests, and the extravagance and variety of costumes, Faris and her companions attracted considerable attention. Faris's costume in particular seemed to occasion remark.

"The king must be here somewhere," Jane murmured. "He'll have to greet his guests."

"Charlemagne," the grand master of ceremonies called.

"There," said Faris softly. "St. Francis of Assisi in a velvet cassock. Who's that talking to him? Alexander the Great?"

"Julius Caesar, surely," Jane replied. "I refuse to believe Alexander the Great had such spindly arms."

During the round of introductions, in which Reed and Tyrian were passed off as fictitious members of the British consular staff, Faris learned that Jane was right, as usual; it was indeed Julius Caesar.

The king showed no interest in Faris's companions, but his reaction to Faris's costume was markedly hostile until it was explained that she represented Smoke.

The king's voice was cold. "Oh, indeed? We thought at first you had chosen to represent a figure from history. Smoke. How original."

Faris looked puzzled. "What figure from history?"

"Joan of Arc," Jane guessed. "She is supposed to have had red hair. Though I never heard she was particularly tall."

"The error was ours." The king thawed slightly. "We did

not think for an instant that Faris portrayed Joan of Arc. However, there was a red-haired woman intimately associated
with the history of this very building. She was exceedingly
tall. We fear we reached a faulty conclusion."

Faris drew herself up to her full height. "If you think that
I consider my grandmother Prosperian suitable matter for a
masquerade with the likes of Columbine and Harlequin, you
are mistaken."

"Our apologies. We confess we are relieved that you did
not wish to remind us of the woman who nearly burned this
entire castle to the ground. Yet we think it was an understand-
able mistake. Your uncle sees nothing amiss in masquerading
as a more remote relation. He was announced as Ludovic Nallaneen, Duke of Galazon. Our daughter, of course, is St.
Agnes."

Faris followed the king's gaze to where Brinker, wearing
Uncle Ludo's armor, his great sword slung at his back, was
looking on with Agnes, who resembled an early Christian
martyr of the most grimly respectable kind. "Perhaps my
uncle is feeling a bit mistrustful of crowds."

"Saladin," the grand master of ceremonies called. "Elea-
nor of Aquitaine."

"If we don't, we're sure he needn't." The king looked
down at his costume with unmistakable satisfaction. As he did
so, Faris realized that the small bird perched on his shoulder
was a stuffed lark, firmly pinned in place against the velvet.
She suppressed a shudder of distaste.

"We wished to come as something a little out of the ordinary," the king continued. He hitched up his silken rope belt
slightly. "It's fairly comfortable, too. An important advantage
at this sort of thing." He was even ruddier than usual. It
seemed as if he had been celebrating longer than the other
guests. He seemed to be having a little trouble seeing through
her veil, for his heavy-lidded eyes scarcely left her face.

As the orchestra struck up the next dance, Jane and
Tyrian slipped away. Faris put her fingertips back on Reed's
sleeve. She didn't want to be left alone yet, particularly not

with the king. "You seem to know all about this sort of entertainment. I've never been to a fancy dress ball before."

"We prefer them, really. Far more comfortable than the usual entertainment, if you know how to choose the right costume."

"No hair shirt, then, I take it?" Reed asked cheerfully.

Very gently, without taking her eyes from the king's, Faris stepped on Reed's toe.

The king gave no sign that he had noticed Reed's existence. "You *will* save all the waltzes for us, won't you?" Dexterously he marked Faris's dance card. "We'll have to greet a few dozen more guests but then we are yours. Yours entirely."

Faris kicked Reed's ankle cautiously and they withdrew together toward the center of the chessboard. Before Faris could speak, Reed led her out into the polka that had just begun.

"You *won't* save all the waltzes for him, will you? It might give him the wrong idea."

"Night and Day," the grand master of ceremonies called.

"Discussing his choice of—his hair shirt might give him the wrong idea, too. How dared you bring that up?"

Reed grinned at her. "How dare you? That's no way for a lady to talk."

He was quite correct. Faris held her peace and concentrated upon the dance steps. Reed was an accomplished dancer, and made the swift whirl of the polka graceful, as well as effervescent.

As the polka ended, the Spanish ambassador claimed her for the galop. Reed surrendered Faris to his punctilious entreaties and found another partner—Columbine. Faris was pleased by, and a little surprised at, Reed's social grace. *If only he doesn't discuss details of costume with her*, she thought.

"Thomas of Bedlam," the grand master of ceremonies announced, with no bored indifference whatsoever. The Spanish ambassador drew Faris out of the press of dancers so they could both take a good look at the newly-arrived guest. Many of the other dancers followed the example he set.

Faris could see nothing very extraordinary about the newcomer. He was a slim young man, tall and dark, in evening dress remarkable only for its excellence of material and tailoring. In no way did he appear to be in costume. He did not appear to notice the interest the other guests took in him. After a casual glance around the cavernous room, he made his way toward the king.

The Spanish ambassador was appalled. "What impudence."

"Why? Because he forgot to wear his costume?"

"Istvan Graelent comes of good family. He has had an excellent education. He cannot plead ignorance. His presence here tonight cannot possibly be excused."

"Why not?"

"He is uninvited." The Spanish ambassador stiffened. "And now the insolent puppy has given his majesty the cut direct. He walked past the king as though he did not even see him. This is an outrage."

The young man had indeed strolled past the king without a glance. He seemed far more interested in the champagne than in his unwilling host. Faris could not help but admire the graceful ease with which he ignored the stir he was creating.

"Does this sort of thing happen often?"

"Certainly not. Surely his majesty will have the young jackanapes removed at once."

The king, however, was listening to Julius Caesar, who was speaking earnestly in his ear. After a moment, the king nodded. He caught the grand master of ceremonies's eye and shook his head. That gentleman relaxed visibly and waved away the guard he had summoned to his side. The king spoke to Julius Caesar, who withdrew looking relieved.

Oblivious to all this, Graelent secured a glass of champagne and began to look calmly around for the nearest tray of lobster patties.

The Spanish ambassador was mystified by the king's forbearance.

"Perhaps the king prefers not to disturb his invited guests

by drawing undue attention to the young man," Faris suggested. "If we ignore him, perhaps he will go away."

"He is a political figure of sorts," the Spanish ambassador conceded. "Perhaps his majesty is wise not to give Graelent's followers any reason to believe their leader is persecuted. Though prison would be the best place for him."

"A young man of good family and excellent education? Surely not."

"You must not let the veneer of good behavior he has adopted tonight mislead you. Though he claims to represent a political faction, he is in sober fact a gangster. His followers are drawn from the most disreputable circles in Aravis: peddlers, students, even the poor. They are little better than a gang of thugs."

"How curious. Don't they call themselves Monarchists?"

"They may call themselves Christian Democrats, or anything they please. The name does not change the fact that they are radicals of deepest dye. Revolutionaries who demand the restoration of a corrupt, deposed regime."

Dryly, Faris inquired, "Which regime might that be?"

Abruptly, the Spanish ambassador remembered whom he was speaking to. He was still trying to repair his diplomatic lapse when the orchestra drew the galop to a close.

After the galop came a waltz. The king was still greeting his arriving guests, but Faris did not lack a partner, for Tyrian appeared beside her. His courtesy matched the Spanish ambassador's desperate gallantry.

Faris put her hand in Tyrian's, grateful that her gloves concealed the dampness of her palms. His touch at her waist was light and impersonal. She tried not to clutch his shoulder in sheer nervousness.

They danced in silence at first. Tyrian was not as accomplished a dancer as Reed. Faris welcomed the fact. She did not feel capable of any flights of high style on the dance floor. Tyrian's touch made her so self-conscious she could hardly remember her steps.

"I don't see Jane."

"She's gone to deal with the lions. As soon as this dance is over, I'll check her progress. When she's ready, I'll return and give you the signal."

"Champagne."

"Right. I wish this mask had larger eyes. It's hard to see you."

Faris glanced ahead as they waltzed steadily on. "If you can't see, how can you dance?"

"No, don't look ahead." Tyrian's muffled voice held an unmistakable note of command. As Faris, surprised, looked back at his mask, he continued more gently. "If we look where we're going, the other dancers won't make way for us. This way, they sense our purpose and let us pass without realizing they're doing so."

"So we may dance where we please, as long as we don't betray our blindness. Fair enough. I won't look ahead."

"Nor will I." Tyrian spoke so softly that Faris scarcely caught the words.

For the first time in her life, Faris found herself an adult in an assembly of adults who were enjoying themselves. Paying attention to her, she discovered to her own amazement, was part of enjoying themselves. And so, despite the task ahead of her, Faris found herself enjoying the ball. As the music buoyed her from partner to partner, she danced on without looking ahead.

The king claimed the fourth waltz. Before Faris could accept, she heard a young man's voice at her elbow.

"I beg your pardon, your majesty," said Istvan Graelent in her ear. "Pray allow a madman to pay homage to you." He swept her a deep and graceful bow. When he straightened, he looked into her eyes. Faris realized he was at least an inch or two taller than she. It had been so long since she had to look up at anyone, the sensation startled her.

Beside her, the king lifted a hand. From all quarters, guards began to gather. Graelent watched their approach with interest. "Are you going to throw me out now? I wondered when you would."

"If you give us the slightest provocation, young man, you'll find yourself in a cell."

Graelent's dark eyes danced. "My bonny mad boys wouldn't like that, would they? I suppose I'd better behave myself."

Faris turned to the king. "Will there be time to ask him a question before the guards escort him out?"

"By all means," the king replied. To Graelent, he said, "Should you offer the slightest impertinence to this lady, it will be our great pleasure to make you regret it."

Graelent inclined his head. "I could never offer impertinence of any sort to my true monarch—whether she is literal or figurative."

While the king mulled that over, Faris asked, "Why did you choose an English song for your party anthem? Have you no suitable songs in Aravill?"

Graelent seemed happy to be asked. "Tom o'Bedlam, your majesty, is a universal figure. It was merely our good fortune to learn the English version of the song from scholars who came to collect our folk songs. How fitting that we should have one of their songs in return for so many of our own."

The guards encircled Graelent. At a sign from the king, they drew him away. He made one last obeisance to Faris and departed.

The king stopped one of the guards and said, "Go tell the orchestra we want another waltz. They've nearly finished this one."

Despite his costume, he cut an impressive figure on the dance floor. Faris complimented him.

"It isn't every king that can risk simplicity. Imagine the German kaiser at a fancy dress ball. He'd come as himself. And he wouldn't have to dress up to do it, either. Those uniforms—*pshaw!*—pure comic opera."

Faris could not quite see what distinction there might be between pure comic opera and his peacock blue cutaway, but she answered as diplomatically as she could. "Yet in Aravis there are a great many uniforms, and if you'll forgive me, some of them are purest comic opera. The palace guard, for example. What is that thing on their helmet? It looks like a scrub brush."

"That's quite a different matter. Military men insist upon uniforms. A king should wear whatever he pleases. It worries us that so many kings are unable to think of anything more pleasing than a military uniform."

"And does St. Francis's vow of poverty please you? You are a rare king indeed, then."

The king said patronizingly, "It's a fancy dress ball. Does your costume imply that you would be pleased to end up as a wisp of smoke?"

"That's different. As I am not a king, I don't claim the right to wear whatever I please."

The king did not seem to notice the amusement in Faris's voice. Instead he tightened his embrace and spun her into a turn that showed her gown to excellent advantage. "You could if you wished."

Faris considered his tone, his eyes, his expression, and decided he must have had more to drink than she'd thought. "But I don't."

The king drew her still closer. "But you could." He allowed the music to carry them into another turn and then another, more sweeping still.

Faris followed his steps precisely, determined to reveal no sign of comprehension. The turns required concentration. She put her entire attention into them. Let him turn until daybreak. If she ignored him, perhaps he would go away.

"You're blushing." The king let the last elaborate turn melt into the final figures of the waltz as the orchestra finished. His voice carried well enough to make heads turn all around them.

"I am not." It took all Dame Brachet's training to keep Faris from staring down at her slippers in embarrassment.

"Then you're flushed." He drew her arm through his. "Come sit down and catch your breath. We know the perfect spot. Have we shown you the library yet? No? We'll go there. It's very quiet."

"I don't need to catch my breath, thank you very much."

"You must, you're more flushed than ever. Let us think a moment. We have it. We'll take the air."

"I don't want any air."

"Yes, you do. We have marvelous air here." The king turned toward the stair, Faris still firmly in his grasp. "Let's go look at the lions."

Faris started to refuse, then saw Tyrian over the king's shoulder. He was holding a full glass of champagne, useless to a man who wouldn't remove his mask. It was time, then. Duty called.

Faris looked up into the king's pouchy dark blue eyes. "By all means," she said, with chilly dignity Dame Brachet herself would have applauded, "let us go see the lions."

14

World's End Close

🐾 IT WAS A simple matter for the king to slip away from his own ball. He led Faris through a room off the ballroom, where white linen-covered tables held silver trays of crab puffs and lobster patties, and into the corridors beyond. Together they strolled freely to the upper reaches of the castle, toward the lion-guarded ruins.

To Faris, the trip was nerve-wracking. She had a good enough grasp of Jane's floor plan to guess at the progress they were making, but she had no way to know where Jane was or what she was doing.

Tyrian would certainly be close at hand, ready to do whatever he thought necessary about the king's presence. But what about Reed? Was he still dancing with his Columbine?

Or had he followed her from the ballroom? Could he be trusted to wait for orders from Faris before he popped out from behind some tapestry to interfere? And what would be best to do with the king? Let Jane perform some magic, if she had any to spare from the lions? Or let Tyrian keep him quiet? Or take him along to the rift?

In addition to these concerns, Faris was distracted by the route they took through the castle. The king was leading her up stairs and along halls which reminded her of her dreams. The twisting passages seemed endless.

"How much farther is it?"

"Oh, not far at all. You aren't tired, are you?"

"Of course not."

"You aren't frightened, are you?"

"Of *course* not."

"Try to be slightly frightened. However well we feed them, they are lions, after all. Slaves to their nature, as man is a slave to his."

Faris doubted that anyone was ever entirely a slave to his nature, unless perhaps one counted Brinker. But she thought it would be as well not to discuss it with the king. "Why lions?" she asked instead.

"Why keep lions, do you mean? Purely to protect visitors to the ruins, rest assured. The throne room fire in 1848 left the upper reaches of the castle in some disrepair. It would be quite possible to meet with an accidental injury there. The lions prevent anyone from wandering freely in the ruins." The king lowered his voice to a nasal murmur. "We will be quite undisturbed."

Faris kept her tone one of bright, though obtuse, interest. "Why not simply repair the damage, instead?"

"Do you see where the windows used to be? That's modern brick work in the arches. We have repaired much of the damage in the upper reaches of the castle."

"But why not repair the throne room itself?"

"Forgive our frankness. Your grandmother left a poor impression on those who knew her. The idea of reclaiming the

room in which she made such a dramatic end fills us with distaste. And even if we wished to, which we certainly don't, we
doubt that we could find anyone willing to make the repairs."

"Fascinating. You will show me the precise spot, won't
you?"

"We can't. Remember the lions."

Faris did not have to counterfeit disappointment. "Oh, of
course." She accompanied the king up a steep flight of steps
and into a narrow hallway. The lamp-lit corridor held a draft
of fresh air, very welcome after the long sequence of stairs and
hallways that had brought them here. "Has someone left the
door open?"

Surprised, the king looked closely at her. "We take pains
to keep the doors locked in this part of the castle."

"Of course. How silly of me."

The corridor turned sharply and stopped at a heavy door.
While the king bent to unlock it, Faris studied the masonry.
Around the door, traces of a much larger arch remained, now
painstakingly bricked shut. She swallowed hard.

The king turned back to Faris. "Curious. It wasn't locked
after all. Someone has been rather careless."

Faris wondered if the lock had given Jane much trouble.
Or had Tyrian opened it for her?

The king opened the door. Beyond was blackness. The
draft of fresh air became a breeze. Faris felt it stir her veil and
flutter at her sleeves. It was a cool night, not cold as a night in
January ought to be. The king crossed the threshold.

"No light?" asked Faris, following.

"We won't need one."

Beyond, the sky was black and the ground was white.
Overhead the gibbous moon hung, overpowering all but a
handful of the winter stars. Underfoot, broken masonry cast
puddles of shadow in the moonlight.

"Oh," said Faris, so softly her breath did not stir her veil.

Across the broad expanse of shattered brick and stone,
Faris saw white walls rising up from the heart of the wreck-
age, faultlessly beautiful, a tower as perfectly made as a uni-

corn's horn. As Faris watched, the brilliance of the tower faded as utterly as if the moon had been obscured by a bank of clouds. In a moment, there was nothing before them but a flat area, perhaps forty or fifty feet across, of shattered brick and stone, ending at a precipice that dropped a thousand feet to the tangled streets of the city below. Beyond the precipice lay a spangle of light against the utter darkness, like dew caught in a spider web.

"Oh," she said again, and walked forward into the moonlight.

"Mind the lions," said the king behind her.

Faris looked around quickly but saw nothing. "Where?"

"They're out there somewhere." He put his hand under her elbow as if to steady her. "It's beautiful here tonight, isn't it?"

"Very beautiful." Faris reached the edge of the precipice and stopped. The spangle of light belonged to the streets of the city below. She watched in silence, identifying the steady glow of gaslights along the Esplanade, the fugitive glint of the Twelfth Night bonfires in the steep, twisted streets of the poor quarter of Aravis.

"Too beautiful." The king drew Faris away from the edge and into the circle of his arm. "One reason we brought you here was to show you this. And to assure you that with us your safety is paramount."

"Was there some doubt about that?"

"We wish to apologize for any inconvenience our younger daughter has caused. Menary has taken you in some enmity."

"Are you referring to your letter to the Dean?"

The king seemed puzzled at first. "Our letter? Oh, that. Certainly, that, too. When we received Menary's news that she needed more money because she was a victim of extortion, we should have remembered her vivid imagination."

Curiosity kept Faris from remarking on this description of Menary's behavior. "That, too? Why? What else?"

"Menary took sufficient time away from her studies to

engage a Parisian firm to execute a commission for her," the
king began, his stately tones ringing through the ruins.

To execute me, Faris thought.

The king continued. "When this came to our attention, we
objected. The commission was canceled. Legal proceedings
have been instituted to recover our fees. We have spoken
sharply to Menary. She will be too involved in her studies at
the Sorbonne to trouble you further. We resolved to apologize
to you. We hope you view us as your friend. Your devoted
friend."

Faris's heart sank. The king's embrace tightened about
her shoulders. She started dramatically. "Was that a lion?"

The king drew her closer still. "We dare them to disturb
us. We would dare anything with you beside us. No, don't
tremble. We will protect you. Only give us the right."

Faris was not trembling. She was shaking with combined
amusement and outrage. She pulled away. "Someone is coming." *Wishful thinking.*

"We are quite alone." The king put his hands lightly on
her shoulders. "We have discussed all this with your uncle, of
course. We are not so old, however, that we don't understand
how you may view the matter. You are young. We know what
it is like to be young. You make us remember—" The king
broke off to yawn. Then, with no fuss, no warning, he sat
down, put his head on his knees, and was silent.

Faris leaned over him. His eyes were shut. His breathing
was deep and steady. She felt almost dizzy with relief.

"You've no notion how difficult it is to cast a spell in this
place." Jane joined Faris's inspection of the king. "He'll do.
Sorry I'm late."

Faris straightened and began to unpin her veil. "Thank
goodness you stopped him. But couldn't you have done it
before he began to propose?"

"I wasn't quite finished with the lions." Jane took off her
scarlet cloak and set it aside, then began to remove her hat. "It
isn't hard to put them to sleep. The problem is to keep them

there. Just when I have things in hand, another bit of something blows past me out of the rift and it's all to do again."

Faris freed her veil and handed it to Jane.

Jane stepped under it and began to pin it into place with Faris's help. "Working magic this close to the rift is like trying to light a cigarette in the rain, while standing with your feet in a bucket of kerosene."

"Sounds uncomfortable," Reed said. Tyrian pushed past him impatiently and joined Jane and Faris. He took off his wolf's-head mask and put it down beside Jane's hat. Reluctantly, Reed came nearer, keeping well away from the edge of the precipice. "Shall I stay here and guard the king?"

"Oh, I'll keep the king with me," Jane replied. Her voice was a little deeper than usual, clearer and softer. She seemed taller, much taller than before, and the height had turned her graceful figure awkward. Beneath the veil, the scarlet of her gown had turned to black, worked with shifting patterns of embroidery. The moonlight made all the embroidery look silver and the veil made all the silver look tarnished. "But I'll have to wake him and the lions soon. I can't keep them sleeping safely *and* control the veil. Not here, at least."

"Promise me, no matter what happens, you won't dance with Uncle Brinker."

"We must go." Tyrian was watching Faris. In the moonlight, he might still have been wearing a mask.

Reed looked anxiously around. "Go *where?*"

"To the tower." Faris drew the key to the warden's stair from around her neck. By moonlight the greenish glass looked dark in her hand. She grasped the key tightly, her fingers tangled in the chain, and started toward the spot where the tower had been. If there was a door, it was her duty to find it.

"If I can't manage all the magic, I'll try to give you a signal before I let the lions wake." Jane bent to touch the king's shoulder. He rose without opening his eyes and let her lead him away. The door closed almost soundlessly behind them.

The moonlight on the broken ground was bright enough to cast shadows. As Faris made her way toward the center of the ruins, the slow return of the tower shifted the shadows around her. Yet she saw no white walls, no surrounding darkness.

Instead, her attention was on the ground before her, where light and shadow shifted into something she had never seen before. Sometimes like the silken play of light on water, sometimes like the embroidery on her dress, sometimes like the stars over Greenlaw on the night of her vigil, the black and silver pattern fascinated her.

Faris could not quite make sense of it, yet she knew there was sense somewhere inside the shifting contrasts. It reminded her of the labyrinth at Sevenfold. It reminded her of the play of color on a starling's feather. It reminded her of the pattern of the rug in the library at Galazon Chase. She followed the pattern haltingly, searching for some center that she could not perceive.

Something behind the pattern shifted. Faris felt something break loose and drift past her. As she watched the contrasts fade, she knew the tower had gone again. And as she watched, the remnants of the pattern shifted one last time and became the pattern of gaslight and bonfires in the dark streets far below. She was at the edge of the precipice. On either side, Reed and Tyrian were poised to pull her back. Blinking as if awakening from sleep, Faris looked around at them, and her voice was ragged. "I can't do it. I can't even find my way to the rift."

"Good," said Reed. "Then we can go home."

"Come back," said Tyrian. "Come away from the edge."

As they stepped to safer ground, Jane's hat exploded. The blast threw them down, deafened them briefly, and dusted them with sand and pebbles, but did them no other harm. Faris spat out sand and rubbed a bruised knee. "I think I knocked something out of the rift."

"Jane said she'd give us a signal," Reed said. "I think she overdid things."

"Back to the doorway," said Tyrian.

They achieved the door before there was any sign of

lions but as Reed swung the door shut, Faris glanced back out into the darkness and glimpsed eyes reflecting the light from the corridor. Then it was down the corridor as fast as they could go.

As they ran, they thumped and brushed briskly at themselves and each other to get the worst of the dust off their hair and clothing. To Faris, the twisting passages seemed endless. The pattern of light and shadow still troubled her vision. She misjudged steps and caught corners with her shoulder. Reed and Tyrian slowed to let her clumsiness keep pace with them.

Finally, in a room off the ballroom, where tables covered with white linen held splendid silver trays of crab puffs and lobster patties, they paused to collect themselves.

"I'll go first," said Reed, adjusting the lace at his cuffs. "I'm the only one who still has a disguise."

"You have three minutes to find her," said Tyrian. "No longer. If you aren't back, we leave without you."

Reed grinned, bowed to Faris with a flourish, and left them.

It was quiet in the refreshment room and oddly deserted, considering the excellence of the food set forth. Faris could not hear the orchestra but she thought she heard voices from the ballroom. It was maddening not to be able to make out the words. With or without Jane, Reed would be back in three minutes.

Faris tried to ignore her rising sense of dread. Jane had promised a signal. But her beloved hat? For all Jane could have known, Faris and the others might have been standing right beside it, waiting for Tyrian to put his wolf's head back on, just at the moment it went off. And just before the blast, there had been that sickening slow shift behind the pattern as something had brushed past Faris. Past her but not past Jane? Surely three minutes could not take so long. Where was Reed? Faris began to pace.

Tyrian, Faris noticed, had unfolded a white linen napkin and arranged it carefully over his arm. The fierce cheerfulness he'd shown in the Boulevard Saint Germain gleamed behind his calm demeanor. As Faris watched, he made minute adjustments to the silver trays, looking as if he had spent all his life in the study of the proper presentation of crab puffs. Finally, he selected a tray and lifted it easily into position. He nodded politely to Faris. "It's been three minutes. I want to reconnoiter. If I'm not back in one minute more, leave for the hotel without us."

Faris started to speak. Tyrian held up his hand to stop her. "Count sixty. Then go." He turned on his heel and walked smartly toward the ballroom, crab puffs on high.

Faris started to pace again.

Before she had counted twenty, Tyrian was back, crab puffs intact. "We must go." Only his wide blue eyes betrayed his excitement. "Jane looks like herself again. I think the king wants to know if she was you all along or if you're both to blame—" Tyrian broke off.

Head held high, dusty shoulders back, Faris walked past him into the ballroom. With a quick, exasperated sigh, Tyrian ran in the opposite direction, as fast as the tray of crab puffs permitted.

In the ballroom, the dancers were drawn up into a gawking crowd just in front of the orchestra, but the musicians were not the source of interest. In a little clearing at the heart of the crowd stood the king, shouting at someone at his feet. "We ask you again. Where is Faris Nallaneen?"

If there was an answer, it did not carry beyond the crowd of costumed onlookers.

Faris crossed most of the chessboard before anyone noticed she was there. When she reached the crowd, she hesitated, wishing for Reed's court sword. She edged and elbowed her way forward on a steady chant of "Pardon me, excuse me, so very sorry."

The ring of onlookers began to yield, whispering. Faris could not help but catch a few of the words. *Witch* was one, *bastard* another. She winced. The whispers rose to a buzz and the crowd melted away before her. Faris found herself within the little clearing.

The king was scarlet with rage. Drawn up to his full height, he made a formidable figure, despite his simple costume. Faris noticed that he no longer wore the stuffed lark on his shoulder. She could not help feeling glad it was gone.

Jane lay at the king's feet, her hands pressed hard to her temples, her youthful face ashen behind the crumpled veil that was now only fabric. Reed knelt beside her, cradling her head on his shoulder. He might have made a picture of eighteenth-century gallantry, but his attention was centered on the king, not on Jane. He looked worried.

Two guards, in full scrub-brush splendor, stood close by. The guests they had elbowed aside in their haste to reach the king were still complaining. Across the clearing, the British ambassador and her husband had stepped toward the king as if to protest. Beside them, Brinker stood, his gauntleted hand protectively on Agnes's shoulder.

Faris walked out into the heart of the clearing and felt the ring of onlookers close behind her. She dared a glance back. No sign of Tyrian. Faris knelt beside Jane and spoke as calmly as she could. "Are you all right?"

Everyone stared at her. For a moment there was no sound in the great room, not a murmur, not a rustle of fabric.

Faris kept her voice prosaic. "Jane, are you feeling all right?"

Jane squinted up at Faris as if the light hurt her eyes. She kept her fingers to her forehead. Her knuckles whitened. Her voice was almost a whisper. "All my cigarettes went out at once. Sorry."

The king's voice was loud and cold. "So—you acknowledge one another."

Faris looked up. "You were looking for me?

"Guard, arrest these women."

"What are we supposed to have done?"

"Treason." He nearly spat at Jane. "She used magic against our person. No doubt you would have done so yourself, had you the aptitude. Instead you set her on. You have conspired to endanger our person."

Faris fixed the king with an icy stare. "Perhaps," she said softly, "you have confused me with one of your subjects. I am the ambassador of Galazon. As such I enjoy diplomatic immunity. So do the members of my staff."

The king's mouth twisted. "You are ambassador of nothing. Your uncle could think of no better lure to fetch you from Galazon. You might with as much right call yourself ambassador of the farmyard. At least that has the ring of truth."

All around them, whispers became murmurs.

Faris kept her voice steady. "Do you think I came to Aravis without looking at my credentials? Whatever your intentions were, my embassy is legitimate." She glanced at Brinker, who looked away.

The king laughed abruptly. "Which is more than you can say for yourself."

Faris began to feel annoyed. It was an emotion she was familiar with. As a relief from her other concerns, she welcomed it. "An old jibe from an old man. I confess I prefer it to your stale flirtations."

The king, ominously calm, stared at Faris, then at the guards. "We have given an order. Why don't you obey it?"

"Protocol, perhaps," said the British ambassador, with icy courtesy. "The Congress of Vienna established certain principles of diplomatic behavior. You cannot set aside the entire apparatus on a whim."

"Very well, if we must continue this farce, we hereby rescind this ambassador's credentials. Guards, do your duty."

As the guards started forward, Faris rose and turned to the British ambassador. She pitched her voice to carry over the rising noise of the onlookers. "Jane is a British subject. I depend upon you, your excellency, to see that she comes to no harm."

Across the chessboard, the outer door was filling up with guards. At their approach the onlookers began to melt away.

The British ambassador gave Faris a crisp nod. The nearest guards faltered before her disapproval. "Steps will be taken," she promised.

Faris found her stern expression oddly reassuring. "Reed, stay with her." Reed nodded as he helped Jane to her feet. Then, to the king, Faris called, "Where do you keep your arrested ambassadors? In the labyrinth at Sevenfold—with Menary?"

The room went still. In the sudden silence, the king stepped close to Faris, trembling with suppressed emotion. He reached out his hand and drew his fingertips very gently across her lips. When he spoke, his voice carried to the farthest corner of the ballroom. "You have a beautiful mouth, when it is closed. If you could have kept it so, we might have done very well together. But as things are, even your dowry cannot excuse you."

For a slow moment, Faris looked into his face. Then she looked past the king to Brinker. Her lips parted, but it took her a moment to find words. "So that's what the taxes were for."

This time, Brinker met her gaze. "You needed a large dowry to compensate for your reputation. Blame yourself, not me. I was simply doing my duty."

"You robbed Galazon to sell me." Her eyes blazed. "I should have killed you when I had the chance."

Brinker smiled. "Probably. Such is the peril of family sentiment. It's a luxury I seldom permit myself."

Beside Brinker, Agnes screamed and pointed. It was a fine, full, operatic scream that ended in the word *lion!* Involuntarily, everyone looked where Agnes was pointing. The silence in the ballroom became pandemonium.

The press of bodies parted for an instant and Faris was able to glimpse the refreshment room. On a linen-draped table, a lioness stood in a ruin of silver trays. Her attention was entirely on crab puffs and lobster patties.

Agnes was still screaming. Someone shoved Faris aside. She caught her balance, and saw that Reed and Jane had nearly reached the door. The king, oblivious of the crowd's panic, moved swiftly toward them. In two steps, the British ambassador had intercepted him.

The crowd closed around Faris again and she turned to

find herself face to face with Brinker. She sprang at him and caught his left vambrace. *"You!"*

Brinker flinched, twisted his arm free, and turned to flee.

Before Faris could follow, someone behind her gripped her elbow. Tyrian's breath was warm on her cheek. "This way." He pulled her back into the crowd.

Regretfully, Faris let Brinker escape. It took all her agility to keep close to Tyrian as he worked his way through the surge of frightened guests. Tyrian reached the nearest service stair and held the door for her. As she darted past him and down the steps, Faris felt a curious lightness of heart steal over her.

Despite her failure to find a way to come near the rift, despite her uncle's betrayal, and the plight of her friends, Faris was glad to be done with her masquerade. Guilt and anger and fear faded before her delight in freedom. Skirts lifted high, all decorum forgotten, Faris followed Tyrian as he made his way along a corridor to the next of his fourteen unnamed staircases.

They came to a locked door. Tyrian produced a lock pick and employed it with the ease of long practice.

"How did you persuade the lions to come to the rescue?"

Tyrian glanced up from the lock. "All I did was squash crab puffs on the floor at every turning on the way—and leave the door open." The lock clicked sweetly and he opened the door. "Thus." He smiled.

Faris smiled back. A small bubble of hilarity had lodged at the base of her throat. It made it hard for her to breathe evenly. "Impressive."

Tyrian looked extremely pleased with her, with himself, with the world in general. His eyes held hers with a steadiness that made her bold.

"Thank you for rescuing me."

"You're welcome. May I claim a reward?"

Faris felt unaccountably breathless. "Certainly."

Tyrian leaned close and murmured, "Tell me where we're going."

Faris blinked. "Out."

"Yes, but then?"

Faris felt the bubble of hilarity grow until she could hardly keep her voice steady. "I haven't the slightest idea."

Tyrian laughed. "That's lucky. As long as we don't look ahead, we should be all right." He held out his hand. "May I have this dance?"

"Of course." Faris put her hand into his. "But I think it had better be a galop."

It rained the rest of the night. Faris and Tyrian had scarcely set foot outdoors when the downpour began.

In moments, the embroidered silk of Faris's gown was plastered to her skin, just as becoming as and rather less comfortable than a burlap bag. Her hair, still pinned in a braided coronet, developed wet tendrils that managed to drip in her eyes and down her neck at the same time. When she could spare a moment to consider her knees and elbows, Faris felt the bruises blooming there, like dark roses. She owed that discomfort to the fall she'd been given by the blast from Jane's hat.

She suspected Tyrian was in no better case. His sodden evening clothes, like his soaked shoes, made squelching sounds as he moved. It was not a pleasant night to be outdoors, wet to the skin or not.

In the first hour after their escape from the castle, she and Tyrian tried to reach the British embassy. It made sense to them to seek Jane and Reed there, and safety as well. But the search parties were out too promptly. Faris and Tyrian found the streets around the embassy too full of the king's guardsmen to risk. In retreat, Tyrian led Faris into the poorest quarter of the city, where the streets were steep and narrow, sometimes connected by passages no wider than a flight of stairs.

There, where the Twelfth Night bonfires were long since burned out, the gutters long since washed clean of the ashes, she followed Tyrian. Despite their damp and disheveled finery, few denizens of the maze seemed to notice them as they passed. None challenged them.

Despite her discomfort, Faris was still possessed of that curious lightness of heart that had come to her at the start of her escape. She was free. There was joy in that. She was not alone. There was comfort in that. Beside her, Tyrian negotiated the labyrinth of the streets with utter confidence. He was following some internal compass, as sure of himself as a cat.

The rain stopped. Faris followed Tyrian, pouncing when he pounced, pausing when he paused. Even in the tangled quarter below the Esplanade, night was giving way to rising daylight. Already windows were open, already laundry was out, stirring gently on lines stretched far above the slick paving stones. There was not much traffic yet. The city was never quiet, but the early morning brought Aravis as close to silence as it ever came.

Faris felt nearly safe, until the sound of marching feet came from beyond the corner ahead. Without slackening stride, Tyrian glanced back. There was enough light to show Faris his grim expression. They both knew their pursuers could not be far behind them now. They had blundered between two search parties.

Faris searched the empty street as she ran headlong after Tyrian. Doors, gates, windows—all barred—nothing of use to them.

Then she saw the locked iron gate at the entrance to one of the narrow passages that connected street to street. It was a very simple lock. Tyrian saw it at the same moment she did. Without a word exchanged, they crossed to it together.

While she waited for him to pick the lock, she noticed the street sign set into the wall next to the gate. *World's End Close.*

Faris touched Tyrian's sleeve. "You told me once that you would follow me to the world's end," she murmured. "Here's your chance."

Tyrian read the sign and smiled angelically. "Come. I've often wondered what it looks like."

After the half-light of early morning, World's End Close was dark. It smelled wet and old and dirty. It was just as cold as the streets outside, but seemed warmer, since it was out of the wind. Underfoot, the worn stone passage was treacherous, running first shallowly up, then steeply down, deep into the hill.

As the descent continued, the passage grew steeper yet, then gave way to crooked steps. Faris kept her hand on Tyrian's sleeve. He led her down the steps unerringly. Once she stumbled and he put his arm around her waist. She caught her breath and her balance at the same time.

Tyrian released her and went on. Faris put her hand firmly back on his sleeve and felt her face and throat grow hot. She was thankful for the darkness.

They stopped to listen, to strain their eyes after a hint of light that would tell them they were moving anywhere but into the heart of the earth. Faris found herself thinking of Hilarion, alone in the darkness beneath his house. "I hope it doesn't go down too much farther," she whispered. "We must be nearly to the three-headed hound by now."

"Listen."

In the distance Faris caught a sound that made her think of the summer wind in the treetops at Galazon Chase: the sound of rushing water. "A waterfall?"

"Not that. Footsteps. Someone is following us."

"Yes, an army of the king's guard." Faris listened intently. He was right. One set of footsteps was coming slowly after them, not far off.

When the steps were only ten feet away, they stopped. A man asked, "Are you two going to stop there?"

Faris wished devoutly for a light. As if in answer to her thought, the newcomer flicked open the shield on a dark lantern. The light it cast showed her the man who carried it. He was small and balding, neither bearded nor clean-shaven, but something untidy in between. He had dark, close-set eyes, bright with interest. His clothes were worn but fairly clean. He carried a pistol pointed at the floor. He studied Faris and Tyrian as closely as they regarded him. If he noticed the pistol in Tyrian's hand, he gave no sign.

After a long moment of silent scrutiny, the man spoke again. "Are you deaf?"

Faris looked at Tyrian. Expressionless, he watched the man with the lantern and the gun. "We're wet," he said finally. "Why aren't you?"

"I'm the Doorman, that's why not. And who might you be, pushing past me to come in here and drip all over the floor, asking me questions?"

"We didn't mean to be impolite. I didn't see you when we came in. Where were you?"

"No, but I saw you, young lady. And I saw your way with a lock, young sir. You opened the door so quick I thought you had a key. But if you had a key, and knew your way, why show no light? Why tiptoe along whispering? And here am I, still wondering." He leveled his pistol at Faris. "You should explain yourselves. And you, young sir, should not point that gun of yours at me."

"It's not polite to point," Faris said gently to Tyrian. He lowered his weapon but made no move to put it away. Faris smiled at the Doorman. "I'm sorry if we startled you. We've lost our way. Can you tell us where we are?"

"You read the sign. I heard you." The Doorman smiled faintly back at her as he lowered his pistol. "It must have been a bonny mad party."

"It was," Faris murmured ruefully. "In its own way, it was."

"Speak up. Tell me who you are or I'll send you back to it. Ah. I thought you wouldn't like that idea."

Tyrian shrugged. "The lady is incognita, and I am unimportant."

The Doorman's smile broadened. Very softly, he began to hum, then half sang, half chanted, *"With a knight of ghosts and shadows, I summoned am to tourney—"*

Faris, on an impulse she did not pause to examine, joined in. "—*Ten leagues beyond the wide world's end; methinks it is no journey.*"

The Doorman beamed. "I like your manners, young lady. I'll let you choose. That's something I seldom do. Will you turn back? Or will you visit us instead?"

"How can I choose where I want to go when I don't know where I am?"

"Why, you seemed such a clever young lady, I thought you must have guessed. You're ten leagues beyond the wide world's end." By the light of his shaded lantern, the Doorman started down the passage. "Come along. You'll be safe with us."

For an instant, Faris hesitated. Beside her, Tyrian was motionless, almost rigid with suspicion. "Do you think they've stopped searching for us yet?"

Tyrian let out a long breath. "No."

"Do you think we should go back?"

After a long pause, Tyrian said reluctantly, "No."

"Do you think we can stay here?"

Tyrian sighed. "Is this what they taught you at that college of yours?"

Faris kept her hand on his sleeve as they set off after the Doorman's bobbing lantern. "More or less."

The Doorman led them through branching passages. Faris hoped they didn't have ten more leagues ahead of them. She and Tyrian were hungry and footsore. Her wet skirts were heavy, and she couldn't seem to stop shivering.

As they walked, the sound of falling water grew louder and louder, until their passage met another at right angles. There the Doorman stood for a long moment, watching the water rushing past, not down a waterfall, but down a flight of steps. Faris glimpsed a handrail on the far side of the torrent. Though stained and discolored, it seemed to her very like the carved balustrade of the castle's white icing staircase.

The Doorman noticed her interest with approval. He

raised his voice to carry over the noise of the racing water. "It's the overflow. Too much rain these past weeks. They've had to open the gates of one of the cisterns above us." Holding his lantern high, he waded out into the torrent. "Watch your step."

Faris watched him, aghast. Beside her, Tyrian walked into the water and reached back to offer her his hand. "There's one consolation. We can't get any wetter."

Stepping carefully after him into the racing water, Faris gasped and winced at the chill. "Colder. We can always get colder."

Already far ahead, the Doorman paused to urge them on. He waved his lantern and called but the rushing water drowned his words.

The steps were steep and very slippery. The icy water shoved at Faris's legs. She set her jaw and shoved back. Her feet began to grow numb. She knew Tyrian was still leading her but she could no longer feel his hand grasping hers. She wished she could reach the stone balustrade. It would be nice to be able to brace herself against it.

The next step was chipped away. Her foot came down on nothing and she lost her balance. Her wet silk skirts hobbled her and she fell, pulling Tyrian with her.

Her last coherent thought, as the current took her completely, was of Hilarion.

15

A Host of Furious Fancies

❧ FARIS WOKE ACHING. She was lying on something hard and flat and cold. With an effort, she put her hand to her breast. The glass key was still there. She was barefoot, her hair unpinned, her gloves gone, her Smoke gown dried into a stiffened ruin.

It took her some time to understand that the light in the room came from silver candelabra. There were two, set at her head and feet. She pushed herself up to look around. The hard surface was the sleek mahogany of a dining room table, long and broad and gleaming with care. The low barrier all around her was chairs pushed in beneath the table. The chairs were polished as carefully as the candelabra and the table top.

The ceiling overhead was too high to give back any candlelight. The walls were as windowless and drab as the walls of a tunnel. The door was unremarkable. The rest of the room was empty. The floor was covered with mud, long dried, cracked, and curled with age. Only the path to the door showed any sign of disturbance. In the rest of the room, mud might have been put there as pavement when Noah's flood receded.

Faris slid down from the table. For a moment the room darkened, and she felt her knees catch and jerk treacherously. She clutched the edge of the table. After a moment, her vision cleared. She hated the crackle of dried mud under her bare feet as she crossed gingerly to try the door.

Locked. Reluctantly, she picked her way back to the table. The chairs looked uncomfortable and she disliked the idea of disturbing more dried mud by moving them. She sat cross-legged on the table top, bare feet tucked carefully under the hem of her battered skirts to warm them.

Faris touched the bodice of her gown again and felt the glass key safe there. Somewhat comforted, she settled down to consider the candelabra.

Suppose the candles had been new when the candelabra were set down beside her. Then she had been there for hours. Yet there was nothing to prove they had been new, nor that they had been there as long as she had. Could she be certain someone would come for her before the light failed? To be prudent, Faris put out all the candles but one, and resolved to light them each in turn for as long as they lasted. It meant she must not sleep for fear the candle might gutter and go out, but sleep had never seemed farther from her.

Faris felt dreadful. She was thirsty and hungry and her head ached. Her scalp burned. The meal she'd had before dressing for the ball seemed a hundred years away. Her elbows and knees were bruised from her night's adventures and she felt stiff in every limb, worse even than sleeping on mahogany could account for.

Her hair had been unpinned and combed, she realized. She examined the surface of the table. Its sheen was unmarred. Her hair and clothes had dried—but not there. That single fact made her feel worse than all the rest together.

She considered shouting. If Tyrian were close enough to hear her shout through a locked door, he was probably close enough to be curious about a locked door without a shout. And anyone else, anyone who might be concerned enough about her waking to leave two full candelabra burning, might be close enough to hear a shout too. She was reluctant to attract that kind of attention.

Faris watched the wax melt down the candle and thought of the books she had read at Greenlaw, tales of the Great Shout, which could open every lock in a kingdom. Jane had tried it with no success one summer afternoon, and had bullied Faris into trying, too. Faris had no more aptitude for the Great Shout than for any other kind of intentional magic. She seemed capable only of accidental magic, the kind that changed matters for the worse.

Perception, Hilarion had told her, and will. Faris stared pensively at the door latch. She perceived the door was locked. *Unlock,* she thought. *Open. Let me OUT. I don't like this place. UNLOCK!*

The latch moved. Faris felt her heart jerk against her ribs. The door swung slowly inward. Then Faris saw the hand on the other side of the latch and looked up to see a slim young man watching her.

"Oh, excellent. You're awake." Istvan Graelent stepped into the room so gracefully that his boots did not make a sound on the cracked mud. He had changed out of his evening attire into plain clothing, cheaply made, save for his spotless white linen shirt and his boots, which had been good once, though much mended now. "I hope you slept well."

Faris stared at him as she considered asking questions: *Where is Tyrian? Where am I? Why MUD?*

Instead she said, warily, "Good morning. I assume it is still morning?"

Graelent smiled at her and set about relighting all the candles. "Morning again, I'm afraid. It is seven o'clock. Unfashionably early, but I thought you might like breakfast." He held out his hand to Faris. "Would you?"

Faris hesitated, then put her hand in his and slid down from the table. "If you let your guests sleep in your banquet chamber, I suppose you must serve breakfast in the dormitory."

He handed one candelabrum to her and took the other himself. "In fact, I do. You grasped our mad methods with ease; I commend you. You'll do well here."

"Here," repeated Faris. She did not follow his step toward the door, but he did not release her hand. Instead, as he turned back, she met his look of inquiry with one of her own. "Where is that?"

"Ten leagues beyond the wide world's end, your grace. Methinks it is no journey."

"Thank you for troubling to get my title right this time."

His smile was piratical, entirely charming. "When I called

you *your majesty*, it was by design, not by mistake. And we Monarchists intend to call you so again."

Breakfast was not served in a dormitory, but in a bed chamber. In the matter of doors and walls and windows, it was a room much like the one in which she'd wakened. A carpet, very like the one in the library at Galazon, had been put down in the center of the chamber, despite the dried mud. There was a four-poster bed, as magnificent in its way as the carpet, a washstand, a desk piled high with books and papers, and a table, set for two. Graelent took her candelabrum and put it beside his on the table.

Faris eyed the four-poster mistrustfully. "This is the first single bed dormitory I have ever seen."

Istvan Graelent seated her at the table and took the chair opposite. "I apologize for letting you spend the night in the dining room. You did not seem to notice the inconvenience. It took time to prepare this bedroom for you." He served her fresh rolls and black coffee, then helped himself. "A few of my papers are still here. I hope you don't object."

Faris drank coffee. It was strong and magnificently hot. The warmth was so welcome she had to close her eyes to conceal her emotion. "Where is Tyrian?" she asked when she could speak again.

Graelent looked interested. "Tyrian? Who is Tyrian?"

"My companion."

"Ah." Graelent sipped his coffee. "We sent him back."

Faris tore her roll in half and looked at the pieces. It was beautiful pastry, drawn from the oven so recently it still held a little curl of steam. But was it safe to eat? She thought of the food in the books at Greenlaw. Pomegranates, for example. Well, if she didn't eat something, she wouldn't be able to leave. Her legs wouldn't take her far in her present state. She ate the roll in four bites.

Graelent gave her another. "He seemed anxious to return to your friends. Perhaps he wished to enlist some reinforcements. A burning spear, a horse of air. That sort of thing."

Faris finished the second roll and drank more coffee. "When did he leave?"

Graelent refilled her cup. "As soon as he saw that you were safe here with us. Another roll?"

Faris nodded. Left to his own devices, Tyrian would have stayed with her until she woke. Only at her order, perhaps not even then, would he have left her. So he was either a prisoner, as she was in this well-furnished tomb, or he was dead. Faris deliberated as she finished her breakfast. If he was a prisoner, she would simply have to find and free him. If he was dead— Faris closed her eyes again.

"You're a restful young lady. Are you always so silent?"

Faris looked at Graelent a long time before she answered. He was young and seemed intelligent. He had a pleasing voice, a handsome face, and his cheer was apparently boundless. It was a great pity his ethics did not match his looks. Finally, she said, "No, almost never. But just now I have nothing to say."

"I see." Graelent contemplated the crumbs that were all that remained of the pastry. "Would you like me to send for more rolls?"

Faris shook her head. "Where would you send? Aren't we ten leagues beyond the nearest bakery?"

"There is a shorter way. I could send the Doorman. He'd fetch us more if you wished. I believe he's taken a fancy to you. He doesn't rescue just anyone, you know."

"Yes, he said he liked my manners."

"He's very impertinent, but very useful."

"Is he your follower?"

Graelent smiled. "One of them. The Doorman is my personal henchman. There are others. But the Doorman is the flower of them all. Isn't there anything else I can send him for, even if you don't want another roll?"

"I would like my shoes back, please."

"By all means." Graelent brought her slippers to her from across the room. "They are finally dry, although I fear they will never be quite as supple as they once were. Your gloves were ruined, I'm afraid."

Graelent knelt to help her put the stiffened slippers on. His hands were very warm on her cold skin. Then he brought her a robe of black wool trimmed with persian lamb, and held it for her to put on. Despite Faris's height, it was too long for her. When she pulled it on over her gown, more than four inches of hem were left to brush along the floor. Behind her, Graelent lifted her hair free of the robe's fleecy collar. Faris felt his warm touch at the nape of her neck and could not suppress a shiver.

"You have already learned the penalty we pay to live here. Winter and summer, the temperature never varies. It is pleasant enough in the summer, but in the winter, unfortunately, we are never quite warm. Until now. Allow me to quote from the English play—" Graelent's breath stirred her hair. *"Now is the winter of our discontent made glorious summer . . ."*

Faris turned to look at him over her shoulder. As she did, he kissed her.

For a moment, Faris was too astonished to move. Then she pulled away. Graelent let her go. With a sweep of her robe, she stalked to the door.

Even as she pulled away from him, she recognized something in herself that she despised. Though the word had not yet been spoken between them, she knew she was his prisoner. She knew that he had lied to her. Yet he did not disgust her. She had liked that kiss. Had her feeling for Tyrian melted something inside her? Was she to be attracted to every man she met? She was disgusted with herself. As she walked to the door, she wiped her mouth hard with the back of her hand.

Graelent reached the door as she did and held the door shut. "I beg your pardon, your grace." His rich voice had gone tenor with embarrassment.

"Let me pass." Faris's voice trembled.

"If we shadows have offended—" Graelent looked mortified.

"I most sincerely beg your pardon. I did not intend to force my attentions upon you."

"Let me out," said Faris, more strongly.

"Your grace, you must consider my chamber your own. And you must believe that I will never enter it again unless at your express invitation. But you cannot leave. I'll go now." He opened the door.

Faris elbowed him in the ribs. For a moment, they struggled side by side, then Graelent succeeded in shutting the door again. He leaned against it and met Faris's angry gaze. "You cannot leave." His voice was back in its own register.

Faris stepped back and drew herself up to her full height. She had to look up slightly to meet his eyes. Her voice still trembled, but now it was with suppressed rage rather than embarrassment. "I think I have been patient long enough. I think I have been the soul of reason. Now I think it's time that you explain yourself."

Graelent scowled. "I must go."

This time it was Faris's hand that prevented the door from opening. "You heard me."

Graelent fell back a step, eyes flashing indignantly. He was a splendid sight, Faris thought, and disgust with herself for that thought made her angrier still.

Before he could protest, she went fiercely on. "What have you done with Tyrian? And don't spin me any yarns about reinforcements because he never needed any in his life. Where am I? What sort of place is this? You have canopy beds and pastry right out of the oven, but look at the state of the floors. Don't you have a broom? What kind of man are you, serving me breakfast in your bed chamber and then *kissing* me? And then *apologizing*? And what do you mean, I *cannot* leave? I shall leave if I like." Faris threw the door open and stalked out.

In the passage outside, she halted. Six paces away, the Doorman stood, his pistol aimed at Faris's stomach. "I heard voices, sir. Is there anything I can do?" His close set eyes were bright, almost gloating.

Graelent slipped past Faris into the passage. Cautiously, he motioned her back across the threshold into the bed chamber. "Do you think it's necessary that he do anything, your grace?"

Faris didn't answer. She took two reluctant steps backward and nearly tripped over the hem of her robe. Graelent swung the door shut. Faris stood so close, it nearly hit her. There was a pause, then the key scraped in the lock. She was alone.

As angry as she was afraid, Faris struck the locked door with her open hand. Almost at once, the lock scraped again and the door opened.

It was the Doorman, his pistol still at the ready. "Are you sure there's nothing I can do?"

Faris did not like his avid expression. She mustered all the dignity she could and looked down her long nose at him. "Why, yes. There is. I would like some hot water, please. Enough to wash in."

The Doorman grinned. "This isn't a hotel, you know. Where do you think I'd get hot water from?"

"You managed it for the coffee."

"Piers makes the coffee, not me. I have my own work to do." He shut the door and locked it again.

"And don't be all day about it either." There was no response from the other side. Faris leaned against the door and let her breath go in a sigh.

Ten leagues beyond the wide world's end, she thought. Perhaps. But she was somewhere in Aravis still. She looked around her prison with a critical eye.

The mud on the floor and the stains low on the wall suggested that the room had been flooded long ago. Yet the water damage was minimal, for walls and floor were stone. Faris studied the masonry. She was no connoisseur of such things, but she thought it resembled the stone work she'd observed in the castle. The balustrade on the waterfall staircase had certainly looked like the one in the castle.

Faris was positive she was either in the castle or very near it, for she had, more vividly than ever, the sense that there was less to the walls around her than met the eye. Even the carpet in the center of the chamber seemed insubstantial. Its pattern of twining foliage, unlike the carpet in the library at Galazon, held constant. But the faded color of the ground behind the pattern changed subtly as she watched, shifting like the colors in a starling's feather.

"I hate it here," Faris said aloud. "I want to go home."

Then, dismayed by her own petulance, she made herself sit down at the desk. There was absolutely nothing she could do but wait. While she waited, she would at least study the papers and books Graelent had been careless enough to leave her.

Graelent's books were well-worn editions of books familiar to Faris: *Il Principe*, *Das Kapital*, and *Entwickelung des Sozialismus von der Utopie zur Wissenschaft*. The margins were filled with notations in a looping, untidy hand. Here and there, the pages were marked with rings of coffee and red wine. All the papers were written in the same untidy script, and stained more freely than the books.

Faris glanced through the papers idly at first, but her interest soon grew. Despite his clumsiness with wine and coffee, Graelent maintained scrupulous accounts. What money came in, what money went out, what he purchased, for how much, were all set forth in detail. What services he purchased and from whom (by code name only), were there as well. When she found a letter from a bank in Vienna, informing Graelent of a generous deposit to an account in Zurich, her eyes narrowed. With a sardonic smile, she studied Graelent's records.

Faris was finished with Graelent's papers when the hot water finally came. A new henchman brought it, a red-haired youth scarcely in his teens. He did not say a word to her, just put the bucket of steaming water down next to the washstand, collected the breakfast things, and left. Faris tried the door on general principle, but it was securely locked.

The next time the door opened, Graelent was there, with

the red-haired youth, who was carrying a luncheon tray. "May we come in, your grace?" Graelent asked.

"Since you ask so nicely." Faris studied the luncheon tray. "And since you come bearing gifts."

The youth put the tray on the table and went immediately to the desk, where he gathered up all the books and papers.

"That will be all, thank you, Piers."

Piers left them alone.

Graelent seated Faris at the table and took the chair opposite her. "Go ahead, please. I've already eaten."

Faris kept her eyes on him. "I ought to make you taste it for me."

Graelent smiled crookedly. "If you wish."

Faris handed him her fork. "Please do."

"With pleasure. All Piers gave me was bread and cheese." With great delicacy, Graelent sampled each of the dishes on her tray. "There. Oh, very nice. Yes. He went to some trouble over this for you." He gave her back her fork.

Faris passed first her wine glass, then her water glass. Gravely, he tasted each.

"Definitely, Piers has outdone himself. I am lucky if I have wine with my dinner." Faris watched him in silence. Her scrutiny made him laugh. "You don't seriously believe I plan to poison you?"

"There are other drugs."

"What a very unpleasant thought. Fear not, your grace, I do not intend to harm you in any way."

Faris prodded absently at the food on her plate. "Then let me go."

"I regret that I must continue to hold you here. Let me assure you, it's for your own protection. There is a warrant out for your arrest. Guards are searching the entire city for you. I do not think it would suit either of us to let you fall into the king's hands again. If my plans go well, however, one day we will be able to return quite safely to the city above." Graelent raised an eyebrow. "If you don't eat that, Piers is going to be very insulted."

"How long must I stay here?"

"I cannot say. But no matter how long or short the time, I hope you will consider yourself not my prisoner, but my guest. Meanwhile, your fish is getting cold."

"Do you often have guests here?"

"You are unique." Graelent smiled again. "You must know that."

Did he know how appealing that piratical smile was? Did he realize how a less sensible person might misinterpret the warmth in his voice? "I know it, but I'm surprised you do. How do you know there is a warrant out for my arrest?"

"I know more than Apollo." Graelent's dark eyes danced but his tone was serious. "I have my resources."

"What news of my friends, then?"

"They are hiding in the British embassy. The king has issued a proclamation. If you are restored to him, he will rescind the orders for your friends' arrest. He promises faithfully."

Eyeing Graelent, Faris decided that the food was probably safe. She sampled the fish. Although quite cold, it was excellent. "So he thinks I'm at the British embassy with them."

Graelent nodded. "And offers your friends their safety in return for yours."

"Typical. But if he really believes I've gone to ground at the embassy, why is he still searching the city for me?"

"He can't be certain. He'll take no chances. Think how embarrassing it would be if you turned up back in Galazon. He brought you here so he could have a look at you before he accepted you and your dowry."

"Did everyone know that but me?"

"We are Monarchists, after all." Graelent looked a little sheepish. "You must expect us to take an interest."

"Why call yourselves that? You believe the king should be deposed." Faris kept her tone light, hoping to sound no more than mildly interested.

"Ah, but why? Because his family deposed the true king—your father. We intend to restore you to your rightful throne."

"You needn't trouble yourself," said Faris dryly.

Graelent grew earnest. "The pleasure will be ours. Indeed, it will be the crowning achievement of many years of hardship and sacrifice. I never dreamed it would really come to this, you know. That we would have the chance to right that ancient wrong."

"Then I congratulate you. How many years of hardship has it been? I would have said you were no more than a year or two older than I am."

"I am twenty-five."

"And a recent graduate of the university."

"Political interests must take precedent, even over scholarship." He sounded defensive. "I was not merely a student, you know."

"Far from it. You are the leading figure of the Monarchist faction—and at such a tender age. How long did it take you to rise to party leadership? Your accounts go back four years. Have you always been responsible for the organization's finances?"

Graelent said cautiously, "I've always felt responsible."

Faris leaned toward him, her voice pitched low. "You originated the Monarchist party, didn't you?"

His dark eyes narrowed. "I merely thought of the name. The movement is as far-flung and as powerful as the working class itself."

"Not quite. I think the movement is confined to a few dozen of your friends. Or do you call them henchmen?" Faris sat back in her chair and studied him while she took a sip of wine. "You invented the Monarchists and you managed to persuade interested parties in the Austrian government to finance you."

Graelent looked disgusted with himself. "I should have sent Piers to fetch my papers long since."

"Very careless of you. It's extremely dull here. And I'd already read most of your books."

He smiled crookedly. "Dreadful, aren't they? But useful

to copy phrases from when it's time to write off to Vienna for a little more pocket money."

"You seem to do well out of the Austrians. Is it expensive to run your own political party?"

"Only when we need to turn out in large numbers away from the university. No trouble raising crowds there, of course, and who is to say who is a Monarchist and who isn't? But when we need a show of strength elsewhere, it can be costly. Luckily, we don't often need to."

"You surprise me."

"Well, the foreign diplomats don't have time to do much beyond their social obligations. With two or three well-scheduled demonstrations, we can impress them all at the same time. And the press are usually content to write about me. I got quite a lot of attention just for crashing the Twelfth Night ball."

Despite herself, Faris enjoyed Graelent's confiding air. He took simple pride in his accomplishments. And he did keep scrupulous records. "How thrifty of you," she prompted.

"I had to order proper evening clothes, of course, but I view that as an investment. I'll get years of wear out of them."

"Do you plan to crash a great many parties?"

"Of course not. I'll soon be able to take part properly, won't I? It's been very amusing, and even profitable in a modest way, but I would never have gone into politics if I weren't genuinely interested in public life. Mind you, private enterprise is tempting. More of a challenge. I could never dare try the Monarchist scheme in a business setting. But politics is where the easy money is."

"I think you'd be wasted anywhere else. Do you have anything in particular in mind? Or haven't you had a chance to look beyond the Monarchists yet?"

Graelent's smile unsettled her. "No need for that. In fact, I'm delighted that the Monarchists are about to come into their full flower at last. How much more worthy an investment we will seem, now that we have you."

"You don't have me, though, do you? And if you tell any-one you do, you'll get a visit from the king's guard."

It was Graelent's turn to lean forward conspiratorially. "But you see, there is one great advantage to having such a small organization, and being so careful about passwords and code names. We keep our location a secret. That means they don't know where we are."

"Nonsense. Any enterprising secret service could have infiltrated you twice over by now. The instant the king has reason to think I've fallen into your hands, you'll find out just how public your location really is."

"I'm willing to risk that. The Monarchists are about to become a very popular political party. All we have to do is keep you hidden long enough to impress the other parties with our growing support. When the coalition realigns behind us, the success of our coup will be a virtual certainty."

"There isn't going to be any coup," Faris said flatly.

"With enough money from the Austrians, there will be." Her obvious discomfiture amused Graelent. "Drink your wine and get used to the idea. You'll enjoy being a queen."

Faris spoke softly and slowly, as though she were ex-plaining something to a small child. "I am not going to be part of this."

Graelent leaned back in his chair and gazed around the room. "We're under the castle here. Did you realize? In the past, when the cisterns were left to overflow, these chambers filled with water. Now they open the sluices much sooner. We seldom get so much as a damp patch these days. A triumph of engineering."

"So that's where the mud came from."

"But if someone opened the wrong sluice, it could be seri-ous. Very serious indeed."

"If it gets too serious, I won't be much use to you, will I?"

"I hope you do not suggest that I would ever endanger a lady? No, I promise that I will do everything in my power to protect you from any peril . . ."

"But?"

"This morning you asked after someone called Tyrian."

Faris pushed her chair back abruptly. "No, don't tell me. Let me guess. You have him locked up. If I don't help you, you'll kill him."

He looked uncomfortable. "You put things so bluntly."

"But accurately."

"Don't look down your nose at me. I've tried to be friendly with you because I thought it would make matters easier for both of us. If you found it possible to be more than friendly with me, well, that would make it easier still."

Faris laughed bitterly.

"But I don't seem to appeal to you in that way, unfortunately. So I must make matters clear. I don't wish to frighten you. I don't think I could, in fact, and anyway, I usually leave that sort of thing to the Doorman. He seems to enjoy it. But you simply must understand your position."

Her fist thumped the table. "No, you must understand yours. You talk about organizing a coup d'etat as if you were about to order a pair of shoes. Stop giving yourself airs. Admit the Monarchists exist only to dupe the Austrians. Or join a real political party, if you're so intent on your career."

Graelent's eyes hardened. "Don't shout at me. You'll have the Doorman in here, and I doubt you'd enjoy that."

"I am not shouting!"

He held his finger to his lips. When she subsided, he continued. "You don't have a choice. The Monarchists will restore you to your rightful throne whether you assist us or not. Do you understand? But if you do assist us, you have my promise that Tyrian goes unharmed. And if you don't—" He broke off and glanced at the signs of past flooding. "I'll let you think it over. Next time I ask, answer carefully."

Faris spent the rest of that day watching wax melt down the candles. Piers brought her evening meal and cleared away the tray afterward. When the last candle went out, there was nothing left to do but shiver, so she wrapped herself snugly up in the heart of the canopy bed.

Faris dreamed.

She was at Greenlaw, in St. Margaret's Chapel, where the air was full of time and silence. She was kneeling. The stones beneath her were cold even through the skirts of her Smoke dress. Her feet were starting to tingle, so she stopped trying to pray and stood up slowly.

There was a firm footstep behind her. She turned and saw Jane, drawn with worry, dressed for a ride, and wearing her borrowed boots. "Where have you been?" Faris asked.

"Finally." Jane looked relieved. "I thought you'd never go to sleep. Are you all right?"

"I'm fine. What's the matter?"

"You'll remember in a moment." Jane took Faris by the hand and led her out of the chapel. "Come along and show me where you are."

They went up steps for a long time, but they were not climbing the steps to the spire above Greenlaw. They were on a staircase of white stone, its spiral as tightly furled as a unicorn's horn. As she climbed, Faris remembered.

"Your hat exploded."

"Something came out of the rift. I've no notion what. It overbalanced me and I lost all my spells at once." Jane sounded cross. "Then it drifted on past and wandered off, lonely as a cloud, no doubt."

"Are *you* all right?"

"I'm fine now. So is Reed. We've been growing fat on the embassy cuisine. How is Tyrian?"

"I don't know. They claim they've locked him up. I haven't had a chance to look for him yet."

"I'll see what I can do when I'm finished here."

The white staircase brought them up into morning, to a rooftop covered with shattered brick and stone that gave them a panoramic view of Paris.

Faris pointed. "There's the Tour Eiffel."

"Ugly thing. Keep climbing."

Faris realized that the steps had turned from white stone to white glass. She climbed on, careful not to lose her footing on the smooth surface. When she looked up again, the city below was not Paris, but Aravis. "I can see our hotel from here," she observed happily.

"I should think so. From up here, we ought to be able to see Sevastopol. Now show me where you are so we can come rescue you."

Faris looked down. The steps had turned to smoky green glass, the color of sunlight in seawater. "Graelent told me the truth for once. I'm down there. The city cisterns. A triumph of engineering."

Jane said something but Faris wasn't listening. She was looking upward, where the steps were made of clear glass. No, Faris realized, not glass. Ice. Very treacherous footing. Yet if she could climb that high, perhaps she could see Galazon. Even from far off, Galazon would be a welcome sight.

At the thought, she could smell dry oak leaves and freshly turned earth. The wind blew her hair into her eyes. She tried to brush it away and failed. She tossed her head, rubbed her eyes, and woke.

Faris was back in the canopy bed, tangled in blankets. For a moment, her eyes stung with tears of disappointment. She blinked stupidly into the darkness. As she woke more fully, she realized what had happened.

Jane had found a way to speak with her and she'd wasted it sightseeing. But if she'd done it once—Faris closed her eyes and tried to will herself back to sleep. She drew a deep breath and shifted in her cocoon of blankets. The mattress rustled beneath her weight. Faris let her breath out slowly.

And went rigid, eyes wide open, straining to see in the dark. There had been another rustle. And she hadn't made it.

Someone—or something—was sitting at the foot of her bed.

Faris made herself breathe. That discipline rewarded her. For as she drew an unsteady shallow breath, she caught a trace of something she recognized, a scent compounded of coffee and smoke and a spice she didn't know. "Tyrian?"

"Yes?" He sounded calm. Of course.

She sat up, tearing impatiently at the blankets. "Are you all right?"

"Yes. Are you?"

The last blanket gave way and she threw herself toward the foot of the bed. Her arms found him and pulled him down. He uttered a soft grunt of surprise. They fell off the bed together, Faris on top. She felt his jaw and cheek rough under her palm and tried to kiss him. Since he was trying to get up, her forehead hit his nose. He made another soft sound that might have been either surprise or pain. She tried again to kiss him and this time she succeeded.

16

Snow Out of Season

IT DID NOT immediately occur to Faris that she had embarrassed them both. At the time, it seemed perfectly natural that she should kiss Tyrian and that he should require a moment to respond.

At the time, she did not spare a thought for Tyrian's situation, lying on the floor under her entire weight. At the time, she did not spare a thought for anything beyond her immediate senses. She couldn't see. There was not much to hear. But touch, taste, and smell engaged her entirely.

After what seemed to Faris all too short a space, Tyrian broke the kiss. He sounded as calm as ever, even a little apologetic. "I didn't mean to startle you."

It took a moment for Faris to gather her wits, so completely had her senses disarranged them. A moment, an endless moment, in which she was so close to him that his breath stirred her hair, and his nearness stirred her entire body.

A moment, and then his careful civility made Faris understand what she had done. Desperate suddenly to release him, she retreated to the bed and huddled in the blankets, mute. Her embarrassment threatened to strangle her.

Tyrian broke the silence, his tone unchanged. "I think I've found the warden's stair."

Thoroughly distracted, Faris did not immediately absorb the significance of his words. She was quiet for so long that Tyrian asked anxiously, "They didn't find the key, did they?"

"No. I have it safe." Her voice was not quite steady. "How can you tell it's the warden's stair?

"I found a door with a lock I couldn't open. If it isn't the door to the warden's stair, I'm disappointed in myself." Tyrian sounded completely matter-of-fact.

Another time, Faris might have resented the bland way he pretended nothing untoward had happened. Now, she could only feel grateful for it. She flung the blankets aside and began to hunt for her slippers by touch. With an effort, she was able to ask almost normally, "What happened to you? Where have you been?"

"I tried to catch you when you slipped on the waterfall stair. I think you must have taken a blow to the head as you fell. You went down without a struggle. Good thing your hair is so long. That's probably the only reason I caught you." Tyrian sounded grim. "By the time I had you safe, you were unconscious, and we were both half-drowned." He hesitated. When he went on, it was with his customary aplomb. "The Doorman took advantage of the situation. He summoned enough help to lock me up. It took me some time to repay him. When I finally did, I took his keys away from him for good measure."

Faris located her slippers and put them on. Thankful for the capacious woolen robe, she wrapped it tightly over her crumpled dress, pushed her hair back, and rubbed her hot face. "How did you find me?"

"I worked my way along the key ring." Tyrian rose and started toward the door. "I was looking for you. It was pure chance that I discovered the warden's stair. When I found a door that neither my tools nor the Doorman's keys would open, I began to think we were finally getting somewhere."

"But how did you know I was here? Did you have to search every room by touch?" As if to punctuate her question, Faris barked her shin on a piece of furniture. Through clenched teeth, she added, "Or can you see in the dark?"

"I knew you were here as soon as I opened the door."

"Oh, really?" Faris reached him at last. "How?"

"For one thing, I could hear a sound—one I recognized from our journey by train from Pontorson to Paris."

Faris thought back, then chortled. "Such a tactful way to tell me I snore."

Tyrian was reproachful. "I'm *not* telling you that you snore. I'm taking some pains to avoid telling you anything of the kind. Let me think. No, it's more of a soft, rasping noise—" He broke off in an unsuccessful attempt to block Faris's elbow to his ribs. "For another thing—" He hesitated.

"What *else?*"

"When I've spent this long working to keep someone safe from harm, I can tell when she's asleep near me. Whether it's dark or not." His words were very soft, intensely serious. He took a step closer to her. Faris felt his breath stir her hair and flinched a little, despite herself. "Whether she snores or not," he added more lightly.

Faris managed a bitter chuckle.

"And when I promise to keep someone safe from harm," he continued, "I mean it. I think you'll understand when you're a bit older."

Faris stiffened. "Of all the patronizing rubbish. What does my age have to do with it? I understand you perfectly."

"So I thought, until a few moments ago. What do you take me for?"

Faris pulled away.

Tyrian went on, sarcastically. *"If love were the only thing, I would follow you—in rags if need be—to the world's end . . ."*

To her astonishment, she recognized the passage. Tyrian was quoting from one of Jane's three-volume novels.

His tone lightened. "If love were the only thing. But we both know it isn't. Love isn't even in the running. Let's not discuss it."

"I don't *want* to discuss it. *You're* the one who brought it up. I never said a word about—it."

Her indignation amused him. His amusement annoyed her. Thinking to alarm him, to put a stop to his laughter, she reached out for him, as if to embrace him again. But he did not seem alarmed. Instead he pulled her close, one hand tangled in her hair. And this time he returned her kiss.

For just a moment, Faris wanted to be the one to break the kiss, to be the one to say ever so calmly, "I didn't mean to startle you."

But in another moment, that thought had floated away for good. Blind in the dark, deafened by the silent thunder of her heart, Faris gave up thinking.

When he released her at last, Tyrian murmured almost spitefully, "There. Now do you believe there might be one or two things you don't understand yet?"

He had stirred her so, it took Faris a long moment to regain her composure. She had not quite succeeded when the revelation came to her—he was shaken too.

Faris paid very little attention to the route Tyrian chose from Graelent's chamber to the door he couldn't open. There was nothing to see, and thanks to Tyrian's natural bent for stealth, very little to hear. She kept her hand in his and moved as silently as she could.

Tyrian's response changed everything for Faris. She marveled at all the time she had spent examining her words and deeds, questioning her conclusions, *wondering* . . . And now everything was different. Underneath her thoughts there was a firm foundation.

If love were the only thing . . . The sarcasm belied the words. Yet Tyrian's voice held music, for her ear at least. His words came back to her, very soft, intensely serious. *When I promise to keep someone safe from harm, I mean it . . . I knew you were here as soon as I opened the door . . . Now do you believe there might be one or two things you don't understand yet?*

Faris reminded herself sternly that she should be thinking about the rift, or at least the perils that might lie waiting on the warden's stair. Instead she was mooning over Tyrian.

Her menial paramour, Brinker would call him. Faris smiled fiercely in the dark. Well, let Brinker say what he pleased about paramours. She'd had to make an idiot of herself, but it had been worth the embarrassment. She wished every idiocy she committed could have such a reward.

Let Brinker say exactly what he pleased. It wouldn't make any difference. All her life Faris had heard talk about her mother's behavior. What harm did talk do?

A cold thought touched her. Unless it made a difference to Tyrian. *Don't look ahead*, she told herself sternly.

Tyrian found the door. He put his hand over Faris's and guided her fingers to the lock. Faris produced the glass key. It fit. She turned it gingerly, afraid it might snap if the bolt were stiff. With a sound as swift and neat as a gambler cutting a deck of cards, the key turned. She withdrew it and opened the door.

Faris went first. It was the warden's stair. And she was the warden, after all. Wasn't she? She tried to conceal her apprehension. Tyrian closed the door after them.

"Lock it again?" Faris murmured.

"I think not. We might need to leave this way. And if we do, we will probably be in a hurry."

They went up stairs built in a spiral as tightly furled as a unicorn's horn. Stairs that had been lost for a long time. The stale air smelled dry and old.

Dust made the footing silent but treacherous. Within a few steps her ankles were coated with it. It was in her slippers. It made her sneeze. The thickness of the dust slowed her down when every instinct she possessed urged her to move quickly, to climb out of that neglected place at once.

After the chill of Graelent's chamber, the close atmosphere seemed very warm. The walls of the stair were some kind of roughly dressed stone, scarcely wider than Faris's shoulders. When she brushed her palm across it, the stone seemed dry and soft. She realized that the dust was there too, that it must be clinging to every surface. She shuddered as she rubbed her hands on her skirt.

Faris felt her way into the darkness. It grew warmer as she climbed, so much warmer that she opened the woolen robe. Sweat prickled her scalp and ran down her neck. The air grew acrid. It seemed to thicken around her. Tyrian touched her wrist and she paused. Her apprehension grew.

Something was very wrong. Tyrian's breathing was heavy, broken. "Smoke," he managed.

It was impossible to see. Yet in her anxiety, in the long moment while Faris put her arm around his shoulders and steadied him, something happened to her eyes, or to her mind's eye. Her exterior vision was blind, yet an interior vision showed her the stairwell opaque with smoke, and the smoke painted with every color fire possessed.

A bonfire in winter, she thought. On the heels of that random memory, instinct brought forth certainty and she knew why that neglected place had frightened her.

With perfect clarity Faris understood that on the warden's stair, time lingered. The rift had been torn long ago, yet that moment lasted still. That moment hung all around her, like the dust in the air. And the air was very hard to breathe.

Faris felt Tyrian's arm close around her waist and realized he was steadying her as much as she was steadying him. Her eyes stung. Her throat ached.

"Back," he croaked.

Faris shut her eyes and let the stair fill her mind's eye. The spiral was as tightly furled as the stair in Hilarion's house. Hilarion, warden of the west. They had climbed the warden's stair, come to a place where there was no more climbing. Nor would there be retreat, not in time to escape the smoke.

Perception and will, Faris thought. And then, *It's a hat as long as I say it's a hat.* Coughing racked her. She kept her eyes closed. No more climbing on this stair. *So climb a different stair.*

Deliberately, Faris shut out her senses and remembered Greenlaw. With loving detail she recollected the stair to the pepper-pot tower, on the way to the spire and the northern anchor. Forbidden territory, presided over by St. Michael and St. Margaret, guarding one another's backs. Forbidden territory and perhaps because of that, a place remembered so fondly and so well. Smoother walls. Broader steps, worn with time.

Time. The air was hot and thick. Faris coughed until her throat was raw. She tasted blood. Tyrian, beside her, was bent double with the effort it took to draw a breath.

Perception. Doggedly, Faris remembered the cool stone, the smooth, silvered gray stone of all Greenlaw, every stair, every tower. She coughed until her knees began to buckle.

Will. And she remembered the dizzy heights, the wheeling of the world as she had once come out of the dimness of the tower stair into the sunlight.

And the world was wheeling around Faris. Tyrian's arm was all that kept her upright on the stair as the darkness shut in again. But it was cool darkness, natural darkness, and the heat failed before a fresh breeze, strong enough to stir her hair and tug at the folds of her robe.

After many years, drafts stirred the dust imprisoned on the warden's stair. At first the dust made it almost as hard to breathe as the smoke had. Then the breeze steadied, the dust settled, and the air cleared.

Faris put her face into the hollow of Tyrian's shoulder and let herself rest there in weary silence. For a while they both drew deep, crowing lungfuls of air, clean air that smelled of Greenlaw and the sea.

"Well done," Tyrian said. His voice was cracked.

"Nothing's done. The rift is still waiting."

"We'll get there."

The steps that brought them up into early morning were the steps Faris had remembered from Greenlaw. The new stair ended with a familiar pepper-pot tower. But the tower door did not open on the heights of Greenlaw. Faris and Tyrian stepped out onto a rooftop covered with shattered brick and stone.

After so long in the dark, Faris was struck silent by the light. She blinked stupidly around as Tyrian moved past her to reconnoiter the ruins of the old throne room.

It was early morning, so early the city below had only just begun to stir. The sky in the east was bright with the coming dawn and the sparse clouds promised a fair morning. The lions ranged in the ruins around them were still asleep.

Tyrian was nearly unrecognizable, weary, unshaven, filthy. Faris found it hard to judge what was bruise and what was grime. He had lost his jacket. His shirt was torn, gray with dirt, collarless, its cuffs stiff with something suspiciously like dried blood. His wrists were likewise stained and looked painfully swollen.

Faris glanced down and discovered she was at least as dirty as he. What she had taken for dust on the stairs turned out to have been ash. Sweat had mingled with the soft gray stuff and the result daubed her like paint. She itched prodigiously.

Tyrian covered the palace door and beckoned to her. Faris left the shadow of the pepper-pot tower.

The sun had just begun to edge over the horizon and the world was changing color from moment to moment. There was light everywhere, so much light that Faris could hardly make out the pattern underfoot.

Faris lifted her eyes. If she watched the horizon, she had her bearings. If she didn't look where she was going, she knew where she had to go. She had seen the way the pattern shifted in the early light. She moved slowly, careful not to lose her footing.

Touch showed her the rift before her other senses perceived it. She felt something alter subtly beneath her feet, as though the pattern were softening. She looked down. She was in the center of a pattern set in white glass against white stone. Beneath her battered slippers, the pattern had changed. White glass had become smoky green glass, the color of sunlight in seawater. The green glass rose into yet another flight of stairs. Wearily, Faris began to climb.

When the green glass became clear glass, Faris stopped. With only reflected sunshine to betray its presence, the stair-case continued up as far as she could see. Faris stood still, eyes lifted. After her time under the castle, the warmth of the sun was welcome, the sky was a fascinating thing. Faris did not mind keeping her attention on it. All around her, she could feel the rift.

This was the moment she had dreaded all along. At last she had reached the rift. Yet she had no idea how to mend it. Whatever she had learned at Greenlaw, it had not prepared her for this.

Or perhaps it had. Faris remembered the pepper-pot tower. Perception and will, she told herself sternly.

She wished Hilarion were with her. She wished the Dean were too. And Jane, most of all.

The ward, she reminded herself. The ward that balanced Greenlaw had two anchors.

Remembering the silence of St. Margaret's chapel under Greenlaw, she thought of the cisterns and passages beneath the castle. Set the lower anchor there, in Graelent's chamber.

Faris let the rest of the structure fall into place, all the while lifting her eyes to the sky. There would be an upper an-chor when she was finished. Until then, there would be only the sky. Not the rift. She would not let her attention stray into the rift.

So far, and no farther, Faris managed to go before she heard a rustle, a small sound, one that she could not put a name to. It might have been the flounce of starched petticoats. It might have been the little sigh a dry branch made as a fire took it, twigs and leaves and all.

Faris knew she was no longer alone on the glass staircase before she turned.

Five steps below her Menary stood, looking around as though admiring the view. She no longer wore a wig. Her own blond hair fell past her shoulders, richer silk than the gray silk gown she wore, which was just the color of her eyes. "What are you doing here?" Menary asked.

Faris scowled. "What are *you* doing here?" The small sound came again. She realized she had heard the rustle of Menary's silken skirts. How long had Menary been watching?

"I've never been up this high before." Menary craned her neck to look upward. "Why did you stop here?"

"Who let you out?"

Menary's eyes were bright. "Someone knocked an extra bit of magic out of the rift for me on Twelfth Night. It overloaded every spell for miles. So I left Sevenfold and came home to see my dear father. He told me you and Jane paid a call here that night." Her small porcelain smile widened. "Do you think there's any connection?"

"Who told you about the rift?"

"I grew up here, remember? I dreamed about the rift in my cradle. It sang to me."

"How very poetical."

"I found it when I was just a little girl. I tried to show the rift to Agnes but she was afraid. She told Father and he told Grandfather. I was punished. From then on, everyone tried to keep me away. They even brought lions to guard it. But I'm not afraid of the lions. I rather like them. They respect me." Menary looked sharply at Faris. "Who told *you* about the rift?"

Faris ignored the question. "You were lucky to get away from Sevenfold. Why come here and risk being sent back?"

Menary looked around and drew a deep breath of sheer contentment. "Isn't it obvious? The power is here."

As Menary gazed out at the horizon, she seemed to absorb the morning light, to take on some of its fire. It brought color to her face and blazed in her hair. "I used to think I would share the rift with Father, but he's afraid of it. He didn't want me to come up here. He's so used to getting his way. I had to put him to sleep. I've put them all to sleep, everyone in the castle. I was in a hurry and it saved arguing. Now I think you should go to sleep too. I'm tired of explaining things."

The wind stirred Menary's hair into a wild pale aureole as she lifted her hands to the sun. So brightly did she give the light back that her fingertips were nearly transparent against the sky. After a long moment, she folded her hands and smiled seraphically up at Faris.

Faris stared back. Menary's beauty made her painfully aware of her own dishevelment, and that made her cross. "How quickly your hair grew. I suppose you must have used some kind of spell on it."

Menary's smile faded. "Why don't you go to sleep?"

"Must you talk like a six year-old? It's so tiresome."

Menary stamped her foot. "Go to sleep."

Faris stamped back. "Make me."

"I am." Menary's eyes flashed. "Oh, I'd like to kill you."

"Yes, so I gather. I dislike you, too, but I don't go around hiring assassins."

"Of course not. Father wouldn't let you."

"What does your father have to say—*oh.*" Faris remembered Brinker's perfidious arrangement with the king. "Believe it or not, I have no ambition to become your stepmother. In fact, I can't imagine a worse fate. The moment I finish here, I'm going home to Galazon."

Menary looked sly. "Finish what?"

Faris put her hands on her hips. "Well, first I thought I'd kick you downstairs."

"You're trying to close the rift, aren't you? I could feel it before. I'm sorry but I can tell you right now it isn't going to work." Menary smiled scornfully. "Don't let me distract you. Go ahead. Try."

Perception and will, Faris reminded herself. Before Menary's blazing power, she felt woefully ill-prepared. She wished for a ring or a wand or any other sort of magical artifact. Even the comforting heft of a poker. *A pointed hat sprinkled with silver stars and moons would be nice,* she thought wistfully. She could not even make impressive hand gestures. All she could do was stand, bedraggled and sullen, on the glass staircase, while she felt the rift gaping all around her.

"Tell me when you're through." Menary looked bored but the malice in her voice betrayed her interest.

The rift shifted. Faris felt the glass staircase soften a little beneath her. Green rose. The clear glass retreated five steps.

Faris sat down on a step and put her hands flat against the glass. It was cold but not slick, more like sea glass than window glass. Faris smoothed her hands across the step, gentling it as if it were alive. The staircase trembled and steadied.

Menary's voice seemed to come from a distance. The condescension in her tone was impossible to miss. "That was nice. Are you finished?"

It took an effort to see Menary, so brightly did the sun shine upon her. Faris squinted. "You did that on purpose."

"You can't close the rift. I knew you couldn't. But it's so amusing to watch you try."

"Keep watching. I was given this job for a good reason."

"Fool. You think you were the first choice? When have you ever had a thing that I haven't had before you and discarded?"

Menary's scorn struck Faris where she did not even know she was weak. "What are you talking about?"

"What do you think? If I'd wanted to be the warden of the north, I would have been the warden of the north. You only get my castoffs."

Faris hardly trusted herself to speak. "You're mistaken."

"Go ahead. Name one thing you've had before I was finished with it." Menary smiled sweetly. "I dare you."

"That's easy." Faris felt her hands curl into fists. The glass was icy against her knuckles. "Love."

"Love? *You?*" Menary's laughter was prolonged. "Oh, do you mean your blond servant? That's really very funny. Do you think I would have let you have him back if he hadn't already bored me? Oh, you're too quaint. Try again."

If love were the only thing . . . Well, it wasn't, was it? "Friendship," said Faris.

"Are you thinking of your time at Greenlaw? At Greenlaw, where I did everything there was to do before you even thought of it? At Greenlaw, where your so-called friends referred to you as the Ferret behind your back?" Menary shook her head, still chuckling. "Is that the best you can do?"

Faris was accustomed to Menary, but in her weariness she found the mockery difficult to bear. It was all true, in its way. She thought hard before she spoke again. "Responsibility," she said at last.

Menary looked puzzled. After a moment, her brow cleared, and her voice grew still more patronizing. "I've tried everything, dear. I'm bored with all of it."

It was finally Faris's turn to be amused. "You don't know what I'm talking about, do you? Whatever you have, you don't have Galazon. You'll never have anything like it, and you wouldn't know how to take care of it if you did. You have only yourself."

Menary's laugh was golden. "I have the rift."

"Do you? Are you sure?" Faris raised an eyebrow and pressed her palms flat on the step. The next wind that lifted Menary's wild mane of hair did not release it. "Are you quite sure?"

Menary's eyes widened. She raised first her hands and then her voice. "Stop!" Still her hair blazed above her like a candle flame. She struggled to escape.

The glass under Faris's hands grew so cold her fingers burned. *Perception and will.* She could feel the rift straining toward Menary's long hair, a blind hunger, like the moth for the flame. *Take it back then.*

Menary cried out as the illusion of long blond hair left her. More beautiful than before, her own hair as fine and short as a child's, she glared at Faris. "Just try that again." Her tone was ugly. "Go on, try. You can't do anything to me. You can only send back the power I took for myself."

Faris did not waste breath on a reply. Into the rift she sent the power Menary had used to satisfy her great vanity. She felt the rift respond subtly, as if eager to reclaim its power.

Had it been anyone else, anyone less tangled in the forces of the rift, Faris's sending would have had little effect. Even so, there was not much to see.

Menary did not scream. She did not lift a hand. She simply went out, as completely as a candle flame. The rift flinched, then gaped for more.

Faris found herself alone on the glass staircase. "You took more power than you knew, perhaps," she whispered into the emptiness.

She could still feel the rift all around her. Sending Menary's power back should have aided the balance. Yet her refusal to surrender the power had sent Menary into the rift along with it. That had upset the balance further. She was keenly aware of the eagerness in the rift. Menary had been best at taking. Perhaps nothing had ever been given to the rift before.

Faris pressed her grimy fingers against the cold glass. What else belonged in the rift? She groped hastily after shreds of the rift's influence.

The mist that wreathed the heights of the castle went in easily. The phantom walls that lingered from the days before the rift was torn went in. The damage done to the fabric of the castle took a little longer. Faris worked until every drifting pattern in the castle, from the floor of the ruined throne room to the oriental rugs, surrendered something to the rift. The balance shifted subtly.

Everything that belonged to the rift was in it. Yet the rift still gaped. In desperation, Faris offered it the memory of her first sight of Aravis, crowned with the ruined heights of the castle, seen from a distance.

The rift accepted something more than mere recollection. Faris kept her memory but once the rift seized it, the memory seemed to diminish. She could no longer envision that familiar silhouette of dragon's spine ridge for herself. She still knew what it looked like, but only as if someone had told her of it. The first-hand knowledge was gone.

The rift still shifted, but much more slowly. As it slowed, the white light grew stronger. There was light everywhere.

If it couldn't be mended, perhaps it could be plugged. Faris deliberated for a moment, then set herself to choke the rift with the city of Aravis, narrow noisy streets lit here and there with Twelfth Night bonfires. She offered the Spanish ambassador's fox hunt, and felt the pleasure she had taken in riding grow stale and remote. She gave her memory of the countryside, the gardens at Sevenfold, the quays at Shene.

She surrendered her ride in the Minerva limousine, her journey on the Orient-Express, and her bruising hours in the diligence with Jane. Sticky dark cake, feathery pastry crumbs, and hot strong coffee were given up, along with the silken fire of cognac.

She gave up the taste of tea brewed far too long—and with relief discovered that no more of Greenlaw College would go into the rift. The wards held steady. She realized no more than stewed tea was hers to bestow. Paris too, safe in Hilarion's wardency, was proof against her efforts to fill the rift.

Faris gave the rift all she could, as quickly as she could, as though she were packing in great haste for a long journey. It took all she had to offer, and took it greedily. She gave up memory and experience as freely as they occurred to her, until the white light dazzled her and she could no longer sense the movement of the rift.

Frowning with effort, scarcely daring to breathe, Faris paused. The instant she did, she felt the white light around her start to splinter into colors. The rift shifted, slowly but remorselessly.

Time. How long had it taken her to send Menary into the rift, and most of her own experience after? Faris had no idea. She might have been on the glass staircase for hours by now. At this rate, she could spend the rest of her life there and not mend the rift.

Faris thought hard. Perception came first, like a cold hand

over her heart. She shuddered, wondering how she would ever muster the will.

"Responsibility," she told herself aloud. She tried to laugh and flinched at the sound she made.

And then she let Galazon, with its high meadows and its deep forests, its frozen rivers and its snow-covered hills, go gently into the rift.

For Faris, the grass in the meadows bleached dry. The wind that stirred the forests fell still. The rivers sank into mud and the hills lay naked in the wind. She felt Galazon become any land, any real estate, any dirt to be bartered, and she caught her breath at the pain.

The balance steadied. The hunger eased. There was a moment of equilibrium that made her heart jump crazily. Then the rift trembled again.

Faris looked down at her hands. The glass they rested on was no longer green but clear, clear and cold. So cold.

"Responsibility." This time she was able to laugh a little, at herself, at the hopes she'd had, at the mere sound of the word. The meaningless word.

Now, she supposed, it was her responsibility to go back and confess her failure. Tell anyone who cared. And then? Go back to Galazon and try to bear existence there? The thought made her stomach twist. Go? *Yes*—anywhere but Galazon. Exile on a ship that never came to land before exile in Galazon.

Or go on up the stair? No explanations. No apologies. No farewells. Just go into the rift.

That should be simple enough. After all, it was her responsibility.

And it wasn't death, or even exile, for she could not die, any more than Hilarion could, and Galazon was already there, waiting for her, within the rift. Yet even so, she was unwilling.

Faris examined her unwillingness. It had to do with a promise, but she couldn't remember making one. She frowned at her hands. There was something she had to do, before she stepped into the rift and pulled it tight around her like a blanket. Something she had promised to do.

The glass key. That was it. She had promised to send the key back to Hilarion. Her hands clumsy with cold, she fumbled at the chain until she pulled the key free. She could leave it where Tyrian would be sure to find it. Because Tyrian would certainly come to look for her. Would he be able to see her, once she was in the rift? Probably not. No matter, as long as she could see him. But could she?

Suddenly it became very important to Faris that she see Tyrian. It was not safe to leave the key on the stair. Stiffly, she rose. She would give it to him herself and see him once more and say—she couldn't think what she'd say. But he would know precisely what she meant. That was the best thing about Tyrian, she decided. He knew her duty as well as she did herself. Or better. He had told her again and again not to look ahead. It was almost as though he had known. The rift was all that lay ahead for her.

She wondered if she ought to have let the rift have her time with Tyrian. But if Galazon itself was not enough, how could her feeling for Tyrian, muddled and silly as it no doubt was, make any difference? And she had given up so much, so reluctantly—*no*. Enough. For now she would keep what little was left her.

Slowly, careful of her footing on the treacherous stair, Faris descended. The steps turned from clear ice to seawater green. Faris looked around.

The sky, so clear at daybreak, was overcast. To the north the clouds were as dark as if day had not yet come. The steps turned from green to white, and Faris had to slow further, for a north wind was pulling at her clothes and pushing her hair into her face.

She reached the ground safely. As she took a step away from the stair, the pattern of white glass on white stone faded. All around her lay shattered brick and stone.

A flight of geese came over, and their high wild song made Faris remember how homesick she had been at Greenlaw, when that sound had reminded her of Galazon. Her memory of homesickness jarred against the numbness that was all that the rift had left her of Galazon.

The lions were awake. In the flat open space that had once been the throne room, they stirred only a little from where they had slept, but they watched with interest. Graelent, Piers and three more henchmen were sitting in a neat row, hands on their heads, before the pepper-pot tower. They regarded the lions anxiously.

Tyrian stood over Graelent and the others, pistol in hand. Until he noticed Faris, he looked exhausted but utterly self-possessed. She saw his expression darken with alarm as she approached. In unison, they asked one another, "What happened?"

Before either could answer, the door to the palace opened. Out spilled half a dozen armed scrub-brush guards, the king with them. Close on his heels was Agnes. A little behind her came Brinker, still yawning.

Graelent called to Faris. "Your majesty! You've returned for us!" Faris scarcely heard him.

At the sight of the pepper-pot tower and the intruders, the guards raised their weapons. The north wind rose, whirling dust everywhere. The king rubbed his eyes. "That proves the rift is gaping anew. This must be Menary's doing. Find the child at once. *At once.* She's out here somewhere. Stop her before she destroys us all."

Agnes, clinging to his sleeve, protested, "She's your daughter. You can't send armed men to capture your own daughter."

Brinker replied, "Unfortunately, at the moment, armed men are all he has."

At the sight of Faris, the king shouted, "Forget Menary. Here's the one widening the rift. Guards! Seize her!"

In crisp unison, the guards brought their weapons to bear.

Graelent's henchmen, including Piers, called out to the guards, "Don't shoot. Don't shoot us." Graelent spared neither the guards nor his henchmen so much as a glance. Instead, he rose and came toward Faris, hands out to her in welcome.

Tyrian blocked his path but Graelent did not seem to notice. He confronted Faris, eyes blazing with excitement. "Your majesty—you've come at the perfect time. *There is a tide in the affairs of men, which, taken at the flood, leads on to fortune.* I quote from the English play."

Faris ignored Graelent. She had to clear her throat twice before she could speak loudly enough to be sure Tyrian heard her over the rising wind. "Tell Hilarion I'm sorry."

Frowning, Tyrian asked again, "What happened?"

Behind him Graelent called urgently, "We are almost evenly matched with the usurper's party. We won't have another chance like this. Come, your majesty. Shall we behold the stars at mortal wars?"

"I failed. I'm so sorry." She put the key into Tyrian's hand and started back toward the rift. She could feel it waiting for her.

Tyrian turned to follow her.

"The witch flees," the king called to his guards. "Stop her! Stop her before she destroys us all, or you are as guilty as she."

Graelent persisted. "Very well. You do not answer. To the wilderness we wander. Come away, your majesty. Down the stairs, your majesty—wait—no—*down* the stairs."

"Halt, Faris Nallaneen," the king roared. "Halt or we bid the soldiers shoot."

Graelent cried, "You dare not fire on our rightful queen."

Faris scarcely heard them. Dimly, she was aware that Tyrian was just behind her. The world had dwindled until only the hunger of the rift was left. There was nothing else before her. The task was clear. The rift.

From a great distance, Faris could make out the voices, faint but clear:

"Ready, aim—"

"For god's sake, no!" That couldn't be Brinker, though it sounded amazingly like him.

"Don't shoot—I surrender!" That was Graelent, face down on the ground, from the muffled sound of it.

Agnes screamed like a doll's teakettle coming to a boil.

What was now unmistakably Brinker's voice, ragged with emotion. "For god's sake, hold your fire!"

"*Fire!*"

Obedience was not perfect, even among the king's guard. Most of the shots went high, by accident or design.

The crash of the guns came from far away. It was no louder than the slam of a door. Faris scarcely noticed it. But Tyrian brought her down in a flying tackle and the world came back with a jolt as she hit her chin on the ground and bit her tongue.

The fall, beneath Tyrian's full weight, shocked her. For a moment she lay still, trying to understand what had happened. Save for her bitten tongue and bruised chin, she felt no pain. She felt nothing at all. Only she could not move her legs. Why was that?

Gasping, she had pushed herself up on scraped elbows before she identified the scalding wetness soaking through her clothes. Then she understood. She was quite unhurt. Tyrian sprawled across her, bleeding.

His eyes were open. When she bent over him, she saw her worst fears confirmed in his expression. He said, as best he could on a ragged breath, "I won't go."

"No, don't go. You can't go." She found the glass key in his left hand. The slender stem had broken. "You have to take the key back to Hilarion for me. I promised."

He did not manage to smile, but one corner of his mouth lifted. "So did I." He looked past her at the sky. "It's going to snow." The words took his last strength.

When Faris pressed his fingers around the broken key, his hand was still. His eyes were empty. When she called his name, he did not respond.

Another flight of geese came over, and another. When Faris lifted her head to look, the north wind had grown much stronger. She pushed her tangled hair back.

The wind had driven the king, Brinker, Agnes, Graelent, and all to shelter. Even the lions had retreated. Faris was glad to be alone. She could feel the rift waiting for her still. A moment, no longer, and then she would go. There really was nothing but the rift before her now.

She felt no pain. Even sorrow was muted by the nearness of the rift. Only the wind touched her. So welcome a scourge, the north wind. She would linger in it a little before she left.

Out of the north she saw skein after skein of the great birds coming. Their call stirred her heart. As she watched, the first flakes of snow began to fall. She welcomed the sting of them on her face. It was just a little pain, but it was something. A token to go with her into the rift.

And still she did not recognize the rush of wind and clouds. Still she failed to perceive the nature of the sudden storm that came out of the north to drive the geese before it. Only when she caught the scent of dry leaves and damp earth on the razor's edge of the wind, did she finally understand.

Last of all the things she had surrendered to the rift, she had called Galazon. Galazon had come.

The blizzard fell like the lid of a white box. Half blind at the heart of the wind-lashed snow, Faris scrambled to her feet.

All around her the shifting patterns of the rift had stopped. She welcomed the sorrow, the pain, the cold that struck clean through her. As the cold struck her, so the cold struck the rift. As it chilled her, so it chilled the rift. The wind buffeted her until she nearly lost her bearings. Was she in the rift? Or was the rift in her?

As the storm reached its height, she set her last anchor far overhead. As sure of her own strength as she was of the north wind's, she sent herself into the heart of the rift. In the heart of the rift, she found the heart of balance, the heart of rest. For a blazing, endless moment, as all pain eased, the world held still around her.

In that instant of equilibrium, she felt Hilarion's presence and, more faintly, two others with him. To Faris, with all her senses occupied, Hilarion's companions seemed to brush past in haste. She glimpsed them only, yet recognized in them great wisdom and great age. Then they were gone.

Hilarion lingered. As if admiring the color and composition of a painting, he hesitated. With the delicacy of an artist wielding his favorite brush, he made a swift adjustment, paused, and made another. Sense of balance satisfied, he withdrew, as if to step back and judge his canvas. Greatly pleased, and mildly mischievous, he regarded his work a moment longer. And then departed.

Faris felt him go: great wisdom, great age, and amusement greater still. Her first thought was puzzlement at Hilarion's reaction. Her next thought was that now she was utterly alone.

The equilibrium held an instant longer. Then Faris felt, as though she felt the deep vibrations of a distant bell tolling, the new wardens of east and south and west, as they took their places in the world. In the heartbeat after the last wardency was restored, the balance altered. Rift healed at last, the world took up its ancient dance once more.

Cold again, half blind again, Faris braced herself against the storm. Slowly the wind began to slacken. The storm eased.

Faint and far off, Faris heard the wild geese, like a high wild song, like hounds hunting. The song stirred her, made her long for high meadows and deep forests. Even if there had been no clouds, she would not have seen the wild geese pass, for she hid her face in her hands. Only her heart could see them go.

17

"I dislike loud noises, particularly in the morning."

⚜ THE WIND DIED. The snow, which had drifted knee-deep in places, began to melt and trickle away, a small sound but steady, more musical than rainfall. The broken surface of the old throne room floor was revealed again, littered with stones, dark with damp. Overhead, the sky was still evenly overcast. But all around the horizon, a ring of clear sky began to show, like a wide blue rim on a gray bowl.

Slowly Faris took off the black robe Graelent had given her. In her ruined silk gown, she felt cold no more. She was numb, but for the dull certainty that she would do the next thing required of her, and the next after that, and so on, until all her duty was done. At the moment, it seemed plain it was her duty to see to Tyrian.

Dead, Tyrian's bruised face held a curious expression. It might have been fear and surprise mingled. Faris tried to remember if she had ever seen either expression in Tyrian's face while he lived. She did not think so, but she could not be sure. The dislocation of grief made it hard to remember. She wasn't certain if her time with Tyrian had gone into the rift or not.

Faris opened his left hand, searching for Hilarion's key. To her consternation, the key she found was whole, not broken. Nor was it smoky green glass the color of sea water. This key was cut of sharp-edged crystal, loop and stem and pin and bit, flawless, and as clear as spring water. The faceted glass gave back the morning light brilliantly. The chain, long and fine as a strand of hair, was unchanged. Faris put it around her neck but let the key hang, unconcealed.

The black robe was large enough to cover Tyrian completely. With great care, she arranged it to shroud everything.

When she rose stiffly to her feet, Faris realized that the lions had returned while she was intent upon Tyrian. She drew herself up warily, lest they try to come near Tyrian, but they merely lay in graceful repose all around her. From time to time, one would gaze with mild interest toward the palace door. None of them seemed inclined to trouble either Faris or the robe.

Brinker ventured slowly out of the palace door. His eyes were grave as he studied Faris.

She was not ready to speak to anyone yet, least of all Brinker. But she could not bring herself to leave Tyrian.

"Is any of that blood yours?"

"Blood?" Faris looked down at herself. "Oh. No." She discovered her throat was raw.

"Are you all right?"

Faris just stared at him.

"Apparently not. I'll take you back to the Metropol."

Faris flinched at his touch. "You wanted me to marry the king."

"I did. I still do. Pity the king detests you. It would be much the best solution. I am sorry he wouldn't listen to me. Unfortunate about your servant. A waste. Still, you're not hurt. That's the important thing."

"You ordered the guard to hold their fire. I won't forget that."

"You noticed my poor effort, did you? You seemed past noticing anything."

"I noticed. Thank you."

Faris's gratitude seemed to pain Brinker. "I dislike loud noises, particularly in the morning. Perhaps we should leave now. You'll probably be quite safe from the guards while you are with me. We can make a discreet departure."

Faris couldn't simply leave Tyrian there. While she struggled to find words her uncle would understand, Agnes emerged from the palace door. She halted a few steps from Faris as one of the lionesses approached her.

"What have you done to my father?" she demanded. "Where's my sister? There's witchcraft at work here."

"There's nothing at work here," Faris replied. "It's over. The rift is closed."

"Ah." Brinker looked warily around. "Where *is* Menary?"

"She's gone." Faris met Agnes's eyes squarely. "I killed her."

Agnes staggered. Startled, the lioness withdrew to a safe distance. As he steadied Agnes, Brinker looked bemused. "Still a natural diplomat, I see," he said to Faris.

"I had no choice. I had to close the rift."

Brinker looked intrigued.

"You killed my sister? You *killed* her?" Agnes fell into a storm of weeping. Brinker attempted to comfort her but she shook him off and retreated into the palace, crying, "I must tell Father!"

"So Menary is dead." Brinker sighed. "Well, I'm sure you had your reasons. Now. This rift. Tell me what you know about it."

"It's—it's difficult to explain. Try to imagine a flaw, a tear in the pattern of the world."

"Oh. Magic, is it?" Brinker looked glum. "I'm afraid I had to promise the king that you're perfectly incapable of performing magic of any kind. He wouldn't agree to the match without my assurance. Something to do with Menary, I take it. After Jane did whatever it was you persuaded her to do, he decided you and Menary were both abusing your powers. He seemed to think Menary wanted to let something out. Something that would make her more powerful than he is. Is that what you were up to?"

Faris shook her head. "I had to close the rift. Prosperian caused it. It was my responsibility." She despaired of putting it into terms her uncle might comprehend.

He was already looking sardonic. "I don't see how that

follows. Can't Prosperian put out her own fires? In a manner of speaking, of course.''

Through the palace door cautiously came a pair of trumpeters. Without taking their eyes from the watchful lions, they played a desultory fanfare. After them, the guards returned, bringing the king, with Agnes hanging on his sleeve.

The king's wrath had given way to shocked silence. He simply stared at Faris and the huddled shape beneath the black robe.

Agnes looked puzzled by his lack of response. She tugged at his sleeve, prompting him. ''Arrest her, Father. You must give the order for her arrest.''

The king's voice was a husk of itself. ''No.''

''Certainly not,'' Brinker said sharply. ''We have had enough misunderstandings here today. It's pure chance we've avoided a most unfortunate incident. No one is going to arrest the duchess of Galazon for anything.''

Agnes was taken aback by Brinker's bluntness. ''You too?'' She turned to the king. ''Say something, Father.'' At his silence, she recoiled. ''Everyone's bewitched!'' She pointed an accusing finger at Faris. ''It's your doing. This is all your fault.'' With a hiss, she sprang at Faris.

Before the lions could pull her down, two guards intervened. Agnes struggled between them until the king realized they were looking to him for direction. At his vague nod, they escorted Agnes away with what dignity they could muster.

Scarcely had they withdrawn than the palace prefect appeared in the doorway, half out of breath, bald head aglisten. ''Your Majesty, here is her excellency, Dame Edith Parry, the ambassador extraordinary and plenipotentiary of Great Britain.''

Almost on his heels the British ambassador arrived, dressed with splendid propriety for a morning call at the palace, in dove gray. The trumpeters bleated dutifully and subsided. The palace prefect withdrew. The ambassador regarded the assembly in silence. Her keen gaze did not fail to note Faris and the figure beneath the black robe.

After the British ambassador came Jane Brailsford, neatly brushed and scrubbed, but still in her red evening gown. Reed, in his somewhat crumpled costume, was beside her.

"You did it! I felt you do it. You've mended the rift." At her first look at Faris, Jane stopped abruptly. "What happened? You look ghastly. Where's Tyrian?" She glanced about at the lions, then saw the stillness concealed by the robe. She paled and looked back at Faris, horrified.

Reed frowned, baffled. "Where? What?" He followed Jane's gaze. "He can't be."

At her friends' expressions of stunned grief, Faris felt her own face twist. Her sore throat tightened.

"With your permission, your majesty," Brinker addressed the king, who was staring numbly at nothing, "perhaps your guards might detail enough men to remove the body." He motioned to the robe. Before Faris could protest, he added, "For honorable burial." To the ambassador, he said, "The king will doubtless make clear how deeply he regrets this accident."

Hesitantly, the king nodded. As the guards responded to his order, Jane murmured to Reed. Reed accompanied them.

Faris watched until the men had borne Tyrian away. There was silence on the windy heights. The lioness sank gracefully down at Faris's feet and began to clean a paw. Faris closed her eyes.

Jane's crisp voice rang out. "Catch her. She's going to faint."

As Brinker reached for her, Faris collected herself. "I will not faint." She swallowed painfully. "I may be sick."

Brinker looked mildly scandalized. "In front of the British ambassador? I think not."

Ignoring the lions, who kept a respectful distance from her, the British ambassador had stepped forward. "Do I address the warden of the north?" Without appearing to notice Faris's distress and dishevelment, she gave her a formidably correct greeting.

Faris braced herself and returned it. "I have that honor."

She glanced down at the lioness. "Although I have not had it long. You find me—and my affairs—in disarray. I will be glad to speak with you another time."

The ambassador gave Faris a look of piercing appraisal. "I understand. You have more important matters to address. But I should like to be able to assure King Edward's government that his embassage here enjoys the good will and protection of the warden of the north."

"You may assure your government that you and your embassage have my entire good will." Faris sighed. "You do understand that I play no part in the government of Aravill?"

"Certainly." The ambassador glanced back at the king, who stood surrounded by the remaining guards. "I am sure the government of Aravill regrets this entire misunderstanding. No doubt all charges against the warden and her friends will be withdrawn. Perhaps the government of Aravill wishes to make a statement to that effect?"

The king seemed to search for words. "I—I deeply regret . . ."

The ambassador looked pained by the king's obvious confusion but said only, "So I shall report." She eyed the lioness, who had moved on to another paw. "With the warden's permission, may I remain? I wish to observe—in the interest of rendering a full and accurate report."

Brinker raised one eyebrow. "There is very little more to observe. Unless you wish to observe us leaving."

Unruffled, the ambassador looked past Brinker. "Yet here is another party who plainly craves an audience with the warden."

Istvan Graelent came forward, brushing a trace of ash from his white shirt cuff. His watchful henchmen lingered at the head of the pepper-pot stair, where they had taken shelter from the blizzard.

"Your majesty—" Graelent intercepted Faris. With finesse, he backed her a step or two away from Brinker and dropped his voice to a conspiratorial murmur. "A word in your ear, your majesty."

"Don't call me that."

Brinker folded his arms and waited, one eye on the lioness. Jane joined him, head cocked at an angle that made it obvious that she was there to eavesdrop.

Graelent took Faris's hand. "Your grace—"

Faris pulled away.

"I must warn you—" Graelent paused and took a portentous look around. "You have enemies everywhere."

Everyone was regarding them with bright-eyed interest, even the lions. Everyone but the king, who had gone so waxen pale that Faris wondered if he would be the one to be sick in front of the British ambassador.

Earnestly, Graelent continued. "Trust no one, your majesty. Yet fear no one. You know who you are to us."

"Why does he seem to have such difficulty with her title?" Brinker asked Jane.

"I offer you my protection." Graelent's gesture took in the pepper-pot tower, the warden's stair. "Come away with me. Accept your place in the world."

"I begin to see why they call him Tom o'Bedlam," Brinker said.

"Quite daft," Jane agreed.

Graelent ignored them. "If you go with them, you go as a pawn. Your time with me under the city makes you mine, Faris, not theirs."

Faris knew there must be a sensible reply to make, there had to be. Something that would end this foolishness. And end it before Graelent told the world, inadvertently or not, that she had been his prisoner.

"Let them reckon us by our deeds. Faris? Your grace?" Graelent seemed puzzled by Faris's silence.

"More trouble with the title," Brinker observed.

Jane stepped close and steadied Faris. "Let me take this one," she murmured.

"Jane—" Faris turned to her friend, wide-eyed with relief.

"Allow me to introduce myself. I am Jane Brailsford. Your name, if I recall correctly, is Thomas of Bedlam."

He replied with simple dignity. "My name is Istvan Graelent."

"Oh, dear. How silly of me. I heard you announced on Twelfth Night but we were never introduced. I was Red Riding Hood. How delightful to meet you face to face at last. Your name has become a byword in the past day or two."

Before Graelent could respond with suitable modesty, Jane continued. "You seem concerned for Faris's safety. Very creditable. Yet I can't help but wonder if you've been paying much attention to current events of late. Perhaps news does not travel so quickly ten leagues beyond the wide world's end, hm?"

Graelent looked suspicious. "Who is this?" he asked Faris.

Jane was all affability. "Oh, I'm no one in particular. Just a friend of Faris's. You seem to be acquainted with Faris yourself. If I may, I would like to give you a piece of friendly advice. Look at Faris. Look at the lions. *Couchant*, I believe the heraldic term is. Mild as lambs as long as no one threatens Faris. Now ask yourself, 'Why?' "

Graelent, frowning, began to speak.

Jane cut off his reply with a chuckle. "My dear boy—my *dear* boy, you have offered your protection to the warden of the north. Look around. Do you think Faris needs your protection when even the beasts acknowledge her wardency?" Jane spoke to Faris. "There. I've done my best to make matters quite clear. If he doesn't take the hint and go away, I recommend that you turn him into a mouse. Perhaps he'll pay attention to the lions then."

Haltingly, the king spoke to Graelent. "The warden of the north has all the protection she needs. She will come to no harm here. Any who think to threaten her—think again."

"Your majesty—" Graelent was addressing Faris, not the king.

"*Go away*," Faris managed to say quite loudly. The world was whirling about her in ever swifter circles. As her knees buckled, she thought of Dame Brachet and her string of pearls.

She heard Jane call out, "Catch her."

No one did. Faris hit the ground and the world went out completely.

Faris woke in a very small, very dark room. That was what she thought at first. As she collected her wits, she realized she was in a bed, an enormous bed, with the brocade hangings drawn. She stirred against the bank of pillows and sat up, blinking. With pleased surprise, she discovered that she was wearing her own well-frayed, familiar nightgown. And her hair was no more tangled than a night's sleep usually left it. Faris let out a great sigh of relief.

The curtain rings clicked smoothly as Jane pulled the brocade hangings back. "Awake at last?" Beyond her, Faris could see that the bed was in a very large room indeed, paneled with more brocade, and a great deal of what must have been gold leaf. It was too gaudy to be anything but genuine.

"Oh, Jane—I had the most horrible dream."

But Jane's expression, grief-stricken, told Faris that her relief was mistaken. It had been no dream.

Faris thought she would strangle before she could make herself speak again. "Tyrian?"

Jane shook her head. "But you mended the rift. There's nothing wrong with the way things work here anymore. You did it. The rift is healed."

Faris felt the numbness that had enveloped her since Tyrian's death falter. She caught her breath at the pain the shift revealed. When the desolation ebbed and she was able to speak again, she asked, "What shall I do now?"

"You will do your duty." Jane looked sad.

"But what is that? I'm out of responsibilities. I've used them all up. Oh, God. What if I live to be seventy? That's another half century—with nothing to do."

"Don't exaggerate. It's only forty-nine years."

"Is it? What day is it?"

"The thirteenth. You're of age. So much for using up your responsibilities. You have a whole new set now." Jane moved around the great bed, pulling back the curtains so that Faris could see the vast expanse of the room.

"Where are we?"

"We're still in the palace."

"My goodness. Is it all this grand?"

"By no means. My room is only about half the size of this one, with ivory brocade instead of rose. Not as much gold leaf, but the ceiling is frescoed—'The Triumph of Love.' Want to swap?"

"Jane?" Faris took another look around at the splendor of the room, frowning slightly. "Are we under arrest?"

"Of course not."

"Why aren't we? You used magic on the king. I killed Menary. Who knows what other crimes the king thinks we've committed?"

"We're honored guests now. Free to go or stay." Jane looked thoughtful. "The old boy seems to have had a nasty shock."

"Where's Brinker?"

"Hovering anxiously in the corridor, last I saw of him. He'll be relieved to hear you've recovered. If you had been harmed, he'd have had to take a very firm line with his majesty—very firm indeed."

"What happened to Graelent? Did they arrest him? Or did you turn him into a mouse?"

"Oh, dear. What a waste of male beauty that would be. No, he recognized the chance to make a quick exit when it came. As you fell into a graceful swoon, he and his lads escaped down the warden's stair. Why? Do you think he should have been arrested?"

Faris shook her head. "It's better this way. Small political parties only grow larger if the leaders are imprisoned. If I were the king, I would arrange to deport Istvan Graelent at once. As soon as he's out of the country, I would make it known that he has diverted party funds to his own account in Zurich. That would cool his followers' ardor."

Jane looked appreciative. "Nothing quite like a good rumor to distract the opposition, is there?"

"Particularly if it has the merit of being true."

"Would you like to advise the king on this matter yourself? He'll probably be relieved to know you're awake at last. I'll send someone to help you bathe and dress while I tell him you'll grant him an audience."

"Wait—"

Jane turned back.

"*I'll* grant *him* an audience?"

"Must I explain it to you, too? Faris, you're the warden of the north."

Faris had bathed and dressed by the time Reed knocked at the door. While the maid who had buttoned her into her black suit hovered watchfully, Faris gave Reed permission to enter.

"The king is waiting for you in the presence chamber. Jane sent me to tell you to take your time. And this is the first chance I've had to give you this." Reed held out a bundle wrapped in black cloth. "I thought you should have it."

"What is it?" Faris put it down on the nearest table— golden legs supporting a slab of porphyry. Reed looked so unhappy that she hesitated. "What's wrong?"

"Nothing. Well, nothing new. You needn't unwrap it. Perhaps you'd rather not. It's his."

Faris knew without asking whom Reed referred to. Gently, she unfolded the rough cloth. Inside the bundle she found Tyrian's pistol, his knife, a set of lock picks. And, crumpled almost beyond recognition, one of the gloves she had worn at the Twelfth Night ball.

She smoothed the glove, turned it over and over in silence. When she looked up, Reed handed her his handkerchief without speaking. While she blew her nose, he wrapped up the personal effects.

"I'll take it away if you'd rather."

"No. No, leave it. I'm grateful to have it."

"Good." He turned to depart. "Jane said you should take your time. I'll tell her you're going to."

"Reed—thank you. May I ask a favor?"

Reed looked curious. "Yes, of course."

"I'm not going home to Galazon just yet. But Galazon can't wait for me. We need to rid ourselves of Lord Seaforth before he makes himself too comfortable."

"Why aren't you going home?"

"It's hard to explain. The rift changed things for me. I need to get used to it before I try to go back to Galazon. Otherwise I'm not sure I can bear it. Anyway, I need someone I can trust. I'd like to send you back. My mother's advisers and the Curia Ducis are no more. But they could begin again. And from them, Galazon might forge a government."

Reed looked baffled. "I'll go if you wish me to, of course. But we have a government. We have you. The duchess of Galazon."

"No." Faris felt the memory of her pride in that title jar against the numbness that was all the rift had left her. "I am the warden of the north."

By the time Faris was ready to leave her opulent chamber, the redness of her eyes had diminished. Brinker was waiting for her in the corridor outside.

"I am relieved to see that you are looking better." He fell into step beside her. "Though I must say black is not your color."

Faris took comfort in the familiar irritation her uncle's manner provoked. "If you must, you must. Have you come to wish me a happy birthday?"

"In fact, I did. I do. Don't look so skeptical. I am not as devious as you would like to think. Where are we going, if I may ask?"

"Nor are you as ingenuous as you would like me to think. I have no idea where you're going. I am going to grant the king an audience in his own presence chamber."

"Feeling better as well as looking better. I am relieved.

Perhaps you have even given some small thought to what role you wish me to play now that you have attained your majority."

"So that's what brings you here." Faris halted. Brinker joined her before an immense seascape. Faris pretended to admire the painting while Brinker regarded her with bemused calm.

"I will be glad to continue in my present capacity as long as you need me."

"A generous offer. In fact, I have given the matter some thought."

It was Brinker's turn to seem absorbed by the huge canvas. "Ah. I thought perhaps you had."

"You and Graelent are not that different. In the end, it all comes down to bookkeeping."

"It does indeed," Brinker said heartily.

"You're cheerful. No doubt you've had plenty of time to cook the books back home. But I didn't spend all my time in Paris ordering clothes. I spoke to our bankers. They were very helpful. Now that I'm of age, I don't think I'll have any trouble obtaining full financial records from them. Full and accurate financial records."

Brinker looked resigned. "What do you want?"

"I want my heir to be raised in Galazon."

"Marry and bear your own heir. Raise the creature where you please."

"I shall never marry."

"You're too young to make such statements."

"How old do I need to be? I'll repeat it annually if you insist."

"You're twenty-one. You will surely have children of your own. In his present queer state, the king might do anything, even marry you. Don't be too quick to dismiss the plans I've made on your behalf."

"Don't be too quick to dismiss the plans I'm making for your daughter."

"You needn't trouble yourself. Ultimately, she is the

king's heir, too. She won't need Galazon once she has Aravill."

"If the child is my heir, she will be raised in Galazon."
Faris hesitated. "If she is my heir. I could choose another from
some suitable family. Perhaps I shall adopt a ward. I wonder if
the Woodrowels could suggest something?"

"The Woodrowels—" Brinker bit off his exclamation. For
a moment he regarded Faris with mute horror, then he spun
on his heel and took half a dozen long strides down the hall.
When he paced back, his jaw was set, his eyes blazing. "You
wouldn't *dare*."

Faris folded her arms. Though she said nothing, her
bemused expression seemed to enrage him.

"You would. It's precisely the sort of thing you would do.
Oh, God! *Now* do you understand why I worked so hard to
arrange matters before you came of age? I knew you'd come
up with some hare-brained notion—but I never thought you'd
be this stupid."

"Agnes is young. I'm sure the two of you will have many
more children."

"Oh, wipe that pious expression off your face."

"So you agree? Prosperian will be raised in Galazon."

"Agnes will never consent."

"I'm certain you can persuade her. I wouldn't care to hold
her responsible for your financial malfeasance, but I will pros-
ecute you both if I have to."

"I made the customary settlements. It was all legal. Perfectly legal."

"Oh, Uncle Brinker. You've taken such good care of me
all these years. Why don't you let me take good care of you
now?" Her words were silken. "I can make things so inconvenient for you if you refuse to cooperate."

Brinker's eyes narrowed. "And if Agnes and I agree to
your terms? What then?"

"Unlike me, you have some talent for diplomacy. I want
you to use it on my behalf. I intend to send you away—far
away—Finland, I think—as my ambassador. Tell Agnes she

has a choice. She may stay in Aravill—*not* Galazon—or she may go with you to—Helsinki."

"Agnes dislikes cold weather."

"She might dislike the alternatives more. Oh, there is just one other thing. You purchased some land belonging to Reed's family."

"Did I?"

"Quince blossom. Don't tell me you've forgotten the quince blossom?"

"Quince blossom? Oh, yes." Brinker's expression cleared. "I remember now. Reed is tractable enough, but his family objected to the taxes long before I began to raise them. They're a garrulous bunch, and related to half the crofters in the duchy. I needed to give them something else to think about."

"If they get the land back, and if you and Agnes agree to allow Prosperian to be brought up as my heir in Galazon, I will take no legal action against you for your financial exploits."

"Done."

Faris abandoned the seascape. Brinker followed her warily. "Surely that's not all?"

Faris looked surprised. "I'm exiling you and your wife. I'm going to raise your first child as my own. What more do you think there should be?"

"You can't expect me to believe you're concerned about that miserable vegetable patch of Reed's." Brinker looked offended. "Why, if you wanted it, you could have just taken it."

"No." Faris stopped and stared at her uncle until he had to look away. "No, I couldn't."

Faris joined the king in his presence chamber. He was alone. As she entered, he was walking slowly along the wall of windows, looking out at the streets below. He seemed older, wearier than she remembered, perhaps because instead of his usual bright garb he wore a neat suit of black. Unconscious parody of her own impulse to wear mourning? She wondered. "You wished to see me?"

He turned to regard her. With the light at his back, it was hard for her to judge his expression but Faris thought his shoulders drooped slightly, as if in disappointment. She guessed this was not the greeting he'd expected. "I understood you wished to see me," he answered quietly.

She crossed to look out the windows herself. It was an unseasonably sunny day, not a cloud anywhere. "Jane thought you might like some advice about Graelent. You'd do better to deport him than to imprison him."

"If you wish him to go free, he shall go free," the king said stiffly.

"I wish him to be exposed for the opportunist he is, no more. And no less. He's a mountebank, but he'll create more trouble if he can convince people that he's being persecuted." She described the method Graelent had used to line his own pockets. "Mock him, don't martyr him."

"You know a great deal about Istvan Graelent."

With an effort, she kept her tone light. "More than enough."

"I told them to give you the finest chamber in the palace. Have they?"

She nodded. "It's very grand."

"You don't like it."

"It's—magnificent."

"You dislike it, don't you?"

"I couldn't. I'm very grateful for your hospitality. Now, may I ask you something? Honestly? How much was it?"

"How much was what?"

"You needn't feign ignorance. Just say you refuse to answer. But I'd like to know the true amount. Brinker does things his own way—even bookkeeping."

"What are you talking about?"

"The dowry. How much does it cost an ambassador of the farmyard to marry these days?"

Obviously nonplused, it took him some time to reply. "I think I must refuse to answer."

"Don't you remember?"

"Why must you know the exact amount? Are you concerned that I might not have demanded enough?" the king asked calmly.

Faris managed a crooked smile. "Oh, I'm counting on you to have demanded more than enough. I'll need to spend some of the money on my maintenance here in Aravis."

"Here? You're staying here?" The king's astonishment flickered and vanished beneath a mask of bland interest.

"I'm not prepared to return to Galazon just yet."

"No?" The curiosity in his tone belied his placid expression. "Why not?"

Faris hesitated. "To mend the rift, I had to surrender much that I value. I am still taking stock of the damage. One thing I lost—" Her words leaped so in her throat, she did not trust herself to continue.

The king looked away. "Galazon."

"Yes."

"I'm so sorry." His voice was gentle, hardly more than a whisper.

She was surprised how much his sympathy moved her. She had to shut her eyes to conceal her response. "I have something else to ask you."

"Ask. Understand, I may have to refuse you again. But ask. I will answer if I can."

"What frightened you so? What did you think I was doing there at the rift?"

"I—feared you would step too close and be lost in the rift forever. Forgive me. I wish to atone for my folly."

"Folly?" Her anger was so abrupt it astonished her. "You call it folly?"

"I have been a fool. What else can I call it?"

"In your folly, you gave the order to—" She broke off, stammering. His calmness enraged her.

"In my folly, I forgot you were—who you were."

"How can you look so blank? Do you even understand what you've done?"

"I gave an order I now bitterly regret. But you were spared."

"You don't understand anything, do you?" She began to pace along the windows. "I gave up Galazon. I let it go into the rift. The rift wanted more. Yet I couldn't bring myself to give Tyrian up too. And then—then you gave your order. Which you now bitterly regret."

Still calm, he managed a quiet reply. "Tyrian won, then. He kept you safe. You hired him to protect you and he did. What better end could he have made?"

Faris turned on him. "Why choose to wear black today, of all days? I know why I'm in black. Why are you? Mourning?"

He looked startled. "One does not wear mourning for a servant."

"You still don't understand, do you? He was not my servant."

He regarded her anger, aghast. "What then? What else could he be?"

Her empty hands shook as she held them out to him. Her voice shook as she replied. "Glove to my hand." Slowly she closed her fists. *"Everything."*

Rage choked her. She left him there, staring numbly out at nothing. Grief and anger drove her through the palace, from the presence chamber to the lion-guarded heights.

On Candlemas, Faris stood again at the empty heights where the rift had been. The sky was cloudy. A steady breeze from the west promised mild weather to come. Far below lay the narrow, noisy streets of Aravis. Faris did not spare a glance down at them. She looked westward. But for the lions, who were fond of her company, she was alone.

The Monarchist party had ceased to play any part in the politics of Aravill. Lord Brinker Nallaneen and his lady wife had departed for Finland. Their child, deemed too young for such a journey, was sent to Galazon with her nurses. Reed escorted them to Galazon Chase, the child's home for the winter months.

As soon as spring came, Reed would take the child and her nurses to Shieling, where Prosperian would be cared for and protected by Warin and Flavia Woodrowel. In return for the child's maintenance, the Woodrowels would pay tribute: one pine bough, once a year. A fresh one.

To secure the castle, the doors to the warden's stair had been locked and bricked shut. World's End Close was sealed and guarded.

The king's silent calm continued. His once-lively social schedule had given way to near isolation. Though this change concerned his ministers, his diligence concerned them more. He seemed determined to review every nuance of his political responsibility.

Greenlaw was still in session. Dame Brailsford's absence could not be excused indefinitely. Reluctantly, Jane had taken her leave a week before.

On Candlemas, Faris watched Greenlaw from the heights of Aravis. Far off, she saw a sleek Minerva limousine roar across the sands of low tide on the spine of paved causeway. With a flourish, the long automobile drew up smartly before the gate.

Before the engine had ceased idling, the little green shutter snapped open. The gatekeeper's grim face was round and red, chapped by the offshore wind. "We have no use for automobiles here."

The driver's door opened and Jane Brailsford emerged, immaculate in her Parisian traveling clothes.

The gatekeeper was dismayed. "I beg your pardon, Dame Brailsford. I thought you were a tourist."

Jane leaned in to address someone still inside the limousine. "Thank you, Charles. I'll send someone down to collect my luggage while I report to the Dean. You're not to trouble about it. I recommend Mère Poulard's for lunch, by the way. Thank you again for the chance to practice my driving. If Uncle Ambrose notices anything fishy about the gearbox, do blame it all on me. Oh, and don't worry about leaving the limo for lunch. I'm sure the gatekeeper will be glad to keep an eye on it for you.''

Disgusted, the gatekeeper slammed his shutter. After a moment, the wooden gate swung open.

Jane walked through the gates of Greenlaw, the visible built of oak, the invisible built of the Dean's will. She crossed the threshold and was lost to Faris's view.

Alone on the heights of Aravis, Faris turned away. Far below lay the narrow, noisy streets. She did not spare them a glance. She felt loneliness welling up within.

From about her neck, she drew the fine chain that held the key to the warden's stair. For a thoughtful moment, she let the key swing and spin, admiring the way its facets gave back the morning light.

The lions looked back toward the palace door. She followed their glance and saw the king emerge. He moved stiffly, almost warily, toward her. With disfavor, Faris noted that he was still wearing black. Pointedly, she turned her back on him.

Faris looked down. Far below lay the city, crowded, heedless, aimlessly busy. She stretched out her hand until the key hung, flawless and brilliant, over the edge.

''The palace prefect told me you were here,'' the king said softly.

Faris did not bother to turn and acknowledge his presence. The effrontery, to follow her here. It must be obvious she wished to be left alone. Quite alone.

''I didn't mean to startle you.''

Something troubled Faris, but she could not identify what it was. She frowned at the key, twisting on its chain as it caught the light and surrendered it.

When she did not answer, he inquired calmly, ''Won't you need that key?''

She spaced her words coldly. ''The stair is closed. If I shatter the key, the stair will remain closed.''

''There may be other doors. And what makes you certain the key will shatter?''

She glanced down at the cluttered streets below. "From this height? Can you doubt it?"

"Who can be certain what Hilarion's key will do?"

More intent on the tone of his words than the sense, she answered almost absently, "It's mine now. And I no longer need it." Then the sense reached her, and she demanded, "Who told you it was Hilarion's key?"

He touched her shoulder with a gloved hand. "Come away from the edge."

At those words, in that place, Faris drew breath sharply. *In that voice.* She remembered that voice. With every bone in her body, she recognized it.

She felt something shift within her as a pattern came clear and clean. Something she could not name came right, as swiftly, as neatly as one might cut a deck of cards.

As she had felt during her vigil, even in the darkness of that last hour before dawn, that all was right with Greenlaw, so she felt now. All was well. Relief drove words away.

Faris willed herself to keep her eyes on the horizon. She would not look at him, *she would not.* She did not need to look. She could feel him behind her. The voice, the touch, the calm competence were all utterly familiar.

Then she remembered Hilarion's swift adjustments, his amusement. She closed her eyes.

At that, as clearly as if he were standing at her side, she heard the words Hilarion had spoken to her in Paris: *I know of no one and nothing that can restore that light once it has been extinguished.* And she heard words Hilarion had never spoken to her at all, but his voice was unmistakable: *I have had so little light in these long years, I am reluctant to let any go to waste.*

Faris understood. She could turn and look or not, it made no difference. When she saw him, no matter how the world perceived him, she would behold him as he truly was: Tyrian. She swayed a little.

"Come back." He drew her gently away from the edge. The warmth of his hand on her shoulder melted something inside her that she hadn't even realized was frozen.

Giddily, she heard herself speaking her thoughts aloud. *"If love were the only thing, I would follow you—in rags if need be—to the world's end . . ."* And then, more light-headed still, *"Ten leagues beyond the wide world's end, methinks it is no journey—"* And then laughter jerked somehow into tears.

When she could speak again, Faris wiped her eyes on her sleeve. She said, almost levelly, "I know you look like him. But no one is as calm as you are. How could it have taken me so long to recognize you?"

His quiet voice held an edge of anger. "I don't just look like him. I wheeze like him. I limp like him. No doubt every function is the same."

His bitterness took her aback. "But you're *here.* Where is he? Has he gone? Or are you in there with him?"

"He was gone when I—arrived. I'm alone in here. Hilarion made that clear. And the arrangement is permanent. He made that clear, too."

"Hilarion did it. *Why?"*

He had to clear his throat before he could answer. "The king intended to kill a warden. Hilarion is—was—a warden himself. He knows what that means in a way you have just begun to understand. The king ordered his men to fire at you. That was reason enough for Hilarion."

"And you?"

"Well, I saved a warden's life. At the cost of my own. Hilarion meted out punishment and reward."

"And you said nothing about it."

"What could I say? I dared tell only you. But by the time I understood what had happened, you were surrounded."

"Talking to Uncle Brinker hardly qualifies as being surrounded."

"Lord Brinker, Jane, and Reed," he countered. "Not to mention that handsome weasel, Graelent. And the British ambassador could surround someone all by herself."

"True."

"I expected you to realize what had happened at first sight. You didn't. So I wondered what Hilarion had intended for us. Perhaps I was supposed to keep silent until you recognized me. I had a hard time concealing myself. And if I had a dinara for every time I heard someone say, 'The king is not himself'—no wonder my hair is gray."

"You fool. Why didn't you tell me?"

"I meant to. I did. Then in the presence chamber, you confided things to me that took my breath away. What could I do? I had to let you go."

"Coward."

"Oh, yes. But remember, I had finally done my duty. It took me a few tries, but eventually I managed to do what Hilarion intended me to do. I saved your life."

"That's not all you did."

"Perhaps not, but my duty was clear, even though I had a hard time carrying it out. At Greenlaw, Menary fooled me completely. In Paris, Jane did all the hard work, and on the Orient-Express too. Remember Copenhagen? It was no fault of mine you lived through the first day at Galazon Chase. Lord Brinker saved you that time."

"Even if he hadn't, it wouldn't have been your fault."

"Oh, no? You don't understand. Do you go to sleep at night thinking, 'Well, that's that. I was warden of the north today.' "

Faris laughed.

"Of course not. I'm different. Guarding you didn't leave much time for sleeping, but when it did, I slept sound. I could tell myself, 'There's another day gone and she's still alive.' Another risk run, another vigil kept, another danger averted. You were my vocation. Don't laugh, I'm quite serious. When I began the job Hilarion gave me, I didn't know what to make of you. Were you a spoiled heiress? A neglected brat? I couldn't see you as a ruler—let alone a warden. I thought you were much more likely to finish up on a scaffold. With me beside you, of course."

"That's curious. I would have said a guillotine, not a scaffold. With you beside me in the tumbrel, naturally."

"You are insanely careless of your safety. It never occurred to you to wonder what would have happened if that bomb had gone off in Paris, did it? And you are insanely responsible about what you've decided is yours. I am yours, apparently. Well, you are mine."

"At last we agree on something."

"At the Twelfth Night ball I finally saw you as you are. Not Smoke. Not the Queen of Swords. Not even the Queen of the Night. When I looked at you, I could see the warden of the north. For the first time, I truly believed you would close the rift. I saw the life you were going to have without me. Or with me only as some distant figure, a valet, a steward . . . someone you felt responsible for. I couldn't bear to look ahead."

"You saved my life on the water stair. And you freed me from Graelent."

"Trifles. By the time the king gave the order to fire, I had no interest in surviving you—or even surviving the rift. I did my job. As a reward, Hilarion gave me another. I have no idea how to go about this one. How does one become a king? I'm not used to having no idea how to go about doing something." He mocked his own plaintive tone. "It is not at all what I am accustomed to."

"Are you quite sure you want to change jobs? I'm not sure I can spare you. Who will protect me now?"

"It took twenty-three lions to do it, but I think my old position has been filled. No, it's your turn to protect me. I don't know anything about being a king. I need you."

"I don't have the credentials to be a king." Faris answered him soberly despite the small bubble of hilarity lodged at the base of her throat. It took her a moment to identify the source of that unaccustomed feeling. Oddly, it was the prospect of responsibility. At the first hint of new responsibility, her heart lifted.

Entirely in earnest, he continued. "But you have the training. It's even in your best interest. Galazon's independence is assured if we manage things properly. If I have a few good years left in this carcass, we ought to be able to make a considerable difference."

His gravity amused her. "You're too young to make such statements."

"Be serious."

"I am quite serious. *Lambkins, we will live.* That's from an English play."

Her levity made him impatient. "Faris, I'm old now."

She drew herself up with all the dignity she could muster, which, between relief and giddiness, was not a great deal. "I don't care how old you are. I care still less how the world thinks of you. I *know* you, Tyrian. And I'm the warden of the north. I can love whomever I please."

"Precisely. You can have your pick of husbands. You deserve better than this old crock."

She did not need to counterfeit indignation. "Husbands? Who said anything about husbands? How many times must I say it? I shall never marry."

"My turn to say it, and I'm serious: You're too young to make such statements."

"So I am *constantly* told. Listen to me. I don't wish to marry." She surrendered her exasperation long enough to add lightly, "Even if I did, I could never marry you. That would make Uncle Brinker far too happy. No, I'll work with you instead."

Her cheerfulness roused his suspicions. "Work with me at what, exactly?"

"You're the king of Aravill now. Together we will set Galazon free. We will do what we can to make Aravill what it ought to be." She grinned evilly. "And we will get every concession we possibly can from the British ambassador in return for the harbor at Shene."

On Candlemas, Faris stood on the windy heights of Aravis and beheld her wardency. The north lay before her, flawless and brilliant. From her vantage point she looked long in all directions. But last, and most lovingly, she turned westward to Greenlaw.

Even on a winter day, the sea was silver. In the distance,

the hills of Normandy were blue. The rising tide came in across the shifting sand like a myriad of rivers running in from the sea. Above the perfect flatness of the bay, the seawalls of Greenlaw rose like a sand castle.

A tidy garland of slate-roofed houses, gardens, and shops marked the village wreathed around Greenlaw's base. Above the village the college rose, gray stone faceted into towers. Above the college rose the spire, and on that height of heights, St. Margaret and St. Michael stood back to back, ready for new battles.